THE SCENT OF MY SON,

IN GOD WE TRUST

BY ADRIENNE MIRANDA

ISBN: 1499664559
ISBN 13: 9781499664553

TABLE OF CONTENTS

TABLE OF CONTENTS

Resources Holy Bible, new international version, Zondervan copyright 1973, 1978, 1984 by International Bible Society.
The NIV Concordance by the Zondervan Corporation. Pastor John MacArthur's study bible. New King James Version Copyright 1997 Word Publishing.

DEDICATION

Dedicated to my Joseph, my precious son who lives on in the kingdom of heaven.

Dedicated to my Jesus, God's precious Son who lives on in the kingdom of heaven.

Acknowledgement

The photograph of my penny pendant was taken by my kind hearted, caring and compassionate friend Dottie Ray.

PREFACE

I have been chosen by my Almighty Father, God, to write this book. My precious son, Joseph Anthony Miranda, was brutally and tragically killed at the hands of another on July 20, 2006. Joseph was 19 years old at the time of his death and just starting to realize all of his hopes, dreams, ambitions and a promising future. He was so full of life, kind, compassionate and had a very strong faith in our Lord, Jesus Christ. I, too, have that same unshakable faith.

The shock, pain and torture a mother experiences when she loses her child are the hardest agonizing sufferings a human being will ever bear. I knew as a little girl that I always wanted to have children and I was blessed with two beautiful sons. Rob my firstborn and Joseph my second. I love my sons so deeply; they are my heart and my life. When we got the sudden and devastating news that Joseph had been run over by an industrial piece of equipment, an earthmover while at work, we were in such severe shock, disbelief and gut wrenching pain that we felt paralyzed.

I was brought to my knees and my tears never stopped as I called out to God for help. I kept calling for my Joseph and wanted to see him but they, the Maryland State Police, told me I could not. Joseph's injuries to his face, head and neck were extremely severe and I was told to just remember my son the way he was.

I knew in my heart that something wasn't adding up by what the police tried to explain to me of how this could have possibly happened to my son. All of my family members felt the same and we knew their homicide and criminal investigation into my son's tragic death left many justified questions unanswered and a multitude of inconsistencies. The police and states' attorneys have not done their jobs and have committed serious malfeasances we alleged as the years went by. We have researched and gathered the proof to confirm what we claim.

I knew that I would carry out my mission and find out who was responsible and why my precious and loving son was so horrifically and brutally killed. I have fought for over seven years now for Justice for Joseph and I vowed to be his voice. My son's death has been confirmed a Homicide by assault by the Chief Medical Examiner of the State of Maryland and his Assistant. A brutal and horrific crime was committed against our son. We know who the perpetrator is. We have all of the facts, science, physics, forensics, etc. that proves my son was murdered. However, no one in the State of Maryland will prosecute the crime. What I have been through is unconscionable and detestable by the law enforcement agencies and the police within the State of Maryland as well as some Outside Unliving employees. They lied to us, withheld reports and documents, never even brought in a reconstructionist and moved our son's legs and arms after his death to disturb the crime scene. The Maryland State Police complied with whatever the owner of Outside Unliving told them to do. His political power and connections they knew were powerful and they felt sure we would eventually go away and be silenced. They were oh so wrong! God is the One and only mighty power. He is just and He is truth. Our Almighty Father God will deliver it all in His way and in His time. Without love, faith and belief in Jesus Christ, our Savior, we are nothing. Glory to you Father, your will be done!

My book titled "The Scent of My Son, In God We Trust" has great meaning for me. The **S** is in Red for the bloodshed of Jesus, Our Savior, and for the words that Jesus spoke throughout the Bible. You will see the words that Jesus spoke in the Bible italicized throughout my book. The word Scent has a dual meaning. I can still smell the sweet scent and fragrance of my precious angel on his clothes, his hemp bracelet and necklace he loved to wear, his cell phone and his leather wallet. There was also one penny found in the pocket of my son when he went home to the Lord.

Joseph never carried change. He was like your everyday teen in that regard. He used to throw all his change in a mug on the dresser in his room. He was full of love, happiness, gusto for life, kind and giving. He had a hug for everyone he met. He was so handsome and always extended to others. He was beautiful both inside and out and truly lit up a room when he entered.

The police gave me an envelope with his belongings in it after he was tragically and brutally killed while working for a landscaping company in Maryland. I was alone, sitting at my kitchen table when I opened the envelope. My tears were glistening in the morning sun that was gleaming through my window. My tears poured and I did not know how to make them stop. I felt so helpless and I yearned to hold my son. I knew my life would never be the same and I prayed for my dear Lord to give me strength and perseverance.

As I held the penny I kept feeling it over and over again and touching the formed symbols, words and copper. I kept saying in my heart, "This penny was with my baby when he went to the Lord." "This penny is my penny from heaven". Then my Lord said to me as I heard my Holy Spirit, "What is the date on the penny"? I turned it over in my hand and the date read 1972. My heart cried out more to my Jesus and my Joseph........"Oh thank you".......you see Joseph was the age of 19 and he went on 7-20. I knew for certain that 1 9 7 2 was God telling me He had Joseph and Joseph was in heaven.

I had the penny made into a circular pendant and wear it always. It lay on my chest close to my heart and it is truly my "penny from heaven".

My story is very, very involved and so compelling and filled with miraculous occurrences that only God could have brought them to me. It has been over the last seven years of my life that I have walked this journey and what I have been able to reveal regarding the company owners, their political connections, their criminal misconduct as well as the criminal misconduct of law officials and law enforcement at every level is unbelievable, appalling, repulsive and unconscionable.

I will keep moving forward until justice for Joseph prevails and all that must be exposed is exposed. My precious son did not die in vain, there is a reason and a purpose for everything on this earth and I will deliver what my Savior directs me to do.

Joseph's story and mine is a true and vital piece of a Mother and Son's life and death that will bring intrigue, tears, laughter, heartache, empathy, revelation and change that must be made. It will come, I am certain of it. I was able to assist in having two House bills passed and I am continuing my crusade for justice for my precious son. I vowed to be Joseph's voice and I will not stop until justice for Joseph prevails.

I would especially like to acknowledge my Brother, Damian Gemma, who has stood beside me this entire time. He is a loving and compassionate uncle, a devoted Brother, a strong Christian and he knows everything that has occurred throughout our inconceivable struggle to obtain Justice for Joseph. He and my sister-in-law, Lisa Gemma, have been so supportive and I am forever grateful to them. I also have made a new friend; a very kind, intelligent, caring and just man within the FBI. He, too, has been with me all of these years and has never wavered in his belief that my son was brutally killed. He is my Brother in Christ and God puts people in our lives for a purpose and a reason while on our journey here.

I believe that through the unthinkable and unconscionable battle these people have put me through and most importantly through the courage God has given me to stand strong and fight the good fight that I may give hope and love to other parents and families so they can have a voice and have their voices heard. Loving, grieving parents need to know that God will in time restore them and He will give them his unfailing love, grace, mercy and strength. I hope and pray that my book will lift them up and they will know the greatness of our Almighty Father and that our beloved children and family members live on in the paradise of heaven. They are with us always and we are never separated from those we love so dearly.

My God has given me the perseverance and strength to carry on and move forward. His love and the love and support of so many that God has put in my path have been miraculous. I pray for Jam's House, Home Sweet Home to become a reality to provide for oppressed children throughout the world.

...JOSEPH ANTHONY MIRANDA TWO MONTHS BEFORE HIS TRAGIC AND UNTIMELY DEATH.
APRIL 22ND 1987 – JULY 20TH, 2006

CHAPTER 1

THE SHOCK, AGONY AND UNBEARABLE PAIN

On Thursday, July 20, 2006, the hottest day of the year, my life as I knew it would change forever. That night I received a phone call from my ex-husband, Bob, the father of my two sons, saying, "Our beautiful baby boy is gone." I screamed, "What, what, what did you say?" He replied, "Joseph was run over and killed by a piece of equipment at work." I ran screaming, crying, searching and scrambling and felt my heart and center had been blown to bits, shattered and left never to be found. I am not able to describe my pain, agony, horror and despair. I collapsed to the floor and begged for my mother and my son, Rob. I cried out for God to please help me. I was home alone. I tried to call my mother, crying to her to come—come quick. She was already crying and said she was coming. I stood scratching the front window and begging for headlights as I held on for dear life to my Joseph's picture.

It seemed like forever, but I finally saw lights coming up my driveway. My siblings, my mother and my friend Matt ran in and tried to hold and comfort me. They, too, were in shock and pain. My tears and screams just would not stop as I cried out, "How could this be? How could this be?" I was on the floor and in trauma, shock and disbelief. I kept calling to Joseph, "Where are you, Joseph? Where are you?" Joseph's best friend from the age of four, Scott, was also there. He hugged me and his tears seemed frozen in time. He sat at the kitchen table, feeling shock, incredible hurt and pain. Scott and Joe were so close all of their years growing up and he was so upset and needed to be with us. My heart was so badly broken and I knew Scott could feel our pain as well as us feeling his.

Bob had called at about quarter after eleven at night, but I had not heard from any police yet. I kept saying, "Where is my Joseph? I need to go to him. I want to hold him in my arms." My older son, Rob, had driven to his father's house and was there when they got the news. He soon came to our home in Lutherville, Maryland, where he and his brother Joseph grew up. When I saw my son Rob, I needed so badly to hold him. Joseph was nineteen years old when this tragic and horrific nightmare happened; Rob was twenty-one.

At about midnight a Maryland state trooper—a corporal, Dan Kitseng—called and asked to speak with me. I was crying and asking him what happened to my son. He just said he really didn't know yet, but Joseph was run over by a Mexican man driving a Bobcat and killed on the premises of the landscaping company where he worked. The spotter tried to stop him, but it was too late.

I kept saying, "I don't understand. How did the driver not see my son? Where is my son? I want to see him." The police trooper told me, "No, you cannot see your son, Ms. Miranda. Just remember your son the way he was." I cried harder and said, "No, I need to hold him. Where is he?" Corporal Kitseng said, "Your son is at the morgue and you cannot see him." The trooper tried to calm me and I tried to hear him. I wanted answers. Nothing made any sense to me. I asked, "What are the police going to do? Who did this? How did it happen? What time did it happen?" He said, "It happened at about four this afternoon." I said, "Why did it take so long for you to contact me or Joseph's dad? It was over seven hours before any of us were contacted by police." The corporal said, "They were investigating." He then asked to speak with another adult and my family members and my friend Matt got on the phone. The corporal gave Matt his work and cell phone numbers and said he would be in touch with me and I could call at any time.

I could not control my tears and panic, got back on the phone with the trooper and asked, "Where is my son? I need to go to him now and hold him." He was hesitant and I then handed the phone to my friend, who is a Baltimore County police officer. He asked, "What are the names of the driver and the spotter?" The corporal told Matt that they would not release any names because it was under investigation. Corporal Dan Kitseng also told Matt that my son was at Elan Funeral Home in Hampstead, Maryland.

I was living a horrific nightmare and felt I would not be able to survive. My mother phoned my doctor and explained what had happened. He immediately called in a prescription for me and Matt went to pick it up. I kept praying to my Lord and Savior to help me. I was on my knees shaking and trembling as the tears kept coming. I knew I would not sleep, so my friend Matt and my son Rob both tried to lie down beside me, each putting his arms around me to try to console me. I cried and prayed the rest of the night until dawn.

When I saw the sun coming through the window, I was still in a state of shock and I wept at what I knew I would have to do. Ruck's Funeral Home would have to be called and I would have to go to choose the casket my baby would lie in and be buried in. I do not know how I got through these days; without my strong faith, I would have not survived.

My phone was constantly ringing as loved ones and dear friends were trying to find out what happened and if they could help in anyway. My siblings helped with phone calls and my mother was trying her best to caress me and hold me up. My brother Dino, his wife, Lisa and his son, Joe, came into my bedroom weeping and gave me hugs and kisses. They, too, were in shock. My youngest brother, Damian, who lives in Florida, was away on business when he got the call and immediately switched flights to come into Baltimore.

All of my family and close friends were there for me with compassion, love, support and such willingness to help. Joseph's best and closest friends were also there the next day trying to comfort me and tell me how much they loved Joseph.

My family set up the time for Joseph's father and me to meet with the funeral director to make the arrangements. My siblings, Joe's dad and my former brother-in-law, Tim, were going to go with us as they had been through the same agony and immense heartache of burying their beloved, Michael, my precious nephew, who was killed also at the tender age of nineteen just seven years before. Michael was killed by an aggressive driver who was speeding, jumped the median strip and was airborne as he went right into Michael's car while he was waiting for a red light on the other side of the highway. Michael never even had a chance and took the entire impact of the car coming at him. We love you Michael with all of our hearts and you are with us always and forever. We know that you and Joseph live on together in God's heavenly paradise and smile down upon us. You will always be our angel boys.

MICHAEL AND JOSEPH TOGETHER FOR JOSEPH'S FIRST CHRISTMAS; THEY WERE SO PRECIOUS AND ALWAYS SO CLOSE.

Michael was killed on April 24, 1999. He was a kind, loving, caring and compassionate young man with such a giving heart. He, too, was handsome and his smile was contagious. His death was so very devastating, shocking and agonizing for all of our family. He and Joseph were extremely close. Joseph looked up to Michael as the older cousin; they were seven years apart. Both of us had two sons. Joseph, being the youngest at that time, always knew Michael would look out for him and they truly had a special bond. The number seven surrounds them. They were born seven years apart, Michael in 1980 and Joseph in 1987, as well as seven days apart, Michael on April 15 and Joseph on April 22; Joseph was killed seven years after Michael—Michael in 1999 and Joseph in 2006—and Joseph went home to the Lord in the seventh month, July. I know they are both together in the arms of Jesus and doing God's work with glorious contentment. They are our "angel boys." You know, in the Bible the number seven means "complete." I know that God has a purpose and a plan for everything. Our "angel boys'" lives were complete here on this earth and God called them home. He wanted them with Him. We yearn to hold and embrace our precious sons yet know where they are, together in the loving arms of Jesus. Lamentations 2:19: "Arise, cry out in the night, as the watches of the night begin; pour out your hearts like water in the presence of the Lord. Lift up your hands to him for the lives of your children."

Lamentations 3:22–27 "Because of the Lord's great love we are not consumed, for his compassions never fail. They are new every morning; great is your faithfulness." I say to myself, "The Lord is my portion; therefore I will wait for Him. The Lord is good to those whose hope is in Him, to the one who seeks Him; it is good to wait quietly for the salvation of the Lord and it is good for a man to bear the yoke while he is young. We are so grateful, Lord, that both Joseph and Michael had very strong faith and loved and adored their sweet Savior, Jesus. We take comfort and solace in this."

On Friday morning, the day after Joseph was brutally killed; I received a phone call from the owner of the landscaping company my son worked for. Mr. Jay Metvet told me how sorry he was about what happened to Joseph and he wanted to offer his condolences. He said he was going to pay for all of the funeral costs and hold a wake for Joseph because there were so many who liked my son. I thanked him for his kindness and generosity. I asked him if he knew what happened to my son and he just said, "No, I really don't." Then he said that he was having a large bell made with Joseph's inscription on it and they would ring the bell every day at noon in honor of Joe. He continued by telling me if there was anything I needed at all to please contact him. He said, "Please work with me, Ms. Miranda. Please work with me." I thought what he had said and how he had said it were peculiar and then he gave me all of his phone numbers. He gave me his work phone, his home phone and his cell phone. He reiterated to please call him if I needed anything. Later I would learn how telling and revealing Mr. Metvet's words would prove to be. The inconceivable travesty of justice was about to unfold. Later that day I also received a phone call from Mick Meanton, the VP of the company, who offered his condolences as well. He said he was very sorry and that Joe was a quick study and very talented. He was very brief on the phone.

On Saturday, that next morning, we were trying to get prepared to go to Ruck's Funeral Home. I was to bring the suit, shirt, tie and other clothing that I wanted Joseph to be buried in. How does a mother do this? You are barely able to stand up, walk, or breathe yet alone shuffle through your precious son's clothing and think what will be the most appropriate to bury your baby in.

I did not even know if I could see Joseph since they had hurt him so badly and the injuries to his beautiful face, head and neck were so severe. My brother told me the funeral director said they were trying but they did not know if we could have an open casket. Somehow, I was able to pick out Joseph's favorite polo button-down, sports jacket, slacks and a tie that he loved and wore often too many special occasions in his young life. That morning before we left, the funeral director did tell us that they had tried but they were very sorry and we would have to have a closed casket.

I was forced to accept that I would never see my precious Joseph again. He went out our front door saying, "Bye, Mom. I love you," as he always did and I ran to tell him I loved him, too, as I always did, but I heard the door close before he heard me. I often now tell myself that I was never supposed to say good-bye to Joseph. I am only to say hello to my precious son when he welcomes me and greets me in heaven. Then I can hold him and kiss him again and tell him how much I love him. I know now for certain that we are never really separated from those we love so deeply; God answers my prayers. They are with us always as we move forward in this life until it is our time for God to call us home. Then we will all be together in the paradise of heaven and know the love, peace, joy and true contentment of eternal life with our Father God and our Lord and Savior, Jesus Christ. *Matthew 7:7 "Ask and it will be given to you; seek and you will find; knock and the door will be opened to you."*

I existed these first few days as only part of a person. I attended the funeral services for my son, although I was not able to see him. Family and friends had prepared beautiful picture boards with photographs of Joseph from throughout his life. You could see his amazing smile, his loving heart, his warmth and affection and how he loved everyone and had such gusto for life. Joseph was very handsome. He lit up a room when he entered and his magnetic personality drew people to him. He had a hug for everyone and loved children. He had shared with me many times, even at the age of nineteen, that he knew he wanted three children and he was going to be the best dad. I smiled and said, "Yes, you will, Joseph. Yes, you will and Mommy will be Mom-Mom."

ROB AND JOSEPH AGES 6 AND 3 SITTING IN FRONT OF OUR FIREPLACE HAPPY AND LOVING.

Rob, Joseph's older brother, had prepared a beautiful montage of photographs and Joe's favorite songs that really captured the heart and soul of Joseph. He had so much love for his family and friends and everyone who touched his life. All of the happy and joyous times throughout his young life were so clearly and vividly depicted that no one could pass by without stopping to view this loving display that was created in honor of Joseph. I still play it and each time I cry, laugh and cry again. I am so grateful that I have this precious gift and I will treasure it forever. The funeral home was very accommodating and set up two DVD players so all who came to show their love and compassion could see and remember how beautiful, precious, loving, funny and happy Joseph was in this life.

I had brought with me one special photograph of Joseph and me together and my love letter to him telling him that I knew where he was and Mommy would be with him and he with me always. I told him I would see him soon and how very much I loved him with all of my heart.

JOSEPH AND I TOGETHER AT FAMILY PARTY; THE LOVE BETWEEN US SO GENUINE AND SO SPECIAL. THIS IS THE PICTURE I HAD PLACED IN JOSEPH'S LAPEL POCKET NEXT TO HIS HEART.

I remember that after the first afternoon of visitation there were just family members still at the funeral home. I stared at the wooden box that my baby lay in and prayed on my knees. I knew I could not see my baby boy because they had hurt him so horribly. I then went into the adjacent room and I kept saying, "I don't know if my Joseph is even in there." No one from our family was ever able to see him due to his severe injuries. I asked my friend, Matt, a police officer, if he would put my picture and my letter to Joseph underneath his jacket lapel next to his heart and kiss him for me. He said, "Of course I will." I waited and watched as Matt walked over to the funeral attendant and asked about my request. I saw the kind man nod yes. Then the gentleman opened up the casket as my family and I stood a good distance away and saw Matt place my special picture and my letter with Joseph as well as a gold cross his father wanted him to have. Then Matt leaned over and kissed my precious son for me for the last time.

I wept with pain and was exhausted from agony, but I knew in my heart and soul that Joseph was home with his Lord and Savior. Joseph had a strong faith in our Lord and was a true believer. His favorite bible verse was *John 3:16 "For God so loved the world that he gave his only begotten Son, so those who believe will not perish, but have everlasting life."* Joseph's favorite book was *"More than a Carpenter"* by Josh McDowell.

That evening from five to seven, the funeral home was packed with so, so many coming to pay their respects and honor my son. I was so deeply moved by our family members and many friends, Joseph's friends, neighbors, co-workers and very kind and caring people from Valley Motors. They all came to show their respect and their sorrow for my loss.

I distinctly recall the owner of the company, Outside Unliving, Jay Metvet and the VP, Mick Meanton and both their wives walking in. They shook my hand and said they were sorry for my loss. I thanked them for their condolences and asked whether the two men, the driver and the spotter, were going to be there. Mr. Metvet said, "Well, he wasn't really a spotter and the driver is not doing well." I just listened and Mick Meanton offered that Joseph was creative and very talented. I asked them, "Do you know how this could have possibly happened?" They just sort of ignored my question and said they didn't know. Then, a little later, the company owner, Mr. Jay Metvet, walked over to me and Joseph's father and handed us a business card. He said, "It was just an accident and all of our employees have their green cards." I was confused and stunned by his remark and gesture and I thought it was very strange and inappropriate. My brother and family members overheard and they later told me they shared my feelings. The card was a Maryland Occupational Safety and Health (MOSH) business card with the words *Brent Timber, Safety Compliance Officer* printed on it. The address was in Hagerstown, Maryland.

JOSEPH IS WITH HIS BEST CHILDHOOD BUDS AS THEY GRADUATED 5TH GRADE FROM TIMONIUM ELEMENTARY SCHOOL. SCOTT ANDRZEJEWSKI IN THE MIDDLE WITH BOW TIE, JOHN DAWSON TO THE LEFT IN SOLID NAVY BLUE SHIRT AND JOSEPH TO THE RIGHT OF SCOTT WITH A BIG SMILE IN WHITE AND NAVY BLUE SHIRT. ALL SO MANY OF JOSEPH'S GOOD FRIENDS AND SUCH GREAT KIDS.

On Tuesday, July 25, 2006, a funeral Mass was held for our beloved Joseph. The church was filled and I was so emotionally saturated with tears as the words of scripture, love, compassion and friendship were spoken by family members and close friends as well as Scott Andrzejewski and John Dawson, Joseph's best childhood friends. How these young men showed me such love, support and honor is truly a blessing. I will never forget the tenderness of their character and the love and compassion in their hearts for Joseph and our family. John read his own loving and beautiful words, saying that Joseph was a blessing to anyone who knew him and he had taught them countless things growing up. Most of all he taught them how to love and how to live every day to its fullest. John also recited a poem by a British poet by the name of *David Harkins* that was so moving. I will treasure their friendship, love and remembrance of Joseph forever. Scott read scripture and also spoke of Joe and he growing up together and all of the wonderful times they shared. All of Joseph's closest and dearest friends have grown into such fine, loving, kind and caring young men. I love them and I am so very proud of all of them. Scott Andrzejewski, John Dawson, Sam Thomsen, Brendan Mayhugh, Kevin Goldstein, Stephen Poggi and Luke Andrzejewski will forever be Joseph's bros and loyal friends. Amanda, a beautiful and loving friend of Joseph's also remains in my heart. She came to my home a few months after Joseph passed and read to me her college paper entitled "Joe's Smile". We sat together as she shared her loving, compassionate, tender and endearing memories of her and Joe when they dated. Amanda is a remarkable young lady, beautiful both inside and out. I will forever treasure, "Joe's Smile", her gift to me from her heart to mine.

Scott, Joseph's best friend, has never forgotten a Mother's Day and brings me flowers and a card each year. He also visits Joseph's resting-place on special occasions and includes Joseph in his life. He had a gold charm made, a crab with Joseph's initials on it, *JAM* and his date of birth to date of rebirth. He wears it always. They used to do everything together as youngsters and especially loved the vacations in Ocean City, Maryland, crabbing out back of our beach home on the bay and playing and swimming on the beach all day. They were inseparable then and such good buddies who became brothers. Scott has given me such strength and support. I love him and respect him with all of my heart.

Joseph was laid to rest at Dulaney Valley Memorial Gardens in our family plot (GEMMA), with his grandfather Joseph Vincent and his cousin Michael Joseph. His headstone reads *Your Loving Heart and Shining Smile Will Light Up Our Hearts Forever, Our Eternal Love.* Embossed in the center of the words is the resurrection cross. As I sat in the chair beside my son's open grave, I prayed and listened to the priest in prayer. The sun was shining and the people seemed to stretch out far and wide over and beyond the green tent. My mother was on one side of me and my siblings and Matt on the other. My brothers, family and best friends were also very close. As the graveside service finished, I kneeled down to kiss the coffin and to tell my baby again how much I loved him and cried out, "Hear Mama, Joseph. I love you. Hear Mama. I love you so much." I knew my Joseph could hear me and I looked up and saw that man's face, Jay Metvet, leaning out of the crowd staring at me. I knew something was very wrong and dark in that man. I kept crying and saying, "I cannot leave my Joseph. I cannot leave my Joseph." It was like I was paralyzed in prayer to my Lord. I held tightly to the two roses I took from his casket flower cascade and prayed. How would I live without my Joseph? The tears would not stop and my mother called to Matt and said, "Matt, get her. Pick her up and carry her." My friend Matt lifted me up and carried me to the limousine. My family members followed and I knew in my heart and soul that Joseph would never leave me. I could feel his presence with me, yet I yearned to embrace him, hug him, stroke his beautiful face and laugh and cry with him. His absence would be unbearable. Inside I was saying, "I don't know how to do this". "Help me, Father. Help me."

While riding in the limousine back to the funeral home, I was seated between my son Rob and my friend Matt. I felt as if my soul and self had left my body and I was suddenly in a conscious state of peace. I suppose I just stared quietly and stopped breathing. I remember my inner soul was in a place of solace and I wanted to remain there. Then I heard frantic voices calling, "Mom, Mom, Adrienne, Adrienne…Oh my God, is she having a heart attack? Help her." They were shaking my arms and I abruptly came back to consciousness. I looked at everyone with confusion and said, "I am okay." *Matthew 5:4 "Blessed are those who mourn, for they will be comforted."*

After the service, we went to the wake, where hundreds of people gathered in memory of Joseph Anthony Miranda, my precious, beautiful son who loved God's green earth and wanted to become a landscaping architect. That was his professional dream. Joseph loved the outdoors and all of God's creatures. From hamster to turtle to fish to bunny to crabs and more as a little guy and then to all of the colorful, beautiful flowers, plants, gardens, trees, shrubs and more—he knew each one by name and origin. He could transform a swampland into the most beautiful garden you ever saw. He was hard working, creative, artistic and very skilled and talented in the landscaping profession. He was so excited about going back to school to get his degree in landscaping architecture, but sadly his dream died with him.

When he was a little guy of about four, he had a pet box turtle that he loved. He played with him every day. One day we were sitting on the front porch just talking. He had his turtle out on the grass and he said to me, "Mom, I really love my turtle. I love the way he comes out of his house and just takes his time and says hello to his friends and then after he eats some grass, he's ready to go back in for a while." I smiled lovingly and then he said, "Mom, do you think he has a TV in there?" I embraced my precious boy and said, "Joseph, Mommy thinks he has everything he needs," and he said, "Yep, so do I, Mom, so do I."

Joseph Anthony Miranda, my angel boy, was born on April 22, Earth Day. God sure knew what He was doing when He brought Joseph into the world He created. Joseph got off the school bus one day running to me laughing and saying, "Mom, they call me Jam at school. You know, because my initials are JAM." I laughed and said, "That is so cute. I love that. But you know it's jam, not jelly…Sweet as jam is what you are." He laughed back.

Ah, my Joseph lived a full life of nineteen years. Such a finite number on what we hope for while on this earth. Although his time was brief, his days here were jammed full—full of love, playfulness, hearty laughter, beautiful giving, fun vacations, sad tears, hard work, congratulations for many accomplishments, a joy of little babies and children, a love for sushi and more sushi. He loved Mom's special crab dishes, crab dip, lasagna, pot roast and tuna casserole supreme and countless birthday parties—oh yes, nineteen. And, oh, how he yearned to be twenty-one—that magical age of rite of passage when he would be all grown-up—but my boy didn't quite make it. However, my boy was spiritually wise beyond his earthly years. He loved Jesus and everyone knew it. He knows all the answers today as he watches over me and all of his family and friends whom he loves so dearly.

Joseph also adored the ocean and the beach and loved swimming, surfing, boarding, jet skiing, boating, crabbing and fun in the sun. Summer was his favorite season. It was in this season of his life that he was brutally taken from me by a criminal act. A horrific, unthinkable, dreadful, violent act by another, a co-worker, stamped out my son's life.

Where would I be without my Lord? He is my rock, my rescue, my restorer and my redeemer. He wipes every tear from my eyes and his compassions are new every morning. His Holy Spirit resides in me, instructing and guiding me every step of the way as I began and continue my crusade for Justice for Joseph. Psalm 18:1–3 "I love you, O Lord, my strength. The Lord is my rock, my fortress and my deliverer; my God is my rock in whom I take refuge. He is my shield and the horn of my salvation, my stronghold. I call to the Lord, who is worthy of praise and I am saved from my enemies."

At the wake there were many family members, friends and coworkers of Joseph from the landscaping company, Outside Unliving. Jay Metvet, the owner, was there but never came up to me. He arranged to have a bus bring in several of the workers of Mexican descent who had also attended the funeral Mass. I know that they were very fond of Joseph and Joseph fond of them.

Within a year, Joseph was promoted three times and became a foreman for the company. He worked on the commercial side instead of the residential side of the business. I knew he liked the workers and he would sometimes say, "Mom, will you make me twelve sandwiches for lunch? I am going to be really hungry tomorrow." I knew who they were for and I smiled and said, "Sure, Joseph." Joseph was popular at work and well liked. He had a hug for everyone and a smile and laugh that were infectious. He could speak a little bit of Spanish and learned a lot about the landscaping business while on the job. He was creative, smart and a quick study. He really had a passion for landscaping and architectural design.

During the wake, I was sitting at a table with my mother and family and again, so many came to offer their sincere condolences. A young man, very kind and handsome, approached me and leaned over to tell me he had something for me. He took a hemp necklace from around his neck and put it in my hands. He said, with a bit of a British accent, "Joe always admired this necklace and would kid with me about how he wanted it. I told Joe in the morning, that Thursday, that I would give it to him by the weekend and it was his. He smiled and it made him really happy, so I am giving it to you for him." I teared up, hugged the young man and told him how sweet, thoughtful and so very kind this was of him. I shared the necklace with my son Rob, who also remembered this very kind gesture so well. It will be an everlasting treasure never to be forgotten. I did recall that Joseph had told me that Outside Unliving did also hire many South Africans and that he really liked the guys. A little later, Earl Magil and Rocky Dipple came over to tell me they were sorry about what happened. I knew that Earl was Joseph's immediate supervisor and Rocky was also a foreman who worked with Joe sometimes.

When they leaned down to talk with me, I asked them if they were there when Joseph was killed. Rocky said yes but that he didn't see anything and Earl just turned beet red in the face and said he was sorry. I asked if the driver and the spotter were there. Rocky said, "Oh, no." I asked how they were doing and Rocky just said, "Not very well." I hugged them both and told them Joseph thought the world of both of them and I thanked them for coming.

I received many gestures of sympathy and empathy and was grateful for the honor and remembrance shown for my precious Joseph. Then, I started feeling extremely tired and felt I needed to go home and try to rest.

My mother agreed and we said our good-byes. The wake was almost over and I knew I had stayed long enough. I did not want to break down into uncontrollable tears there in front of everyone.

We arrived home and I put on my pajamas and wanted to try to sleep. My mother stayed with me. I was still in a fog, but the reality of my broken heart and the agonizing pain throughout my insides was unbearable. Many of my closest family members stayed, too, to help in any way they could. I was so emotionally and physically sick. That week, close family and friends brought food and beverages to my home and were so kind, but the thought of eating made me sick. I had no appetite and all I could do was cry, pray and hold Joseph's picture, my Bible and my loved ones. I was feeling as if a cannonball had blown my entire body to bits.

On Friday morning, July 28, I received a call from the lead investigator with the Maryland State Police, Corporal Kitseng. He was the same man I had spoken with the night that Joseph was killed. He asked how I was doing and told me they still did not know exactly what happened to Joseph. I told him I had a lot of questions and nothing they said made any sense to me and my family. He did tell me that they concluded Joseph was driven over forward. I said I had now seen a picture of a Bobcat and it was completely open in the front. How would the driver not have seen my son in front of him?

I confirmed with him, again, what the piece of equipment that ran over my son was. He said it was a Bobcat skid loader, model G873. I asked how the driver had not seen Joseph, who was five feet eleven, when it was broad daylight. He just said, "I don't know." He told me it was being investigated and they would know more when their tasks were completed. He said he could not release the names of the driver and the spotter and that I should sue the company. He said, "You can't sue us or me because we have immunity." I said, "What? Who is talking about suing? I want to know how this could have possibly happened to my son." I was sobbing and asked him who else was there with him at the scene. He said several other troopers were and that Trooper Hudock arrived first. I asked if there were any drug tests taken on the driver and the spotter. He said no. I asked about the interviews of the two men. Corporal Kitseng told me that the driver was of Mexican descent and they had to bring in an interpreter. I asked, "Who was the Spanish interpreter for the driver?" Corporal Kitseng told me that it was Sergeant Detective Monroe. I asked, "Were you there when he was being interviewed?" The corporal just said he was coordinating other tasks but he was sure that the driver was interviewed.

As more facts and truths unfolded, we would later learn that Sergeant Detective Monroe was never at the scene on July 20, 2006 and that he does not speak Spanish. He was not the Spanish interpreter who interviewed Antoine Ruberra, the driver of the Bobcat. In the next months and beyond, we would realize all of the lies, distortions of truth, crime scene manipulations and disturbances that the Maryland State Police and Outside Unliving employees were guilty of. It was unfathomable and unconscionable.

I said to Corporal Kitseng that in the *Sun* paper there was a tiny article in the middle of the paper written by a reporter named Arwin. He wrote that the driver felt my son tap him on the shoulder before he began to back up and asked to use the Bobcat and that he then backed up and did not know Joseph was still there. How was it possible that he had backed up over my son's head, face and neck? I asked whether a reconstruction had been done. Corporal Kitseng said no. I said, "What? No reconstructionist was brought to the scene? Why?" He said, "Crime scene photographs were taken and there was still a lot to do." I was crying and asked if I could please meet with him and said that my family and I had so many questions. He scheduled August 15 for the meeting. "I asked him where we would meet and he said at the Westminster Barrack and then gave me the directions. I told him I was bringing some of my family members with me. He said come with any questions I had.

Also that day, my friend Matt went to drive Joseph's Jeep Cherokee, still parked at Outside Unliving's parking lot from the day he was killed, back to my home. My brother took him so Matt could drive it back. While Matt was there, the MDSP also met with him and gave him and my brother an envelope with my son's belongings in it that were taken from his pants pocket. Matt returned and parked Joseph's jeep in my driveway and then he and my brother came inside and handed me the white envelope.

A bit later, after Matt left and while my mom was still sleeping, I sat alone at my kitchen table. My tears were glistening in the morning sun that was gleaming through my window. My tears poured out and I did not know how to make them stop. I saw on the outside of the white envelope the word *evidence*. I opened it and through my agony, I removed my son's black leather wallet, the landscaping blueprint of the job he was overseeing that day, his cell phone and one penny. Joseph never carried change. He was like your everyday teen in that regard.

He used to throw his change in a mug on the dresser in his room and always said, "You know, Mom, I like the bucks—the big bucks."

CHAPTER 2

THE SWEET SCENT OF MY SON, MY PENNY FROM HEAVEN

I opened the envelope and held the penny. I kept feeling it over and over again and touching the formed symbols, words and copper. The first words I saw were *In God We Trust* and I kept saying in my heart, "This penny was with my baby when he went to the Lord. This penny is my penny from heaven." Then my Lord said to me as I heard my Holy Spirit, "What is the date on the penny?" I turned it over in my hand and found that the date read *1972*. My heart cried out more to my Jesus and my Joseph…"Oh, thank you, Lord"…You see, Joseph was the age of nineteen and he went on July 20 (7/20). I knew for certain that *1972* was God telling me He had Joseph and Joseph was in heaven. I wept with joy through my suffering heartache and got on my knees for my Savior.

Then I held Joseph's black leather wallet and his cell phone. I, too, touched and felt them and I could smell the sweat and sweet scent of my son, my Joseph. I opened his cell phone and put it next to my ear and my face. It was so soothing to me, just holding his belongings and knowing he was right there with me. The sweet scent and fragrance of my precious son was consuming me and I could feel his love and life. The aroma of extravagant love was so pure, so lovely that it took me to the veined alabaster vase that flowed from Mary's broken heart at the cross. His scent became more concentrated and potent enough that our Lord's scent lingers to this day. The heavy and heart-wrenching smell of our Savior's sweat and blood and the hard reality of His imminent death mingled with my tears and the love that spilled from His broken and beaten alabaster body. Oh, how I love my Jesus; it is only through Him and in Him that I survive. I still, to this day, hold and caress Joseph's belongings and many of his favorite shirts, hemp wristbands and rope bracelets he wore. Joseph's scent is forever a part of me and he, too, lives on in me and through me. I opened my son's black wallet and saw a ten-dollar bill and some cards as well.

I took out a white card with Joseph's signature on it and the signature of someone with a foreign-looking name. I could see that there was very small blue print on the card and some kind of code. There was also a two-year eligibility for the card. It kept bothering me because I had never seen any kind of card like it; it was not a business card and I needed to know what it meant. Later, I called my brother Damian and with a magnifying glass read to him the letters and numbers of the code in blue.

He searched it on the web and then said to me, "Adrienne, this is for NAFTA." I said, "The North American Free Trade Act?" He said yes and then continued by explaining that this code allowed the named person to cross the border and enter into Mexico. I loudly said, "What?" Why in God's name would Joseph have a card obtained for him by Outside Unliving to cross the border and enter Mexico? My brother agreed it was worrisome and more than strange and we were both very upset and completely astounded.

That week I kept going over in my mind all of the conversations Joseph and I had had. We were so close and discussed many topics as well as his job with Outside Unliving. Then it was like a red flag went off in my head and I started to weep in agony.

I distinctly recalled that Joseph came home one day from work, washed up and came down for dinner. He was seated at the kitchen table as I was standing at the kitchen sink and stove preparing our plates.

I looked over at him and saw he had his head down, resting on his arms. I could see that he seemed to be distraught. I walked over and sat down at the table and said, "Joseph, what's the matter, sweetheart?" He kept his head down and said nothing and just kind of sighed. I put my hand on his arm and said again, "Joseph, I know something is bothering you. Please tell Mommy what is wrong." He looked up at me and hesitantly said, "Mom, Outside Unliving does *bad things*." I said, "Joseph, what do you mean? What are you saying?" He just put his head back down and I could tell he did not want to go into any detail. I again said, "Joseph, you need to tell me what you mean by *"bad things"*. Joseph just kept his head down and would not talk. I knew when not to keep pressing him. I then got up from the table, picked up our portable phone, handed it to Joseph and said, "Joe, you are telling me that Outside Unliving does bad things and if you can't even tell Mommy what they are, then you need to call Outside Unliving right now and resign."

I walked back over to the sink. Joseph then came over and put the phone back on the cradle. He turned me and put his arms around me. He kissed me right in the center of my forehead like he always did and said, "Mom, don't worry. I will be fine." "I am only staying till the end of the summer so I can collect a few more paychecks and then I will quit." He said, "You know that I want to be a landscaping architect and I am going to go back to school in September." "Please, Mom, don't worry, I will be fine."

Less than two months later, my baby was crushed to death at the hands of a co-worker and I have all of the proof of what the owner, other employees of the company and the police did to try to cover up the violent and brutal murder of my son.

Earlier that year, Joseph had walked in the door smiling and said, "Mom, Outside Unliving is doing a job at the White House." I said, "What? The White House?" and he said, "Yep." I just said, "Wow, Outside Unliving must really be growing and getting bigger." He answered, "Yeah, they are." This was when Bush was in office.

It felt like my head was spinning but I knew that God was with me. He was showing me my way and He has given me this crusade and journey that will bring purpose and truth, His truth. I would come to know that *Matthew 19:26 "with God all things are possible"*. I had the aforementioned penny made into a circular pendant and I wear it always. It lies on my chest close to my heart and it is truly my "penny from heaven."

I noticed the blueprint that was in Joseph's pocket was the landscaping architectural plan for the job he was working on and overseeing that day, July 20, 2006. Days later, I began to study it and saw that it was for the Windsor Mill Middle School. This school was the first STEM school in our nation. *STEM* stands for *science, technology, engineering and math*. The STEM initiative began that year and is still a primary goal for the education system in the United States.

I thought it was interesting that Outside Unliving was able to win such an important contract and when I noticed the federal contractors, the general contractor and the architectural contractor and knew how huge these companies were, I was surprised. I knew Outside Unliving was a midsize landscaping company, but I thought they only did jobs throughout the state of Maryland. I did not realize that they had opened an office in Ijamsville in 2003 and were greatly expanding.

My story is very involved, intriguing and so compelling that as you read you will at times be shocked with disbelief and at other times you will give thanks and praise to our Lord and Almighty Father, God. I have witnessed firsthand miraculous occurrences that only God could have brought to me. It has been over the last seven years of my life that I have walked this journey. What I have been able to reveal, through the Spirit's guidance, regarding the company owners, their political connections and their criminal misconduct as well as the criminal misconduct of law officials and law enforcement, at every level within the state of Maryland, is unbelievable, appalling, repulsive and unconscionable.

I will keep moving forward until justice for Joseph prevails and all that must be exposed is exposed. My precious son did not die in vain, there is a reason and a purpose for everything on this earth and I will deliver what my Savior directs me to. Proverbs 3: 3–6: "Let love and faithfulness never leave you; bind them around your neck, write them on the tablet of your heart.

Then you will win favor and a good name in the sight of God and man. Trust in the Lord with all your heart and lean not on your own understanding; in all your ways acknowledge him and he will make your paths straight."

Joseph's story and mine are true and vital pieces of a mother and son's life and death that will bring renewal, tears, laughter, heartache, empathy, revelation, justice, God's truth and change that must be made. It will come—I am certain of it. All glory and honor is His.

Without faith we have nothing and without justice there is no peace. Our God is a just and true God and everything happens in His way and in His time. We must be in a personal relationship of love with our Lord and show Him what is on our hearts. *Matthew 22:37–38 "Love the Lord your God with all of your heart, soul and mind, this is the first and greatest commandment."* He already knows our hearts, but He yearns for the love of His children. God is Love. Show Him and tell Him how much you need Him and give all of yourself to Him. He is the way, the truth and the life. There is power in prayer. He has given us the promise of eternal life in His kingdom and I am certain heaven is real.

On August 15, 2006, Joseph's father, Bob, Lisa, my brother Dino, my mother and I attended the meeting at the Maryland State Police Westminster Barrack. The only person present to meet with us was Corporal Kitseng. We introduced ourselves, shook hands and took seats at the table in a conference room. After we sat down, I pulled out the picture of Joseph that Corporal Kitseng suggested I bring so he could get to know Joe.

He had told me during our phone conversations that he wanted to learn all about Joe—what he was like—and really expressed what seemed to be sincere interest, compassion and concern. During the meeting, we asked many questions pertaining to his investigation and listened carefully to Corporal Kitseng's replies. He explained how Joseph was positioned underneath the Bobcat and how he lay in relation to the Bobcat. I specifically asked him if anyone had physically contacted or put their hands on my son. Corporal Kitseng said, "No, no one touched him or pushed him." I asked, "How do you know for sure?" He said, "I am sure because I asked. I asked the spotter and the driver and they said no." I said, "I do not believe this,

Corporal. It isn't making any sense. Please ask again." He said, "OK, I will ask again." My sister, Lisa, asked about the photograph that showed where Joseph was positioned in relation to the Bobcat. She asked if Corporal Kitseng could somehow block Joseph out and bring us a printed copy of the photograph to view so we could better understand what may have happened. He complied and left the room and returned with the print copy of the photograph as requested. We all hesitantly looked unsure of what we might see due to Joseph's severe injuries and then looked deeper.

When we were then made aware of how Joseph lay on his stomach completely underneath the Bobcat and where his head, arms, legs and feet were positioned and situated in relation to the actual size of the Bobcat, we were in disbelief. The small space in between the two left tires and the minimal height of nine inches beneath the undercarriage was alarming. When we were told Joseph's legs were sticking completely out the back of the Bobcat and the left tire was behind Joseph's left armpit, we were in shock. We said to the corporal, "The physics make no sense." "How could Joseph be on the ground, parallel with and underneath the Bobcat with the left rear tire behind Joseph's left armpit, if the Bobcat was driven over Joseph in a forward motion?" "If this is what happened like what you told us, Corporal, the left rear tire would be in front of Joseph's head, not behind his head, shoulder and armpit." We stated that this Bobcat, model G873, would have cleared Joseph and the tire would not be where it is. The left rear tire would be in front of Joseph's left shoulder. "Do you see what we are saying?" we asked.

The corporal looked at us, appearing somewhat puzzled. We continued to ask very pertinent questions, but Corporal Kitseng did not seem to have any logical or reasonable answers. When I told him more about conversations I had had with MOSH and asked him again if we could please know the names of who was involved in the incident of our son's death, he was reluctant. He then proceeded to tell us that Mr. Brent Timber of MOSH had left a message on his voice mail that he did not understand. We asked, "What did the message say?" He promptly picked up the phone, dialed a number and allowed us to listen, firsthand, as he played Mr. Timber's message on speakerphone. We sat astounded at what we heard. To summarize, Mr. Timber said they (MOSH) were finished with their investigation, the incident was ruled an accident, there were no citations given to the company and he would not release some of the employee statements given during his interviews, for fear that these employees might lose their jobs. He continued by saying he knew the family wanted the names of the employees involved and he didn't care what Corporal Kitseng did regarding that—they were done. Obviously, Mr. Timber was insinuating that certain employees of Outside Unliving had made negative remarks about the company. The tears streamed down my face and Corporal Kitseng conveyed he would do all that he could for us. We then, of course, asked for the names and he gave them to us. The name of the driver of the Bobcat was Antoine Ruberra and the spotter was Pete Coldwin. As we gathered our belongings, notes, the one copy of the aforementioned photograph and our aching agony that consumed the room, I thanked him and asked him if I could give him a hug. He let me and as we flowed out of the barrack, I recall him saying, "Sometimes it takes years and years before you find out what happened and cases are ever solved." I extended my appreciation again and said I knew he would be on it and we would find the truth.

Now the red flag that was waving in my face was the bloodshed of my precious son. The revelation of what I would begin to know as my reality, my life, unveiled with each passing day. I searched and delved deep for truth and I could feel the Holy Spirit working in me, guiding me specifically in His purpose. Truth was the very least my Joseph deserved. We had to wait more than six weeks before the police would even give us the names of the two men involved in Joseph's death. We realized that we never did receive one message, flower, sympathy card, or any acknowledgment of Joseph's death from Pete Coldwin or his family. There was absolutely no remorse or attempt to offer any extension of sympathy to us and Joseph's family—not a single gesture.

In our hearts and minds, this said a lot about who these people were and continue to be. They are obviously troubled and their response was certainly cold and heartless.

As essential facts, evidence, physics, science, information and proof unfolded before my eyes, I remained relentless in digging further in order to confirm the underlying wrongdoing and evil in the wretched, wicked cover-up and the vicious, heinous killing of my sweet son.

JOSEPH GETTING READY FOR A WRESTLING MATCH AT TOWSON HIGH SCHOOL. HE WAS VERY STRONG, AGILE AND SKILLED. HE WON SEVERAL AWARDS FOR "WRESTLING". HE WAS ALWAYS FOCUSED AND HAD A GREAT TEAM SPIRIT.

In early September, I noticed a message left on my son's memorial page that was set up for his family and friends on MySpace. The message referenced Outside Unliving and the VP of the company, Mick Meanton. I sent a message back to the young man and thanked him for his kindness and remembering Joe. I noticed he had also worked for Outside Unliving, so I gently asked if he would please contact me to talk. He wrote back that he would and gave me his cell phone. I would soon learn his identity and that he knew Joseph from high school. Joseph was a graduate of Towson High School and was on the wrestling team. He became quite skilled and performed well. I really learned a lot about all that was involved not only physically but psychologically in the sport of wrestling. I went to all of Joseph's matches and would be amazed at the focus, strength, skill and techniques that were required. Joseph was very lean, strong and agile and I could see he really knew the sport and felt passionate about his performance. He really loved those years of wrestling for Towson High and he improved not only on the mat but academically as well. He was on the honor roll, felt a brotherhood with his teammates and loved and respected both Coach Yoska and Coach Simmons. Joe shared a heartfelt fondness and friendship with his coach, Phil Simmons. Phil taught Joseph so much about wrestling and would also go hiking with him and on outdoor excursions. They had a special bond and I will forever be grateful and appreciative for all of the kindness, teaching, support and guidance Phil Simmons gave to my son. Joseph won several awards and medals and was honored for his success in wrestling. I was proud of him and could see how hard he practiced and worked to give it his all.

MOM GIVING JOE A BIG CONGRATS KISS FOR HIS HIGH SCHOOL GRADUATION. HE WAS SO EXCITED AND OVERJOYED TO GRADUATE AND I WAS SO VERY PROUD OF HIM.

Joseph and Scott hugging each other on their Graduation Day; they were both so very happy. Joseph will always remain in Scott's heart and Scott in Joseph's.

This young man who sent his Myspace message was very sorry about what happened to Joe and provided other names of other employees who he knew worked on the same day Joseph was killed. I learned after speaking with him that he also went to Towson High and wrestled. He informed me about Outside Unliving's business practices and that they had a fake company set up for illegal immigrants. He had wanted to quit the company a few weeks prior to Joseph's death and added that the company had serious safety issues and did not care about their employees at all. He was able to provide some names for me that proved to be very helpful—for example, Jack Brodeman, Dick Stilling, Rocky Dipple, Ocar Raviera and a few others. He also said that he had heard five people saw what happened but he didn't know who.

He said that he did not work directly with Joe but saw him often and knew that he was promoted to a higher-level position, a foreman. He told me Joe was a great guy and a hard worker. He had only heard something about Joe being hit by the rear or back of the Bobcat when he was killed.

He also knew Pete Coldwin, the so-called spotter and said he had tried to call Pete several times on his cell phone after Joe was killed but Pete would never pick up.

Upon receiving this information from this employee who had just quit Outside Unliving, I immediately called Corporal Kitseng to tell him about it. The corporal wrote down the names and said he would follow up with me as soon as he checked it out. I also recall the young man telling me that he remembered one of the supervisors, Sammie, who was there on July 20, was leaving Outside Unliving after thirteen years of employment. It ended up being the case that Corporal Kitseng never did find or talk to Sammie. His police report just said *NFD*, meaning "not found." However, later, in November of 2007, when I finally received the police reports in piecemeal format, I saw Sammie's name right on the Outside Unliving's employee list. He was the only Sammie they had employed there. Corporal Kitseng had possession of this list for four months after Joseph was killed but somehow could not find Sammie's name on it when it was right under his nose. This is just the beginning of the outrageous, inept, useless, clumsy, incompetent, unskilled and unjust investigative process used throughout the criminal investigation of Joseph's death. Needless to say, laziness and malice combined with idiocy of certain MDSP in the criminal investigation of my son's death was a recipe for disaster. What will be revealed over time—what I was put through by these corrupt, lying, deceitful and malicious Maryland State Police—you will find unconscionable and detestable. They tried so hard to beat me down over and over again as well as ridicule me. They withheld crime scene photographs from the medical examiners, withheld crucial investigative reports done by an expert homicide detective in their own agency and would not polygraph the suspect, Pete Coldwin. They were ordered to conduct the polygraph and knew Coldwin lied repeatedly about what happened to Joseph the day "he" brutally and intentionally took his life, but they did not. It would all unfold with each passing day, week and month. I first tried to put my faith and trust in them to do the right thing and get to the bottom of how my son was tragically killed, but just the opposite actually occurred.

In mid-September I received a phone call from the lady who had helped us with Joseph's funeral arrangements at Dulaney Valley Memorial Gardens. She had been so kind, compassionate and responsive to us. I could sense in her voice that she was shaken up a bit and hardly knew how to begin her conversation with me. I listened as she told me that Mr. Michael Meanton from Outside Unliving had called her and was very abrupt and rude. He told her to make sure that Joseph's five thousand dollar death benefit from social security be sent to him. He emphatically told her to not contact the family about this. He continued, "We paid for the funeral costs and twelve thousand dollars was more than enough." "I want that check for five thousand dollars sent to me."

I knew she was upset but felt that she had to inform me. I thanked her for letting me know and I just said that if that is what is supposed to be, then so be it; it is fine. Again, I just felt that these people were lying, greedy slime and I was not surprised. I knew they were covering up the heinous crime committed against my son so there would be no repercussions or anyone looking deeper into their company and their practices.

We learned that Trooper Stan Huddak was the first to arrive at the scene from the MDSP on July 20. He took pictures of the crime scene, talked with some employees, detailed how Joseph lay underneath and was positioned in relation to the Bobcat and called for a criminal investigation. Weeks had now gone by and fall was approaching. I had heard nothing back from Corporal Kitseng about his follow-up tasks and the name I had provided. When I would leave messages, he would not return my calls. One day, Detective Sergeant Buck Monroe, the assisting detective, told me, "Corporal Kitseng has been in training and you are not the only case we have." I said, "I realize my son's case is not the only one you have, but I have been very patient and Corporal Kitseng said he would get back to me last week. What kind of training is he in? Homicide and detective training?" Sergeant Buck Monroe said yes. I asked, "How long has Corporal Kitseng been in homicide work?" and he answered, "About three years." I asked if he would please give my message to him and please call me to discuss other information I had just received from MOSH. He said he would.

It was really starting to sink in for me and my family that the MDSP had put a rookie homicide detective on my son's brutal and violent case, when they had so many seasoned, experienced, highly skilled detectives who had worked criminal cases for years. I wondered why they did this. It wasn't right. On the day Joseph was killed, July 20, 2006, both the MDSP and the Baltimore County Police arrived at the scene. Joseph was killed on a dirt road that ran right through Jay Metvet's property of about ninety acres. At this location he had also had his mansion built and it was where his offices were located. Both agencies arrived because each thought Joseph had been killed in their jurisdiction. You see, the Baltimore-Carroll County line runs right through the property and the Baltimore County Police thought it was their scene to investigate. However, we later found out that the MDSP never even used a GPS to determine the correct jurisdiction and that they allowed the owner, Jay Metvet, to make that determination. This is outrageous. Mr. Metvet had no authority, in any way, to determine the jurisdiction of my son's death. However, for some reason, it was good enough for the MDSP.

Later, as my story unfolds, you will see the intense effort that I was consumed with to have a survey completed to accurately determine the correct county my son was killed in. I will tell you now that it was not Carroll County but Baltimore County where my son lay bleeding out in the burning hot sun on a dirt road and where they left him underneath that Bobcat for four hours. You wouldn't do that to a deceased animal in the road. I was trying so hard to stop my tears every day, but they would not. Each morning I awoke with a knife right through my heart, trying desperately to get through another day. My tears flowed 24-7 and I wiped them with the grace of God's mercy. I told Joseph, "I know he lives with Jesus and watches over me. I know, Joseph, that you want me to find peace. I will my precious. I trust in God our Father and it is His will be done. All glory and honor is His."

Before Trooper Huddack even arrived at the scene, an officer, Tom Feebus from the Hampstead Police Department, arrived. He agreed with Mr. Metvet about the jurisdiction. It turns out that Officer Tom

Feebus had no business being there at all. It was not his crime scene or jurisdiction in any way, shape, or form, yet later we will see that this Hampstead officer Feebus remained at the crime scene until nine in the evening. Here again was another peculiar and more-than-unusual practice of a police officer remaining at a crime scene investigation that he had no authority or jurisdiction over whatsoever. I would later find out when I called the Hampstead Police Department and spoke with a nice woman who worked in administration that Officer Feebus was no longer employed there. He resigned in September 2006 and went to work at Recreation and Parks in PA. I asked her if she would have access to his notes turned in for his work hours on July 20, 2006 and she said she should. So after I had introduced myself and said I was trying to gather information about the crime that occurred on July 20 on Saint Paul Road, she said she understood. She came back to the phone and said, "Yes, I have pulled up Officer Feebus's notes for that day and that address and it reads that he arrived at Saint Paul Road at half past three and then left after ten minutes when he was informed it was not his jurisdiction." I thanked the woman and thought of how strange this all was. Officer Feebus had outright lied about the time he worked that day and where he spent it in his written report submitted to the Hampstead Police Department.

I was learning in my heart and soul that so many people had covered up, lied, created confusion purposely, blamed the victim (my son) and committed criminal misconduct on so many levels and they were sure they would get away with it. Nothing was adding up. And I was sure they would not get away with it. I knew for certain that God was giving me a very specific purpose and that He had His plan in what ways truth and justice would be revealed. As a Christian woman, I know that my Lord will only put upon me what I am able to handle. He knows my heart, my brokenness, my grief and everything under heaven. Almighty God gives each of His children their own unique gifts, talents and abilities and He uses us as His instruments to fulfill His purpose. I know there will be a greater good from all of the trials, tribulations and suffering. Who of us knows better than Father God about pain, agony, suffering and grief for one's child, as He gave His only Son, Jesus Christ, to be tortured, beaten down, ridiculed, whipped, chained and nailed to a cross with thorns through his head and a sword through his side to be crucified to death to save us. His promise to us is true and everlasting so that we may know and love our Lord and Savior intimately and follow Him as His Holy Spirit dwells in us and guides us in His purpose. I know that this is my truth. My Jesus, My Beautiful One whom I adore—I will follow you all the days of my life and am certain your presence is with me always. I know my Joseph ascended right into your loving arms when he exhaled his last breath and then in the blink of an eye inhaled with rebirth into your heavenly kingdom that does, indeed, await all of your loving children.

In late October 2006, Corporal Kitseng called me to follow up. He said that he did talk with Joseph's friend on the phone and that yes, his friend gave me the information I passed on. He continued to tell me he did speak with Jack Brodeman and he said it was fine for me to call him. The corporal gave me Mr. Brodeman's phone number.

He continued saying that he drove over to Outside Unliving with two other Maryland State Police officers and that they stayed outside talking with Antoine Ruberra, the Mexican driver of the Bobcat, while he went in the office and tried to keep the VP, Mick Meanton, occupied. The corporal said, "We talked about everything and when he tried to ask him about his employee Omar Raviera, Mr. Meanton said, "I have a lot of people named Omar and I don't know who you are talking about". Corporal Kitseng then told my brother Damian and I, in separate phone conversations, that Mick Meanton then told him to get off of his property. I proceeded to ask the corporal, "Since you are conducting a criminal, homicide investigation, does he have the right to order you off his property?" The corporal didn't really answer. I asked, "Can't you get the payroll records or employee lists for the business?" He said, "I can try, but they may have to be subpoenaed." I said, "Please try and at least please get the employee list for Outside Unliving through June, July and August—especially July, when my son was killed."

During my research for the company, I noticed a frightening, unsettling photograph on Outside Unliving's website. You see, my beautiful, handsome son was driven over by a 7600-pound steel vehicle, a Bobcat model G873. Joseph was found lying flat on the ground, on his stomach, completely underneath the Bobcat. Both of his legs were sticking straight out the center of the back of the Bobcat. The left side of Joseph's head, face and neck had been completely run over by the rear left tire of the Bobcat and crushed, but Joseph had no broken bones below his neck. His face was completely disfigured and distorted on the left side, his brain matter was extruding from the top-left portion of his skull, (note) the brain matter of my baby was undisturbed and the rear tire ended up behind his upper left shoulder and his armpit. Since his brain matter was undisturbed this proves that the tire never moved in a forward motion back over Joseph because the brain matter would have been crushed or damaged. The picture on the company website was of a handsome young man's face, similar looking to Joseph, but the complete left side of his face was missing. There was no JPEG number for the photo, just the name *OUjpg.000* and when I saw it, I became very upset; it frightened me and was extremely disturbing.

I showed other family members and they, too, were upset and taken aback. I do not know if this was some kind of strange and eerie artwork or sculpture, but neither I nor my family had ever seen anything like it and it was too demonstrative of Joseph's horrific injuries. I will tell you now that there are people involved in this heartbreaking nightmare that I have been living who are cruel, hateful, sadistic, mean, evil, criminal and malicious. Also, you will see as you continue reading the deep, hideous and repulsive criminal misconduct, lies, deceit, cover-ups and manipulations perpetrated by police, law enforcement, local and regional states attorneys, the company employees and certain personnel within the state of Maryland at every level, including the highest. What is going on in the state of Maryland is reprehensible and detestable and must be stopped.

In early October, I had made a call to Mr. John Feilding, the secretary for the Department of Labor, Licensing and Regulation (DLLR) in Maryland, under Governor Robert Ehrlich's executive leadership at that time. I explained to Mr. Feilding my circumstances and our fight for justice for Joseph. I said that we insisted on getting answers and the truth. He was very compassionate and listened intently. He said he understood and shared with me that he, too, had lost a child. I was humbled and sorrowful with him and I knew he felt empathy for us. Mr. Feilding told me he would definitely get in touch with the supervisor and have him contact us for a meeting. I expressed how deeply I appreciated his response and promptness.

In mid-October, I did finally receive the MOSH documents, safety sign-in sheets and two Outside Unliving CDs provided by them for MOSH compliance and their so-called investigation. I also received the written statements given to the MOSH Officer Brent Timber by Pete Coldwin and Antoine Ruberra, the driver and the spotter. I noticed as I searched each document that the written statements given by Pete Coldwin and Antoine Ruberra made no sense—they were completely contradictory—and Pete Coldwin admits he pushed and pulled my son Joseph. This was what I needed to start to understand what actually happened that dreadful day. It was evident that Pete Coldwin had made physical contact with Joseph the day he was killed. I immediately left a message for Corporal Kitseng because he was not picking up. Later that night he called and I told him what the documents in the MOSH package revealed. I asked, "Do you have the MOSH reports?" and he said he did. "Well, don't you see where Pete Coldwin says he pushed and pulled Joseph?" He just said, "I haven't bothered to look at the MOSH reports." I could not believe his aloofness. I repeated, "Pete Coldwin pushed and pulled my son on the day he was killed." "You need to look at the MOSH reports." "When my family and I met with you on the fifteenth of August at the barrack, you told me no one put their hands on Joseph and you knew because you asked." "I requested that you ask again and you said you would." "You need to do this to get to the truth of how my son was killed." "You need to interview Pete Coldwin again." He said, OK, and that he would get back to me.

I continued going through the MOSH package sent to me upon my request. I found hundreds of safety sign-in sheets with all of the Hispanic names whited out by Outside Unliving. My brother and I looked at each page and sure enough, we found Omar Raviera written on the sheets the week before Joseph was killed; we watched both CDs for compliance and not one of them had anything about instruction in safety or one function or activity pertaining to safety. Outside Unliving did have its own safety policies and handbook and in it the rules and requirements state that all equipment must have backup alarms and that all drivers of any equipment must have a driver's license. We allege that the Bobcat involved in the killing of my son had no backup alarm and Mr. Antoine Ruberra had no driver's license. Yet MOSH did not issue one citation to this very unsafe and dangerous company. After Joseph's death, we learned this same Bobcat remained in use to be driven every day, taking the risk of causing severe injury, serious disability, or even death to another employee.

The Maryland Occupational Health and Safety (MOSH) department in the state of Maryland is completely inept, useless, incompetent and deviant. In its own policies, practices and manual, it states that in a catastrophic event the closest MOSH office is to respond. My son lay crushed to death under a Bobcat skid loader, bleeding out profusely in the burning hot sun and they left him there for four hours until a MOSH inspector came from West Virginia. When I asked the MDSP and MOSH why they did that and didn't call the Baltimore MOSH office, just twenty-five minutes away, they just looked at me dumbfounded. The MDSP said Rod Chimpall, the director in Hagerstown, made that decision and that that was MOSH, not them.

When I asked for a meeting with MOSH because I had many questions and I wondered what their role was in determining if an incident where a person has been killed was a crime or not, they were a bit reluctant but then agreed to a meeting. The corporal had already told me that when MOSH arrived so late, they had already removed Joseph because it was over three and a half hours that he had laid there. The corporal also told me that when the MOSH inspector Brent Timber arrived, he never touched the Bobcat at all. He never turned it on; he did nothing to inspect it. All he did was walk around it and then went to talk with the owner of the company, Jay Metvet.

I could hardly believe what I was hearing. I was already in such emotional, psychological and physical agony that I did not know how much more outrageous and unending injustice and lack of due diligence and duty that I could handle. These people sounded like a bunch of unqualified idiotic, lazy cops and the MOSH inspector sounded like a pencil pusher who knew nothing about equipment inspections.

In late October, I received a letter from Mr. Carl Loory, the deputy commissioner for the Division of Labor and Industry. He extended an opportunity for us to schedule a meeting with MOSH and their representatives who were involved in Joseph's death investigation. He said he had to talk with some others and he would get back to me in the near future with some dates. I thanked him and said that this did need to take place because we had many questions for MOSH about their conduct during the death investigation of our son.

On October 23, 2006, my family and I made a trip to Ocean City, Maryland. We had a beach home there on the bay at 117th Street. All the boys—Michael, David, Rob and Joseph—loved it growing up as they spent their summer vacations there. My sister and I kept the beach house for years and have so many wonderful, loving and treasured memories of all of the fun in the sun our boys and we enjoyed. When Michael, Joseph's cousin, was killed in 1999, my sister, Lisa, dedicated a special tree in the memorial park that was started right there on Jamestown Road, which is at 117th Street. We all attended the dedication and watched Michael's tree grow and bloom beautifully each year.

JOSEPH WAS HIS HAPPIEST IN THE SUMMER MONTHS CRABBING OUT
BACK ON THE DECK IN OCEAN CITY AND AT THE BEACH. HE LOVED
EVERYTHING ABOUT GOD'S OCEANS AND SEA CREATURES.

ME HUGGING MY PRECIOUS JOSEPH ON OUR DECK IN OCEAN CITY......HE WAS SO
HAPPY AND LOVED BEING AT THE BEACH AS MUCH AS WE COULD GET THERE!

Today, the memorial park is filled with various kinds of beautiful trees and each one is dedicated in memory to a loved one that cherished Ocean City and all of its treasures. Before that piece of land became a memorial park, our boys and our family would walk that property up to the beach. We walked by thousands of times and often the boys would play sports—soccer and football—and laugh and play like such free spirits and with love for those summer days. How they all loved the ocean, the beach, the boardwalk, the rides, the waterslides, the bay, the boats, jet skiing, fishing and crabbing. Joseph especially loved crabbing and would sit on the dock of the bay, when he was a toddler, for hours. He grew into a young man who learned a lot about crabbing, sea creatures, fish and dolphins and loved always being around the water. He loved to swim, scuba dive and surf and of course loved Maryland steamed crabs, sushi and all kinds of seafood.

At this time and on this day, we were dedicating a special tree in memory of Joseph. I recall going to Ocean City a few weeks before the dedication to have everything prepared for all of our family to attend and to choose the special tree that Joseph would want. Joseph loved music and the first song on his iPod before he was killed was the medley of a musical version of *"What a Wonderful World"* and *"Somewhere Over the Rainbow"* by a Hawaiian artist who played the ukulele. Joseph always loved the words to *"What a Wonderful World"* and I remember that when he was twelve and we were driving in the car, I had the radio on and was singing along to this beautiful song with Louis Armstrong. Joseph listened to the words and then said, "Mom, what is that song called"? "I love it." I told him it was called *"What a Wonderful World."* He smiled over at me and said, "I love the lyrics and I want that song played at my wedding when I get married." I smiled and said, "I know, Joseph. I love this song to and it has always been one of my favorites." Joseph also loved the band 311 and one of his favorite songs they wrote was *"Beyond the Gray Sky."* It is a very meaningful and beautiful song and throughout the lyrics the word *candle* is sung. Joseph had already purchased his ticket to attend the 311 concert in September of 2006 with all of his friends, but sadly he did not live long enough. Joseph's brother, Rob, somehow connected with the lead singer and their agent and conveyed to them Joe's story. They told Rob how very moved they were and that they would do their best to give Joseph Miranda a shout-out from the stage before playing *"Beyond the Gray Sky"* and they did just that. All of Joe and Rob's friends and so many more were overjoyed at the concert and you can hear their hearts and love for Joseph and 311 as Rob recorded it all. When Rob played it for me, I knew Joseph was right there and he did not miss the concert; his spirit joined in and was present for all of the jubilation. I will never forget 311 for their compassion, love, concern and honor in remembering Joseph in their music and their hearts. They will always be so very special to us.

Joseph always liked candles and candlelight whether it was around our home or our fireplace or when we were roasting marshmallows or having a special dinner.

I recall meeting with Mr. Purneil, the coordinator and director of the memorial park. He was such a kind, gentle, faith-filled and compassionate man. When we met I told him about Joseph's and Michael's tragic and untimely deaths at the age of nineteen. I said that I wanted to choose the perfect tree that I know Joseph would want and I have talked to him and prayed about it.

Mr. Purneil showed me four specific trees that had just been planted and were ready for dedication. He took me to each one and detailed the origin of the tree, its name, how tall each would grow and whether they blossomed. I listened intently and in my heart I was saying, "Joseph, give me a sign and show Mommy which one you want." As we walked together over to a beautiful, deep-green pine, Mr. Purneil said, "This tree is an evergreen pine. "It is known for its rich green color and strength and it will grow more than thirty feet tall up toward the sun and blue sky." "See these seedlings, he said?" "They are called candles." And right away I knew in my heart and soul that his was the tree Joseph had chosen. He continued, explaining that these candles then become cones and that the pinecones flourish every year. I started to cry and thank Mr. Purneil as I told him, yes, this was the tree and why. He then prayed with me. Now,

Joseph's memory tree is beautiful, healthy, strong and tall. Over the last seven years, I have taken one of the pinecones from the tree and placed it in a special place for Joseph. The memory plaque underneath his tree reads, *Joseph Anthony Miranda 1987–2006* and *Your love and vibrance will forever be reflected in the warmth of the sun, our eternal love.*

I pray love, love, love it is right here; let's smile together, my sweet son. I hold you and I hear you so close that I may sleep and close my eyes with your smile on mine. Let's rest together, Joseph; a stronger day awaits—I am certain of it. Watch over Mommy, my angel son and I will do better to be ready and worthy to receive you and my Lord, reaching out to help me along my way. Together we are reunited in His promise and still you live so vividly and perfectly in my heart. For now I know that God tells me my heart is not really broken. For my heart is you, Joseph and my Jesus and you are more alive than ever. My Holy Spirit has taken over and will carry me where I need to go. I thank you, sweet Jesus, for lighting my way; I love you so deeply that I will obey. May all that I seek be good and right and reveal to me your truth and miracles that you will to prevail. I pray, I listen, I seek, I grow and I see. Behold my spirit, Father and enrich my soul to please you, Lord. May my Joseph assist you to work through me in my journey; I will never leave him and you will never leave me. Have mercy on me, Father and know that I trust in you with all of my heart, soul and being. Love is the strongest power in the universe and you, Father God, are Love. It is this miraculous gift of love that you have given me and my son. Praise be to you, Father, as I bow my head in prayer and my tears are swallowed up by your ever-present grace and compassion. Amen. Alleluia.

During September and October 2006, I was making many phone calls to try to find legal representation. Joseph's father and I first met with a well-known attorney in Towson, Maryland and reviewed all of the circumstances with him. At first he seemed very interested, but then after we were jerked around, misinformed about statutes in Maryland and put off due to his busy schedule, we realized that he was only wasting our time. I continued, determined to find a good, decent attorney who would stand up with us and help us.

I continued making phone calls every day and writing letters. I spoke with an attorney in Washington, DC and explained as best as I could, in summary to him, all that had happened and was taking place. He set up a meeting with my sister, my brother and his wife, Joseph's father and me. Attorney Cutler and his investigators were very compassionate and listened intently to what we had been told about my son's death. We explained that the Maryland State Police was acting strangely, nothing was making sense and everything scientifically and forensically proved that Joseph was backed up over and killed. Yet the MDSP still kept telling us Joseph was driven over forward.

In the MOSH package I received there was an invoice from where the Bobcat was purchased. It showed the year and model of the Bobcat G873, the specifications of its manufacturing and that a backup alarm was "to be installed at a later date." This was very essential to our case because we presumed that this Bobcat involved in the death of my son had no backup alarm on the day he was killed. It is mandatory and policy that all vehicles that have an obstructed rearview must be equipped with a backup alarm. We already knew that when the MOSH inspector, Mr. Timber, came all the way from West Virginia as my son lay in a pool of blood crushed to death by the rear left wheel, he did nothing. Mr. Timber never touched the Bobcat or checked to see if a backup alarm was installed and functioning properly or if any of the mechanics of the Bobcat were faulty. All he did was walk around it and then went to talk with the owner, Jay Metvet. Then, after a few interviews, they closed their investigation, calling it an accident and not issuing one citation to Jay Metvet and his company.

CHAPTER 3

BEYOND HUMAN COMPREHENSION

I showed the invoice to Attorney Cutler and his team and they were very disturbed and said, "No one ever checked to see if there was a working backup alarm?" We said, "No, we are certain of it, no one ever checked." They immediately wanted to know exactly where Outside Unliving was located and Attorney Cutler drafted a letter to the company saying they would be representing us and they would like to meet with them. Their letter was completely ignored, but they visited Outside Unliving anyway. While there, they saw the Bobcat model G873 that said *YARD* on it in black letters and they checked the serial number. They had waved down the Mexican man who was operating it that morning and spoken with him briefly. He confirmed himself to be Antoine Ruberra. When they asked him if the Bobcat went "beep, beep, beep" when backing up, he shook his head and said no. They then observed the driver operating the Bobcat in a reverse motion and heard no backup alarm. This occurred on November 1, 2006, just three and a half months after Joseph was brutally killed.

In November, I received a phone call from Corporal Kitseng telling me he did meet with Pete Coldwin. He said they met in a BB&T Bank parking lot. He started to tell me that he asked Pete Coldwin about pushing Joe and Mr. Coldwin said he never said that. The corporal said, "It is in the police report and the MOSH report and you cannot take back something you already said." Pete Coldwin asked the corporal, as they sat is his police car, "Am I going to be arrested?" Corporal Kitseng assured him he was not and said he needed to know more about the pushing. Pete Coldwin told the corporal that he and Antoine Ruberra were loading dirt into a dump truck and Joe Miranda came up and said he needed to use it. Pete Coldwin said, "No, we are not finished and you will have to wait." He then said that Joe Miranda tried to jump in the Bobcat and pull Ruberra out and he had to grab the end of Joe Miranda's shirt and pull him to tell him to stop. Pete said he got irritated and told Joe, "We are not done—wait, I said." Pete Coldwin continued and said, "A few minutes later was when the Bobcat was moving forward and Joe Miranda ran up next to it and jumped up on top of the left front tire and his foot slipped off and he fell between the two left tires. I think his foot got stuck underneath the tire. After I put my hand across my neck to signal Antoine to stop, he got out and saw Joe underneath the Bobcat." Pete Coldwin said he tried to stop Antoine but it was too late. Pete Coldwin said, "I went into the office and said, "Joe Miranda is dead." The corporal asked Mr. Coldwin, "What did you hear when it happened?" Mr. Coldwin said "it sounded like a watermelon being squished." The corporal continued and asked Mr. Pete Coldwin if he would be willing to take a polygraph test. Pete Coldwin replied, "I don't really like the polygraph, but if and when you ask me, I will let you know."

I was in shock and knew something was very wrong and Pete Coldwin was lying. The corporal said he was going to submit the necessary paperwork to administer the polygraph test to Mr. Coldwin and he would be in touch. He also said he was still working on trying to get the employee list of the company. I thanked him and said OK. I now knew for certain that I had to find an attorney to help me. We had started hearing so many negative remarks about Outside Unliving and their business practices and nothing was making any sense.

During this time, I had asked my sister to call Ruck's Funeral Home. In the few police reports I had received from MOSH, they used the term *decapitated.* On July 20, the owner, Jay Metvet, said he was out in the field and someone came screaming that someone had been decapitated. I was crying so hard and needed to know if this had happened to my baby. My sister called and spoke with the funeral representative and he assured her that while Joseph's injuries to his face, head and neck were very severe, he was *not decapitated.*

I had started doing research on the company and the owner through the Internet to see what I could find out about them. This ended up being a daunting but very necessary task. Each day there would be a piece of information that would connect me to another fact about the company, its owner, its top-level employees and its business and additional businesses. It was like connecting the dots of a disturbing maze and then finding all the puzzle pieces to put it all together.

In early December, I finally received a phone call from Corporal Kitseng and he said he could not tell me anything except that "there could be more serious charges." I said, "Corporal, please help me to understand better what you are saying. Are you going to make an arrest on Pete Coldwin?" He just said, "No, I cannot tell you any more at this time." I asked if they had done the polygraph test on Pete Coldwin, but again Corporal Kitseng would tell me nothing. He just ended the phone call and said he would get back to me in a few weeks.

All of December went by and I heard nothing from Corporal Kitseng. I started calling and would get no answer on his phone line. I left messages for him to please return my call and give me an update. But he did not and I was just ignored.

Now was the Christmas season, my first Christmas without my sweet son. All around me was Joseph. I was hurting badly. I could only think of how much Joseph loved everything about the holidays. "Where is my Joseph?" I cried out again and again. "Oh Lord, help me heal and surrender my agony to you." The pain was heavy, so heavy. I was not able to decorate, bake, shop, put up a tree, or sing carols, not without you, Joseph, though I knew deep in my heart that where he was, so was Jesus. I think of how we used to decorate the tree and you and Rob would help me every year.

Psalm 34:15–19 "The eyes of the eyes of the Lord are on the righteous and his ears are attentive to their cry; the face of the Lord is against those who do evil, to cut off the memory of them from the earth. The righteous cry out and the Lord hears them; he delivers them from all their troubles. The Lord is close to the brokenhearted, they may have many troubles but the Lord delivers them from them all." Your special ornament, since the age of three, was Rudi, a precious little red velvet reindeer with a smile and a tiny red nose. You loved him so much and even last year when you were eighteen and Mom was decorating, you still said, "Mom, where is Rudi?" as you did every year. You were lying across the couch eating some toll house cookies and you got up and placed him exactly where you wanted him on the tree. You and Rob treasured that every year. Remember Rob's was the Superman ornament that lights up and turns from Clark Kent to Superman in a phone booth? Oh, how much joy and fun we had over the Christmas season. I could not take Rudi out this year or even put up my manger, but the Lord knows I was on my knees to him. I became so sick I stopped breathing and Mom-Mom and Aunt Lisa called 911. The paramedics came and took my blood pressure and hooked me up to some kind of monitors. They were so kind. I recall them asking me if I was going to take my life. I said, "Oh no," through my tears. I told them that if I did that, I would never go to heaven and see my son. They answered, "That is right, Ms. Miranda. That is right." I recall holding tightly to Jam, the little cuddly pup that you gave me for Mother's Day. Remember, Joseph, how much I loved him when you gave him to me? He has a red heart on his floppy sweet ear that says *#1 Mom*. I still sleep with him and your T-shirt that I encased in a pillow. Holding Jam, your pillow and my Bible was the only way I could sometimes close my eyes and get rest.

I see your face light up, Joseph, and I am able to find you. I can feel you right next to me. I close my eyes and I see you everywhere. My cheeks feel your kiss and my arms your embrace. You tell me, "I love you, Mom and I hold on with grace. The grace of my Father will carry me these days and I love the gift of my Savior's birth on this Christmas morn. He came and called you my sweet son. He carried you home and I wait to come. I pray to Jesus to ease my pain and give me the strength I must have for our sweet Rob, your brother. I know how much you love each other. I love my two sons so very much. There is a plaque that sits on my foyer table that reads *there's a special place in heaven for the mother of two sons.*

I sometimes felt your little kicks as I just lay there and felt your precious, miraculous life in my womb. It is a joy, tenderness and special love that only a mother can know. The bond of mother and child is one that can never be broken or separated. We are never really separated from those we love so deeply. This I know, Joseph, as I feel your presence and rest in your sweet scent and fragrance. Jesus said, *Matthew 16:20 "All authority in heaven and on earth has been given to me. And surely I am with you always even to the end of the age."*

A new year, 2007, was approaching and what would be revealed to us was beyond human comprehension, but God gave us the courage and fortitude to stand convicted in His truth. In January 2007, I called the Westminster Barrack and asked to speak to the head person in charge. They said that would be Lieutenant Don Rickerts. They put him on the phone and I introduced myself to him and explained the purpose of my call. The lieutenant said that he was sorry that I had not heard back from Corporal Kitseng and he was not at all familiar with the case. I asked him if he would please look into it for me and that I had been very patient. He listened and said that he understood and would call me back the next day.

Lieutenant Rickerts did phone me the next day to follow up. He said that they were still investigating my son's case. I said, "Lieutenant Rickerts, my family and I have so many questions that remain unanswered and the contradictions and inconsistencies are numerous and very troubling and we must find out what is going on in the investigation." I asked if we could meet with him. He said OK. We scheduled a meeting for January 15 at the Westminster Barrack and he said he would tell Corporal Kitseng and Sergeant Buck Monroe to put it on their schedule. I thanked him and said, "We will see you then."

Meanwhile, after many calls and conversations, I found an attorney who said he would do his best to help us. Attorney Greg Mills was very kind and compassionate and had gotten a lot of information from me as to where we were with everything from the Maryland State Police as well as the MOSH investigation. I told him we were still waiting for a call back from the deputy commissioner, Carl Loory, to set up a meeting with MOSH. We had so many questions for them as well. Attorney Mills understood all of this and agreed to attend the January 15 meeting with the Maryland State Police. I was hopeful that with some legal representation we would now start to get some answers that made sense.

The next week I did later also receive a letter from MOSH to set up a meeting with them for January 20, 2007. I called Mr. Loory and told him that day would be fine and he gave me directions to where we would meet in Baltimore County.

I had been talking with so many people trying to find out where to go for help. One day I happened to talk with Mr. Gary Klusmay, who was with the state of Maryland comptroller's office. He was so kind and really listened about all that had happened thus far pertaining to Joseph's tragic death and the MDSP and MOSH investigations. We had stayed in touch and he agreed to attend the MOSH meeting set up for January 20, 2007. I was so appreciative and felt I was finally finding competent, good people who would be supporting us.

On January 15, 2007, the meeting with the Maryland State Police was held in the Westminster Barrack. In attendance was Bob Miranda, Joseph's father, Betty Gemma, my mother, Robert Miranda Jr., our son, Dino Gemma, Lisa Napoli, Rick Caparosa, Attorney Greg Mills and me.

We entered the barrack and said who we were and why we were there. A state trooper asked us to have a seat in the waiting area. Lieutenant Rickerts came out and introduced himself. Our attorney, Mr. Mills, introduced himself to Lieutenant Rickerts. We waited in the lobby for over a half an hour while troopers scurried and doors opened and closed. The Maryland State Police then took our attorney, Mr. Greg Mills, into a private room and spoke with him. We thought it was unusual and just waited until they were finished.

Prior to the meeting, I had asked Lieutenant Rickerts over the phone if Trooper Huddack would attend. I said, "He was the first to arrive at the scene and I would like him present at the meeting." The door opened and our attorney, the other troopers and Lieutenant Rickerts came out. They took us into a large conference room to be seated. Lieutenant Rickerts outlined some rules. I then asked if we could record the meeting so we would have it on tape and we would be able to refer back to it. He agreed. We went around the room and introduced ourselves. I then asked if Trooper Huddack was joining us and Corporal Kitseng said, "No, he could not make it."

We began to listen for an update and knew Attorney Mills was expecting to view the crime scene photographs that we were too fearful and broken to see and he also wanted to read the witness and suspect statements. Attorney Mills had been instructed to put his request in writing prior to the meeting. You see, Corporal Kitseng had faxed him a form requesting that he put in writing what and why he was attending the meeting and what documents and records he would need in order to assist us. Our attorney, of course, complied.

Dan Happman, an attorney who worked for the attorney general of the state of Maryland, had to see our attorney's written request. Evidently, he denied our attorney's request and Lieutenant Rickerts explained that he could not see these documents and photographs because the case was still under criminal investigation. Attorney Mills reasonably explained that in order for him to accurately assess our case he would need to have a reconstruction done since the MDSP had not done one. Therefore, he would need to see the crime scene photographs and read the police reports and statements made. Both Lieutenant Rickerts and Corporal Kitseng said he could not because it was an ongoing criminal investigation. Our attorney then said, "Can I at least look at the photographs here at the barrack?" They told him no. We were very disappointed, hoping that maybe Mr. Mills would finally get the reconstruction performed and completed for answers. Again, we were let down. During the hours we met in the conference room, we asked many reasonable and justified questions and still did not get any answers. Nothing they told us added up or made sense except that Joseph was horrifically killed and we knew it was at the hands of others. I pleaded, "I have waited six months and no one will tell me anything." Attorney Mills spoke up. "I think it only reasonable and fair that you provide a reconstruction for the family."

When we mentioned MOSH had done no inspection, impounding of the Bobcat, no reconstruction Sergeant Monroe said, "That is not us. That's MOSH." I said, "You say MOSH. MOSH says you. Either way it was never done. Why was this not done for my son?" As the tears started pouring, I cried, "Why, why did you leave my baby in the dirt, in the burning hot sun, under seventy-five hundred pounds of steel for four hours? Why no forensics? Why no drug tests? Why no other employees questioned? Why no citations given? Why no charge of at least assault? Why no polygraphs when there had been so many inconsistent and contradictory statements from these two men? My boy was physically attacked, pushed and pulled around dangerous equipment and then backed up over and crushed to death. There are only backup tread marks in the photograph I saw. Why no prints, forensics, or evidence collected? Corporal Kitseng, did you follow up on the names and all the leads I gave you? Did you contact and interview Omar and Juan Guadala?" He said, "Who is Juan Guadala?" I said, "What? I gave you his name and explained to you that he was the one who ran down to Jack Brodeman and pulled him to run to Joseph. Did you not ask Mr. Brodeman about this when you interviewed him? You told me I could call Mr. Brodeman and I did. I thanked him for talking with me because no one at Outside Unliving would tell me anything. I asked Mr. Brodeman, 'How in God's name could this have happened to my son?'"

It ended up that every time we asked a question, Corporal Kitseng would just answer, "I am not going to discuss anything about the case." It went on and on, only for me to realize they seemed to have done next to nothing. Lieutenant Rickerts then said I should put all of my questions in writing and send them directly to him and they would do their best to answer them. I cried and said, "We all took our day". "We took time away from already planned obligations to be here." I said, "This meeting was planned." "Why can you not answer any of my questions?" "Did you get the employee list from Outside Unliving?" The Maryland State Police only came up empty again and again and repeated that this was an ongoing criminal investigation and they could not tell me anything. I said, "I don't understand; I am Joseph's mother." "We are his family." "Why can you not tell us anything?" I said, "I have been more than patient for six months now and we must have answers." They just wanted to blame the victim. My son did not jump up on any tire and then twist himself underneath a sixteen-by-nine-inch space between the two left wheels and the undercarriage of the Bobcat. I said, "What you are claiming is impossible." "We know Joseph had no broken bones below his neck—none." "It is in the autopsy report and you have seen it."

Unbeknownst to us, the Medical Examiner had changed their determination of Joseph's manner of death from being an accident to "Undetermined, with a strong possibility of homicide." We would find out about this very crucial information later. All the while, Corporal Kitseng, with the Maryland State Police knew it and knew it on the very day of this meeting but would tell us nothing, nothing at all.

From January 2007 until July 11, 2007, my communications were to be only with and through Lieutenant Dan Rickerts. I felt relieved that he was my contact and not Corporal Kitseng. I e-mailed Lieutenant Rickerts all of the questions we had as he requested; there were forty-one in total.

You see, I had spoken with Jack Brodeman in September and it was somewhat informative but also upsetting for me. He was one of the supervisors whom Joseph worked for. Joseph had gotten three promotions throughout the year he was employed at Outside Unliving. They promoted him to a foreman. As I said, Joseph was a quick study and he was familiar with landscaping. Mr. Brodeman told me that in a few years Joseph would have made project manager and that he was smart and hard working. When I asked him what he could tell me about the incident, he was forthcoming to a degree. He told me that he was at the south end of the property at the rear of the office where the garage bays were. Mr. Brodeman said that someone came running to grab him and pull him to where Joseph was. I asked him, "who". He reluctantly said, "Juan Guadala." I asked, "How did he know to come and get you? What did he see?" Mr. Brodeman said that Juan was Mexican and spoke very little English but he came screaming and pulling him up to the roadway. Mr. Brodeman continued that when he got to the scene, the Bobcat was still running and Joseph lay dead under it. He told me that at first he did not even recognize who it was and then called Joseph's cell phone, which rang in his pocket and that was how he knew it was Joe Miranda. He went on to tell me that Joseph's jugular vein was exposed and he put his hand on it to take a pulse but knew Joe was dead. I cried and asked him to please stop and to not be so graphic. I knew the injuries to my son's head, face and neck were severe and horrific. I could not bear to hear such details. I tried to calm myself as Mr. Brodeman continued. He said he knew the driver was Antoine Ruberra and the one looking out for trucks going by was Pete Coldwin but he did not know how it happened. I asked how long he was there that day and if he had talked to anyone else. He told me he was there all day until MOSH came and that he did talk to the police because he spoke Spanish and could translate for Antoine Ruberra. He said he had to go and I asked if he would please meet me for a cup of coffee one day just to talk. He said he would have to think about it. I said OK and thanked him for his time. I asked if it would be okay if I phoned him again and he said "yes".

I did remember that he did not attend the funeral home or the funeral for Joseph even though he worked with him every day. When we hung up, I had a strange and peculiar feeling that Mr. Brodeman was not telling me entirely what he knew; he had seemed a bit uneasy. I knew that I wanted to talk with him again and I hoped he would meet with me in person.

Over the next several months, I spoke with Jack Brodeman four times. At no time would he meet with me in person. After I had received the MOSH report and some of the photographs from after they had removed Joseph from the scene, I studied them closely. I could tell through a magnifying glass that there were only backup tread marks and that the dump truck that Ruberra and Coldwin were loading dirt in had been driven forward. I could plainly see where the chain from the rear of the dump truck lay on the road and that behind the dump truck there were fresh forward tire tread marks. This confirmed for me that someone had driven the dump truck forward after Joseph was already killed.

You see, several employees had disturbed the crime scene and tried to create the illusion that the Bobcat was traveling in a forward motion when Joseph was killed. They not only drove the dump truck forward but also dragged my deceased son's right foot forward about four inches after he had been killed and still on the ground. They moved his left arm up and later Jay Metvet was at the scene with a broom. He claimed in his deposition, taken four years later, that he was trying to swat the flies away. In a criminal investigation no one is to go near or cross the yellow tape but the Maryland State Police allowed Jay Metvet to do so.

I will expound more on all of the horrible, unlawful, atrocious actions that Metvet and his employees, as well as police, did to cover up the truth of how my son was killed as you read on. Their actions are heinous and criminal.

I am so grateful to all of my family who showed their love, support, care and concern for me. They knew, too, that Joseph's death was no accident and the lies and torment that I was being subjected to were appalling. I truly had no appetite at all and trying to eat made me feel worse.

I must have lost about fifteen pounds and did not realize it. My mother and family members kept saying, "Adrienne, please try to eat something. You are already weakened and sick." I thank God for my dear and loving Aunt Marion and Uncle Moonie. My uncle is a wonderful cook and I really believe his homemade chicken and lentil soup kept me alive and surviving. His soups were about the only thing I could eat and keep down. He would bring a fresh batch over each week for my mother and I. May God bless them always; they are so dearly loved and appreciated.

CHAPTER 4

HIS LAST BREATH OF LIFE AND BLAMING THE VICTIM

On January 20, 2007, the MOSH meeting was held. We were still working with Attorney Mills, who attended. I was also present along with Bob Miranda, Betty Gemma, Lisa Napoli, Dino Gemma, Rick Caparosa and Mr. Gary Klusmay, the gentleman who worked for the Comptroller's office. Representing MOSH were attorney Casey Wilfry, Greg Loory, Rod Chimpall and Chase Dileo. We were shocked when we found that Brent Timber, the MOSH inspector at the scene of my son's death, was not present. We asked, "Where is Mr. Timber? "We have many questions for him." Attorney Wilfry replied that that was precisely why he was not present; he was the one we knew you would have the most questions for. We, again, could not believe what we were hearing. We, of course, kept feeling like we were being forced into a ferocious battle with these people as we were in extreme pain and agony and just trying to find answers and the truth of what happened to our child. This meeting was unproductive and their answers to our questions were absurd and bizarre. How they were able to sit there and actually give us their confounded, stupid answers remains unforgettable and outrageous. For instance, we asked why Mr. Timber didn't ever inspect the Bobcat that crushed our son. Mr. Chimpall replied that he didn't even know what a Bobcat was and that Mr. Timber knew nothing about Bobcats. We said, "Then why send him?" They just looked at us and said he was the only inspector available at the time. We said, "Why didn't the MOSH office in Baltimore respond to the scene?" "They are only twenty-five minutes away." "We read in your policy and procedure that in a catastrophic incident the closest MOSH office is to respond." They just looked at us with blank stares. We asked, "How can MOSH make a determination of accident while the case is under a criminal investigation by the police?" Mr. Loory said the police report would supersede their findings. We asked, "Why was Outside Unliving not given any citation?" "It is our understanding that the Bobcat had no functioning backup alarm." They said they were not aware of that. We said, "Wasn't it your job and duty to ensure that the equipment was safe and the company was complying with MOSH workplace mandates?" They answered that by the time Mr. Timber got there from West Virginia everyone was gone except the company owner. We said, "The owner, Mr. Metvet, would surely have known where the keys were to his Bobcat that had just killed one of his employees." "In your report, it says Mr. Timber did meet with Mr. Metvet when he arrived and we know the police were still there." Again they had no answer for us. We asked, "Are you aware that Outside Unliving employs many illegal immigrants?" They said, "What do you mean?"

I pulled out all of the safety sign-in sheets from Outside Unliving's so-called safety meetings. All of the Hispanic signatures were whited out. You could look at all of the weeks and clearly see the white outs. Attorney Wilfry said, "Oh, they are their Social Security numbers." I got up from my seat and walked them over to her and said, "No, Ms. Wilfry, they are not. Look at them." She just looked and then gave me a sort of nasty look before looking over at Mr. Chimpall. Mr. Klusmay then said, "Adrienne, bring them over and let me look at them." I said, "Of course." Mr. Klusmay looked at the many pages and said, "Yes, indeed, they are definitely names whited out."

Our attorney, Mr. Mills, did say, "It does not make sense that you send an inspector all the way from West Virginia and that on top of that he does not even know what a Bobcat is." Again, they offered no explanation. We asked, "when Mr. Timber went back four days later on July 24 and interviewed the driver of the Bobcat and the spotter why he did not take an inspector who knew about Bobcats or why he could not have at least asked to observe the Bobcat moving in reverse to see if there was a functioning backup alarm." Again, they just said they did not have enough inspectors for that. Mr. Loory, the deputy commissioner, then wanted to close the meeting and told us he would get back to us. We left knowing that what MOSH conducted throughout their investigation into safety in the workplace at Outside Unliving was appalling. The MOSH practices and careless disregard for human life and its reason for existing in the state of Maryland was a downright disgrace. There are serious issues with OSHA and MOSH regarding workplace safety, accountability and corruption.

I left that day once again feeling the magnitude of the pain and misery put upon us by these worthless, rude, ignorant and incompetent employees of the state of Maryland. Their distortions of truth, blatant lies and twists and turns were ominous. As more time passed and they kept trying to beat me down, I only came back stronger. We would later be trying to cope with withholding of police reports and crime scene photographs. The unfolding of repeated, deliberate barefaced lies and untruths, sinister actions and obvious defiances that continued on and on to exorbitant, sickening levels of victimization was and remains disgusting. But I will continue in strength and my faithful answer to His call. Jesus says, in Revelation 2:7, "To Him who overcomes, I will give the right to eat from the tree of life, which is in the paradise of God."

For most of the next few months, January through April 2007, Lieutenant Rickerts and I had some e-mail communication, but most of it was only to inform me that the MDSP was still investigating and he did not have any updates for me.

In April, I decided to contract my own forensic reconstructionist and engineer. I researched on the Internet and found Mr. Roy Gink, who had excellent credentials and was very familiar with industrial equipment and earthmovers—Bobcats.

We spoke on the phone and I explained where we were in the process of the criminal investigation with the MDSP and what MOSH had done and not done. He was surprised that the police did not bring in a reconstructionist on the day Joseph was killed but assured me he could help me. He sent me a contract that outlined his process and procedures and his fees. I agreed to the contract and over the next several weeks, Mr. Gink was able to study and assess the photographs taken by MOSH of the crime scene on their CD and in their reports. I also updated him on what we knew about the case and that the two men involved had contradictory stories of what occurred on the day Joseph was killed.

After many hours of study and assessment, in the end, Mr. Gink sent me a written document and an e-mail of his conclusions. He stated that Joseph was already flat on the ground and the Bobcat backed up over him in a reverse motion. He said nothing else added up or was possible and it was impossible that Joseph was driven over forward. Joseph was also not driven over twice and anyone could see that if Joseph was standing on the top of the left front tire while the Bobcat was moving forward, Joseph would have ended up in the bucket. He confirmed what we knew was the only physical, factual, scientific and forensic assessment and facts of how Joseph was killed.

So how did my son get prone and lying on his stomach just prior to the Bobcat backing up over him and crushing his head, face and neck? Again, Joseph had no severe injuries below his neck, no broken bones below his neck and no injuries to his feet. You could not do what Pete Coldwin claims happened even if you were a contortionist midget. It is impossible given the sixteen-inch space between the two left tires and the metal-box undercarriage of the Bobcat that was nine inches from the ground.

Pete Coldwin thought he was sly and cunning, but he is a devious, hateful, jealous, coldhearted criminal who intentionally put my son in harm's way, surely knowing Joseph would be severely disabled or dead. We believe he was out to kill Joseph given the weight and huge thickness of the tires on the Bobcat and that he knew the exact motion and maneuvering of the Bobcat as he had observed Ruberra loading and unloading dirt eight times before Joseph even arrived in the area. It was a repetitive, recurring motion of the Bobcat traveling forward and backward to load and then unload dirt. Coldwin knew how Ruberra drove the Bobcat—his tempo and pace—and when Coldwin was deposed later, he actually drew it on the site map and could speak to each motion and how and when the Bobcat moved forward and then backward. He did not realize how he was telling on himself, but so much came out in his deposition that it was the final testimony that sealed for the chief medical examiner and his assistant that Pete Coldwin was a killer and Joseph's death was, in fact, a homicide by assault. All of the proof, facts, physics, science and forensics are evidence as well as Pete Coldwin's own testimony under oath when he was deposed. Of course, he is a calculating liar over and over again. But all of the evidence proves he was lying repeatedly and he caused the brutal and horrific death of my son.

Remember, Pete Coldwin, the spotter, said that he thought Joe's foot got stuck under a tire. Well, that surely did not happen. Mr. Pete Coldwin also said Joe ran up to the Bobcat as it was going forward and then he jumped up on the top of the left front wheel and his foot slipped off. He said that then he fell underneath and between the two left tires and was crushed.

Mr. Pete Coldwin is a pathological and compulsive liar. Why lie if you have nothing to hide? In addition, the driver of the Bobcat, Mr. Antoine Ruberra, said that Joe, whom he called Jose, walked up and flagged him down that day after he had brought the bucket down from unloading in the dump truck. He said in his police report that Jose leaned in to ask him if he could use the Bobcat because they had to load trees. Mr. Ruberra's report said that the machine was loud but he could hear Jose and he asked, "Jose, can we finish loading one more bucket of dirt," to which Jose agreed. Mr. Ruberra then saw Jose walk past the open cages on the left side to wait and this was the area where Pete Coldwin was standing. Then Mr. Ruberra said he waited a minute and then proceeded to back up, turning the wheels to the left. He finished backing up and just before he was going to drive forward, Pete Coldwin came up to the left front of the Bobcat signaling to Antoine Ruberra to stop by moving his hand across his neck several times. Mr. Ruberra did not even turn the Bobcat off and jumped out of his seat. He then saw Jose (Joseph) crushed to death underneath the tire and bleeding out profusely.

We later heard that Mr. Ruberra started screaming and crying, pounding his fist on his chest and begging for a priest. The police reports say Mr. Coldwin just went into the front office and said Joe Miranda was dead.

There is no question whatsoever that Pete Coldwin pushed, knocked, shoved, or harshly punched Joseph off his feet, propelling him directly into the oncoming Bobcat to his death. This is no different from throwing someone into an oncoming train to his or her death. This is a deadly, brutal and heinous crime.

Joseph had his back to Pete Coldwin and didn't even know what was coming. There was no pushing contest or altercation. Joseph was even drinking a Dr. Pepper soda and had it in his hand. There was no time for a fight and Joseph was not angry or irritated; Pete Coldwin was the one who was angry and irritated—just look at the police report. Also, Pete Coldwin did not have one mark, bruise, or injury anywhere on him. He is a killer and a liar and he had not an ounce of remorse. I cannot even imagine what my precious son experienced or felt or if he knew he was about to take his last breath of life.

Where is the truth and justice? It is all in the concrete evidence just waiting to be tried in a court of law. But no one in the state of Maryland will prosecute and do the right thing. Again, the political corruption, criminal misconduct and violation of our human and civil rights are so extreme that it is an abomination of humankind. I will not tolerate this gross and disgusting injustice against my precious, innocent son who did nothing except go to work that day, do his job and follow the instructions of his supervisor, Earl Magil. He was brutally and horrifically murdered at the hands of Pete Coldwin and justice must be served.

Outside Unliving and its continual lawbreaking, criminal actions, obstruction of justice and underhanded business practices must end. They think they are powerful enough to get away with anything they choose and they have—even the murder of a nineteen-year-old, hardworking, kind, caring, bright and promising young American.

But do not be so sure, Outside Unliving. The day will come when your deep, greedy, gangster pockets will not survive. You and all those involved in your cover-up tactics, schemes, deceit, concealing and document fraud will be exposed. You will have to answer and be held accountable in a court of law. It will happen; it is only a matter of time. I know who my higher power is and He is a good and just God. I do not know who your higher power is—we can only speculate—but you will not see victory. I am suited up with the armor of God and I am His warrior against evil. I will follow His instruction and when confronted with fierce wrongdoing and forced into battle, my God will bestow His power upon me and I will be the instrument He calls me to be. His belt of truth will bring revelation and action as all will be sealed up in His victory. Ephesians 6:10–14: "Finally, be strong in the Lord and in His mighty power, Put on the full armor of God so that you can take your stand against the devil's schemes, for our struggle is not against flesh and blood, but against the rulers, against the authorities, against the powers of the dark world and against the spiritual forces of evil in the heavenly realms. Therefore, put on the full armor of God, so that when the day of evil comes, you may be able to stand your ground and after you have done everything to stand, Stand firm then. Stand firm then with the belt of truth buckled around your waist and with the breastplate of righteousness in place."

I remain in the light and as hard as all of you in this state have worn me out, beat me down into the ground, mistreated me, deceived me, bribed me, exhausted me, sickened me and emotionally tortured and tormented me throughout my agony and grief, you will fail and hopefully someday repent to our Lord and Savior.

Everything happens in the Lord's time. He is perfection and His purpose is for all that is good. Romans 8:28 "And we know that in all things

God works for the good of those who love him, who have been called according to His purpose."

All my family and I have ever asked is for you to perform your jobs and your duties and show due diligence to bring truth and justice. It is very sad and disgraceful what has gone on in the state of Maryland and continues to remain swept under the rug and ignored. Well, no more will that be the case. The highest authority and power has spoken and His truth and justice will prevail. Psalm 33:5 "The Lord loves righteousness and justice; the earth if full of His unfailing love."

We knew that Lieutenant Rickerts, my contact with the MDSP since January 2007, was staying quiet. We also knew that the homicide investigation into Joseph's death was very disturbing and their continual response that Joseph was driven over forward was absolutely wrong and made no sense. Nine months had now passed and we needed to talk directly to the medical examiner who performed the autopsy on Joseph.

I asked my brother, Damian Gemma, to make the call. Damian had stayed very close to the information given to us thus far and he also was well aware of all that was going on and not making any sense. Damian, Joseph's uncle, was very close to Joseph all of his life and in my son's teen years, he would often visit and vacation with Damian in Florida. They shared a wonderful bond of love and Joseph met so many of my brother's friends in Florida and was loved by all of them. They all took Joseph's death extremely hard and to this day they pray and stand by us for justice for Joseph.

The call took place on Wednesday, March 7, 2007, in the late afternoon. Damian had actually already made a call to Dr. Ali to inquire about the postmortem report on his nephew, Joseph Miranda. Dr. Zabiullah Ali was very cordial and informative. He offered his condolences to our entire family. Damian thanked him and he could tell he had real compassion. Dr. Ali explained that he had met with a detective and a trooper on October 24, 2006, but did not have the file in front of him. He asked him to hold on while he retrieved the file. He came back to the phone and Damian could hear him rustling through the papers. He said, "Bishtall—that is the name of the detective," and that another trooper assisted the MDSP detective at their meeting. Dr. Ali said he had his card in his desk and he would make sure he would get the assisting trooper's name as well. Damian told him that on behalf of my sister and my entire family we were so thankful to him and for all of his efforts. He asked Damian what questions he had for him and how he could assist. Damian asked him about the Bobcat and how after seeing one of those Bobcat models last August he could not believe that what happened was even possible. He said, "What the police are stating is not consistent with the other evidence at the scene." Originally the police had given Dr. Ali only one picture, he explained to Damian and he had very little to go on. Dr. Ali added, "In the first report it was "reportedly an accident." Even though my son's death investigation was warranted and confirmed as a criminal investigation by police on the day he was killed, Detective Monroe advised the trooper who was submitting the paperwork to the medical examiners to report it as an accident and to send only one photograph among the ninety-one crime scene photographs that had been taken.

Dr. Ali explained that Joe had substantial injuries to the left side of the head, face and neck but did not suffer any injuries to his hips, legs and feet and that made the witness account impossible. "I believe there was foul play," Dr. Ali said. He said, "I don't understand where the police are. They said they would be back." Dr. Ali questioned, "Where are they?" He explained that the very same day, October 24, he went to his chief medical examiner and showed him all the photographs the detective had brought and his report proving foul play. They both reviewed and studied the evidence they now had and agreed to list the death as *Undetermined with a strong possibility of homicide*. He added that Detective Bishtall showed him how the witness account was completely impossible.

Damian asked him if he thought Joe had seen the vehicle coming and if there was any time to be able to get out of the way. He answered, "I am not sure you understand what I am saying. I am not sure Joe was even conscious to be able to move out of the way." Damian stopped right then and realized what Dr. Ali was inferring. As far as he was concerned, he knew that Dr. Ali did not think anything about his nephew Joseph's death was accidental. He asked if he could talk to him again and he agreed. My brother, Damian, hung up the phone and cried.

When Damian phoned me and told me all of his conversation with Dr. Ali, I broke down in tears. I knew in my heart he was confirming everything we knew and all of our disturbing suspicions about the Maryland State Police and their so-called homicide investigation. As hard as it was for me to realize what they had done and their stupid and ignorant avoidance of me and all of our questions, it only made me stronger. Their actions were and remain completely unacceptable and we knew there was a dreadful reason why they would exercise such abuse upon me and my family and engage in such severe misconduct.

If you will recall, when we went with our attorney, Mr. Mills, to meet with the Maryland State Police on January 15, 2007, at the Westminster Barrack, they knew that Joseph's death had been changed from being considered an accident to being undetermined and that Joseph was prone and then backed up over but the police would tell us nothing. I knew I would forever keep the vow that I made to my precious, beautiful baby and would work day and night to get to the truth and justice for my son.

My brother made a second phone call to Dr. Ali on March 22, 2007. He wanted to ask some specifics regarding the findings of the OCME as well as the report of the detective. Dr. Ali picked up and they exchanged a greeting. Dr. Ali then said he had a speaking engagement that evening so he might have to be somewhat brief. Damian thanked him once again for it seemed like he was the only person exhibiting follow-through and due diligence. Dr. Ali asked what specifically he could assist with. Damian told him we wanted to know more about the meeting he had with the MDSP detective Bishtall and the process involved in the OCME's changing of the death certificate. Dr. Ali stated that the process would have to officially take place within their legal department but that the death had already been changed to undetermined. "Regarding the findings, it is all in the letter," Dr. Ali said. "What letter?" Damian replied. "You mean to say you don't have the letter?" Dr. Ali answered. "No, we do not know anything about any letter," Damian said. At that time my brother could literally and actually hear the disappointment in Dr. Ali's voice. He further explained that he had written a letter to the Carroll County state's attorney urging further investigation. He asked Damian to hold on for a moment while he went to retrieve the letter.

A few moments later, Dr. Ali returned and began reading the letter. He outlined and highlighted how the witness statements were untrue and completely inconsistent with the crime scene. He explained that the witness who acted as a spotter stated the Bobcat moved forward over Joe but there were only backup tread marks and a forward motion was completely inconsistent with the scene and especially Joe's lack of injuries to the lower extremities—most importantly the lack of injuries to Joe's legs. He continued that there was reportedly a struggle for control of the machine and that there was pushing and pulling of the victim, Mr. Miranda. Moreover, Dr. Ali added that there was probable foul play and a strong possibility of homicide but until further investigation could be completed the death would be listed as undetermined.

Dr. Ali said that he wrote the letter in early February about seven weeks ago and that he did not speak to Mr. Bines, the state's attorney, but he did speak with the deputy attorney, a Mr. Doggett. "I am sorry, Damian, that your family has to go through all of this," Dr. Ali stated. Damian thanked him once again and told him he would immediately call his sister, Adrienne, to inform her of this letter. He hung up with Dr. Ali and then phoned me.

My brother called and explained everything to me. I knew I had to find out about this letter and also what the state's attorney, Jeremy Bines, in Carroll County was doing regarding my son's case. They had not called me at all and I needed an update.

I found the phone number for the Carroll County State's Attorney's Office and I also knew if Jeremy Bines would not answer or come to the phone, then I could ask to speak with his assistant state's attorney, David Doggett, especially since I knew Dr. Ali had talked directly to him about the letter urging for more investigation and stating that my son's death had now been changed from being considered an accident to undetermined with a strong possibility of homicide.

That week I called State's Attorney Jeremy Bines and when I asked to speak with him, the secretary asked my name. I told the secretary and she connected me to his assistant state's attorney, David Doggett. I introduced myself to Mr. Doggett and said that I was trying to get an update on my son's case, Joseph Miranda. Mr. Doggett said there was no more information and the police were almost finished with their investigation. I said, "What do you mean? The MDSP tell me that my son's death is still being criminally investigated and I would like to know what Mr. Jeremy Bines has done. I know that you have received a letter from Dr. Zabiullah Ali, the medical examiner who performed the autopsy on my son and he is urging further investigation and has changed my son's manner of death to undetermined." Mr. Doggett said, "Yes, that's right. I have the letter." I said, "Mr. Doggett, will you please read it and tell me what it says?"

He first laughed when I spoke of my son and was nasty, rude and callous. He read a few sentences about Dr. Ali's request for further investigation from the letter and then stopped and said, out of the blue, "Do you realize that this company thinks you are going to sue them for everything they've got?" I was shocked, hurt and devastated by his response and said, "What? Mr. Doggett, who is talking about suing? This is my son and I am just trying to get to the truth of how my son was killed." David Doggett was so rude and ignorant in his words and his tone and kept talking about suing the company. I said, "Mr. Doggett, I have not sued anyone and I do not understand why you are so interested in the financial status of Outside Unliving. I am trying to confirm the position of Joseph and the statements made by the spotter." Mr. Doggett was not interested and yelled at me. I started to cry and said, "I cannot listen to any more of this and I have to hang up now." When I got off the phone, I knew this wretched, wicked force was against me and with each passing day and week, I would learn more about the living nightmare I was experiencing and how I needed so badly to obtain some legal representation and contact my senator in Baltimore County to help me.

On April 23, 2007, I made a phone call to Senator John Roaching's office. Senator Roaching represented Baltimore County. I explained everything that had happened and asked him if he had seen any of the local newscasts and newsprint articles about my son's death and the case. He said he vaguely remembered but he would do a search and get updated.

After I told him all that was going on and all that had occurred in addition to the horrible treatment and lack of follow-up that I was getting from the MDSP and the criminal investigation of my son's brutal death, he assured me that we could meet and that he would do everything he could to help us. Senator Roaching asked me to send him all of the questions—forty-one in total—that I had sent to the state police upon their request and I did.

Those few weeks, Senator Roaching was in and out of the office. His aids, Jennifer and Marc, were very helpful and understanding. Jennifer confirmed for me that they did receive all of my questions that I had written and sent to the Maryland State Police and that Senator Roaching would be reviewing them.

I spoke with Senator John Roaching a few times on the phone and during that time, he informed me that he was able to speak with Jeremy Bines and the Maryland State Police. He said he had asked and they had both agreed, to set up a onetime meeting where both the State's Attorney's Office and the Maryland State Police would be in attendance with, of course, Ms. Miranda. The senator also asked and Mr. Bines again agreed, that a representative from his office be at the meeting as well. The senator would like to be there personally, he said, schedule providing, but if it was impossible given the date that they chose, a representative from his office would be there.

I already had been told by Lieutenant Rickerts that a meeting would take place once they were finished with their investigation and that Carroll County State's Attorney, Jeremy Bines, would lead the meeting along with the MDSP investigators. I knew it would be coming up, but I did not know when. Each time I emailed Lieutenant Rickerts, he would just tell me they were still investigating and they had also put senior investigators on the case. I asked, "Will this upcoming meeting give us a chance to ask our questions that have never been answered so the state's attorney can review the case in its entirety, including Dr. Ali's findings?" Lieutenant Rickerts said "yes".

The senator also suggested that I may want to bring an attorney with me to the meeting, though he was not sure if he had to clear that with State's Attorney Jeremy Bines. Senator Roaching said, "If you do want to bring an attorney, please give me his or her name and I will contact the State's Attorney's Office and make sure that it is okay." I informed the senator that I was beginning to talk with Attorney Karl Frinze and I would let him know if he would be able to attend once we knew what the date was.

Through my hundreds of calls and letters, I reached the Maryland Victims Crime Unit and the supervisor gave me the name of Attorney Karl Frinze and said that he was very good working on homicide cases and with families who have been victimized. I thanked him and felt at last that there was an attorney who would maybe help me. Again, no other attorneys at that time had any interest in helping me.

In addition to the fact that I had finally obtained representation from an attorney, the local media in Maryland was very supportive. Several newscasts and interviews with me were held in my home with WBAL and WMAR, as well as stories in newsprint from the *Baltimore Sun*, the *Examiner* and the *Towson Times*.

I met with attorney Karl Frinze and brought him up-to-date on the investigation. He had seen the newscasts on TV and had read some of the newsprint. He was, at first, very kind, compassionate and supportive and I felt like prayers had been answered.

We e-mailed often and I conveyed to him that Lieutenant Rickerts was still deliberately withholding information from us because it was an ongoing criminal investigation. It apparently did not matter that I was Joseph's mother and I was trying to help them with everything I knew regarding Joseph's friends and coworkers, my son's statements before he was killed and how the MOSH report was so absurd and completely incompetent and made no sense. Lieutenant Rickerts still said he would let me know when they were complete with their findings and that my family and I would have the opportunity to ask our unanswered questions.

On April 22, 2007, the birthdate of my son, Joseph would have turned twenty. Yes, he was born on Earth Day and he innately loved God's earth and landscaping. He was born at 6:07 a.m. in 1987 and I was only in labor for one hour. I will never forget that. With the birth of my Rob, I was in hard labor for thirty-four hours. I told myself I would not scream from the indescribable pain of childbirth because if I did, I would lose it and I so badly wanted to have natural childbirth. I was finally ten centimeters dilated and the doctor told me I could push. Thank God that I barely had to push for Rob's beautiful head was already crowning and they immediately took me and their dad into the delivery room. Rob was so healthy and beautiful. He weighed eight pounds and eleven and three-quarters ounces and was born at 11:22 a.m. He was perfect and strong. God's miraculous gift was laid upon my stomach and then wrapped in a warm blanket and given into my arms. We cried with joy, happiness and so much soulful contentment. Rob was born on August 16, 1984.

You see, when I went into labor with Joseph, I thought it would at least last twenty hours. But no, when they wheeled me in the labor room and saw my breathing, the nurses looked at me intently. I asked if I could please sit in the big rocking chair in the room because it felt better to sit than to lie down. At first they said "okay". Then the head nurse came in and looked at me still doing my breathing exercises and said, "Mrs. Miranda, I think you need to lie up here on the bed because you are about to deliver." I said, "What? I'll probably be here at least twenty hours in labor." They took my arms and said, "Come with us, Mrs. Miranda," and I dropped my drawers as they laid me on the bed. The nurse took a close look and examined me and all of a sudden it was like a speed-up film with nurses running everywhere; they threw Bob, my husband, a blue robe and cap to put on and the next thing I knew, my obstetrician ran in and was delivering Joseph. It was like Joseph said, "Get out of my way. I'm coming through." And sure enough he arrived at 6:07 a.m. and was perfect and beautiful. Again, God blessed us with His gift of a healthy, precious, beautiful baby boy. We were overjoyed and so thankful. These were the happiest years of my life and my sons captivated my heart. I love my sons with all of my heart and all of my being. I always knew, even as a young girl, that I wanted to be a mother.

On this day that Joseph would have turned twenty years old, I wept. I cried nonstop, but how beautiful the sun was shining and how blue the sky and the soft breeze was all around me. I then felt Joseph all around me and knew he was right here with me. As I put my twenty red roses in his vase, tied his birthday balloons and attached my love card to the stems, I kneeled and prayed to my Lord. I asked Mother Mary to hold my Joseph in heaven on this mother's special day, the day of his birth, for he had been reborn to Jesus and God our Father. My baby boy lives on in the heavens of our world and in the hearts of all who love him. I sent kisses and more kisses. I said, "Joseph, do you remember how Mommy would ask you as I stroked your forehead, 'Do you have any idea of how much I love you? I mean any idea?' Well, of course I know you know and always knew how very much I loved and adored you and Rob and always will." My Joseph now knows all the answers that we must wait for until we are called home. My journey continues but not one moment without my Lord and Savior, my Joseph and my pouring out of tears.

Psalm 56: "Be merciful to me O God, for men pursue me; all day long they press their attack, many are attacking me in their pride. When I am afraid, I will trust in you. In God, whose word I praise, In God I trust; I will not be afraid. What can mortal man do to me? They plot, they conspire, they lurk and they watch my steps. On no account let them escape. Record my lament, list my tears on your scroll—are they not in your record? Then my enemies will turn back when I call for help. By this I know that God is for me, my God whose word I praise, in the Lord whose word I praise, in God I trust only. I am under vows to you God. I will present my thank offerings to you. For you have delivered us from death and my feet from stumbling, that I may walk before God in the light of life. Have mercy on me, O God, have mercy on me. For in you my soul takes refuge. I will take refuge in the shadow of your wings until the disaster has passed. I cry out to God Most High, to God, who fulfills His purpose for me. God sends his love and his tenderness."

This spring, Luke Andrzejewski, Joseph's friend and Scott's brother, did landscaping work for me. He mowed the lawn and edged beautifully. I always loved to garden and the blooms of springtime always gave me peace and solace. One of my favorite magnets on my refrigerator reads *every flower is a soul blossoming in nature.*

One morning I was drinking my coffee and looking out my kitchen window toward the back.

There is a large blossoming tree there and near it I had hung on my wooden fence a guardian angel that my sister-in-law, Lisa, gave to me. She said, "Adrienne, Joseph will forever be your guardian angel. Lisa and I are so very close and bonded in sisterhood. I love her and she has stayed with me every step along the way of my journey and my brokenness. She has given me her love, support, tenderness and intellect and has shared her faith with me.

So, now, on this morning I noticed Luke digging under the angel and laying down rocks very carefully. I walked out back and saw that Luke was making a special prayer garden for Joseph.

He said, "Ms. Adrienne, every morning when you look out the window drinking your coffee, you can say your morning prayer to Joe." I saw that the rocks were laid into the shape of the cross under the guardian angel. I cried and hugged Luke tight. I told him how much I loved him and that Joseph knew what he had made. To this day, I have my morning coffee and look to the cross in prayer to my Lord and Savior. We have now added a beautiful heart made from white rocks around the cross and each year I plant red impatiens or petunias in the heart. I often walk my angel gardens that I love—I have built many around our home—and I pray and give thanks and praise to my Almighty Father. I tell my son how much I miss him but that he is always with me. Every summer a tender white butterfly flutters all around me and follows me as I pray and sometimes sing.

LUKE AT AGE 4 STANDING IN THE MIDDLE OF SCOTT AND JOSEPH; HOW THEY
ALL LOVED ONE ANOTHER SINCE CHILDHOOD AND ALWAYS WILL.

My sister-in-law, Lisa, also has a beautiful sister, Tricia, who is also loving, kind, compassionate and spiritual and gave birth to our perfect, beautiful angel, Grace. Grace was born on August 31, 2006, just forty-two days after Joseph went to the Lord. Our little Grace is heaven-sent and she knows Joseph; even at the age of three, when she would come over and we would have our "best girl parties," she would look closely at Joseph's picture and kiss him. She said, "Aunt Nonnie, I know Joseph." My sweetheart Grace has so many times given me love, affection and rest for my soul and spending time with her has brought me healing. I love her beyond measure.

ALL OF JOSEPH'S BEST BUDS SCOTT, JOHN, SAM, KEVIN, ME AND
BRANDON AT THE MEMORIAL HELD FOR "JOE'S GARDEN". THESE
YOUNG MEN ARE KIND, CARING, COMPASSIONATE AND WILL ALWAYS AND
FOREVER REMEMBER JOE. THEY HAVE BEEN A BLESSING TO ME!

During the month of April, we had a celebration of Joseph's life and began a memorial fund to build a garden at Annie's Playground in Harford County, Maryland. Annie was a five-year-old little girl who was killed by a drunk driver when she was coming out of her day at the circus with her family in Baltimore City. This sweet little angel was carrying her balloon and so full of excitement and then her life was stamped out.

Her playground is absolutely beautiful with state-of-the-art swing sets, castles, slides, bridges and dream houses. There are also picnic benches for families to sit with their loved ones and friends and take a lunch or snacks while having fun in the sun with their little ones. We wanted to build "Joe's Garden" there. Since Joseph was a landscaper and also loved children, we felt it was the perfect place to honor and remember Joseph. About five hundred people attended the fundraiser in memory of Joseph and we are so very grateful to them. Today, along the border of Annie's Playground, there is a large sign that reads *Joe's Garden*. Joseph's father and his family were very instrumental in putting all of this together as we ate, danced, held a silent auction and held one another up in love and honor of Joseph. During the event, my brother, Damian, went around to folks and asked them to sign a petition we had put together that enumerated the facts of Joseph's death and demanded that justice be brought. He collected five hundred signatures in total. Many were from other friends and family who could not make the event and many were also from friends and loved ones who attended. Later, in a newscast by WBAL, we held up the petition to the cameraman after explaining its purpose and what we hoped to achieve to the reporter. The petition was sent to Governor Martin O'Malley, AG Douglas Gansler, Senator Ben Cardin, Senator Barbara Makulski, Robert Ehrlich Jr., Superintendent of Police Terrance Sheridan and many other top officials in Maryland.

Today, Joe's Garden is filled with beautiful hostas, daylilies, roses, hibiscus, tulips, a beautiful cherry blossom tree and some tropical flowering plants that Joe also loved.

There are picnic benches facing Joe's Garden that have the names of other teens who were killed or had passed. Beyond the garden is an open field for teens and young sports enthusiasts to play soccer and football and exercise their athletic potential. Annie's Playground is truly a blessing.

There is a very special bench under a tree that faces Joe's Garden that reads *In loving memory of Michael J. Napoli*, Joseph's cousin, whom he adored and who also went home to the Lord at age nineteen, seven years prior to Joseph. My family, friends and I visit often and continue to plant annuals at times and make sure Joe's Garden is thriving.

During this first year, we were broken and devastated. I knew that the MDSP investigation was beyond inept, strange and inconceivable. I had the map of the parcels and the property of where my son was killed. I knew in my heart I had to visit the place where my precious son took his last breath on this earth. I knew, again, from the police reports and photographs that MOSH had sent me that there was a very specific, distinct tree that paralleled with where my son was killed. I could even see it on the enlarged map I had received from the Board of Public Works. This tree was just a few yards directly across the road from where Joseph lay underneath the Bobcat.

It was a rainy afternoon, late in the day—around four. My mother, Betty Jane Gemma, Joseph's dad, Bob Miranda and I decided to drive out together. I took with me my flowers, my prayer card and my shattered heart. We found our way into the grounds of Outside Unliving and parked where we knew Joseph's death had occurred. I saw the tree, knelt down and placed my flowers and prayer card against it. I was crying so hard that my mom came over and tried to pick me up and then Bob, my mother and I all stood in the very spot where Joseph lost his life on that dirt road and wept. We held one another and the tears just poured out of us.

As we were holding one another and trying to gather ourselves to walk back to our car, a man came out of the Outside Unliving office, looked at us and smirked and laughed. We could not believe the evil ground that we knew we were standing on. I shuddered and said, "Who are you? Who are you?" and he just kept smirking. I then took the tape measure that I had brought with me and went over to the same exact model G873 Bobcat and measured the distance between the two left tires and the undercarriage. Sure enough, it was sixteen inches between the tires and the undercarriage sat only ten inches from the ground. As I walked back to our car in the rain, I knew that I was sure the man who was smirking at us was Rodney Schwib. He was the man who in the police reports tried to bring another industrial vehicle to lift the Bobcat off of Joseph even though they knew my son was already dead. Thank God that trooper Stan Huddack had stopped him and said, "Get that thing out of here. You are not to move or touch anything." Again, the one good, decent man with the Maryland

State Police that they would never allow me to talk to came through and did his job despite the others.

I had found Rodney Schwib's address in the phone book and saw that he lived in an apartment off of Cranbrook Road, only about ten minutes from my home. I drove there many times and saw his Outside Unliving truck parked there. Then one day while I was sitting in my car around the bend but still in view of his apartment, I saw him come outside and get in his truck. I remember him distinctly and sure enough it was this same man who was smirking and laughing at us while we grieved and cried over Joseph's place of death. My heart was telling me there was wickedness and evil in this company and in this man. Rodney Schwib also happened to be Pete Coldwin's supervisor at the time Joseph was killed.

I remember when we were driving back I noticed the large *Welcome to Baltimore County* and *Welcome to Carroll County* signs on Route 30. I remember thinking that where Joseph was killed in relation to the signs would indicate that Joseph was killed in Baltimore County, not Carroll County. I also remember that my brother, Damian, when he was visiting from Florida in the winter, had also driven up Route 30, Reisterstown Road and he, too, insisted, "Adrienne, those road signs show that Joe was killed in Baltimore County, not Carroll County." We knew something was not right and we remembered that on the day Joseph was killed both the Maryland State Police and the Baltimore County Police arrived.

Trooper Hudock thought for sure Joseph was killed on the property of Outside Unliving on the Baltimore County side. However, he was just ignored and the MDSP never even used a GPS to determine the correct jurisdiction. You see, the Baltimore-Carroll County line runs right through Joe Metvet's property and he was the one who told the MDSP that Joseph was killed in Carroll County and that he knew his property lines.

Joe Metvet had no authority whatsoever to determine the jurisdiction of my son's death.

Yet the MDSP just went along with him and let him make that decision. Due to the fact that in Maryland, while there are twenty-three counties and each has its own county police department, Carroll County did not. The police to be called to a crime scene or any type of unlawful disturbance and homicide are the Maryland State Police. We feel certain that Joe Metvet and Mick Meanton had their connections with the MDSP. As I continue it will be very clear to you as well.

As I continued my e-mail communications with Attorney Karl Frinze, I explained this to him about the county lines and jurisdiction and he said we would have to look into it. I said, "OK, but this is all very strange and we do not even think they have the correct jurisdiction of where Joseph was killed."

I began doing research on plats, parcels and MapQuest diagrams of the dividing lines in Carroll County and Baltimore County. When my brother, Damian, came up again to visit, we both took all of the information I had gathered and went to the Towson Public Library to search land records and the origination of county lines in Maryland. Everything we found confirmed that Joseph was killed in Baltimore County and not Carroll County. I copied documents and took them home for my files.

We were now in May 2007 and during this month I continued working day and night and gathering as much information and evidence as I could about Metvet and his numerous companies. I had even sent letters to Governor Martin O'Malley requesting a response from him and a meeting with him. I was just ignored and after about six weeks, I received a letter from Mr. Alfred Tiller saying they were sorry for the loss of my son and offering their condolences; that was all that it said.

In June 2007, Detective Rickerts e-mailed me to say that the MDSP homicide and criminal investigation of my son's death was finished. He said that they would be setting up a meeting very soon with Carroll County State's Attorney Jeremy Bines and the Maryland State Police (MDSP). He assured me at this meeting that my family and I would be given the time to ask any questions that we had and after the meeting the state's attorney would be making his decision. I thanked him and said OK.

I alerted Attorney Karl Frinze and told him as soon as I had the date I would let him know since he had assured me he would be attending the meeting with me. I also notified Senator John Roaching's office so that they would know that a date would be coming soon.

On July 4, 2007, the call finally came and Lieutenant Rickerts informed me the meeting was scheduled for July 11, 2007 and would be held at the Carroll County courts building. He told me over the phone that State's Attorney Jeremy Bines would be there along with Lieutenant Colonel Tim Copsinger with the Maryland State Police. He said, "Major Don Calisin is also supposed to attend, but I do not know if he will. It doesn't matter if you bring an attorney, a senator, or whoever, but I will not go against Lieutenant Colonel Tim Copsinger. He is second in line from the superintendent and he is an attorney." I was shocked by his tone and his statements. I said, "I thought you said that we can ask all of our questions and they would now be answered." Lieutenant Rickerts just said he was telling me the way it was and that was that.

On July 5, 2007, I received an e-mail from Detective Monroe saying that because of time constraints for the meeting on July 11 and because the meeting was for only one purpose, they did not need or have the time to look at the report from the reconstructionist we had hired, so we shouldn't bother bringing it. Things were constantly becoming more obvious to us.

Prior to the meeting, I had notified WBAL of the meeting on July 11 and given them the place and the time. They told me they would have a reporter waiting outside so they could interview us after the meeting. I thanked them for their diligence and said OK.

CHAPTER 5

THE MEETING OF MALICE, DECEIT, COVER-UP AND CORRUPTION

It was now July 11, 2007 and those who attended the meeting were Carroll County State's Attorney Jeremy Bines, Joe Deemonic, Lieutenant Rickerts, Corporal Kitseng, Detective Monroe, Lieutenant Colonel Tim Copsinger, Attorney Randy Apestein, Senator John Roaching, Jennifer Levi, Damian Gemma, Dino Gemma, Bob Miranda, Adrienne Miranda, Attorney Karl Frinze, Lisa, Sherry Bley, Rob Miranda Jr., MDSP Bryan Perry and several other unidentified men in plainclothes who sat behind us in chairs. We could not see them, but the police and Jeremy Bines could see them from where they sat.

We went around the room and introduced ourselves and then Lieutenant Rickerts opened the meeting with "We only have the room for one hour and this investigation has been deemed an accident." We were in total shock and dismay. We did not understand why Lieutenant Rickerts would convey the conclusion of the criminal investigation rather than the state prosecutor, Jeremy Bines. I said, "Lieutenant Rickerts, this is not what you had promised me at all. You said that we would be able to ask all of our questions and you would do your very best to attempt to answer them and then, at a later time, State's Attorney Jeremy Bines would give us his conclusion as to whether or not to prosecute." Then, the first words out of State's Attorney Jeremy Bines's mouth were "Are we being taped?" Lieutenant Rickerts assured him there was no tape recording. Lieutenant Rickerts was forceful and said, "I will not allow an argument or any further discussion on the conclusion. It is what it is."

As we all sat in shock at the conference table, here is what continued to occur in that large meeting room and what we had to endure. We spoke up. "We still have many unanswered questions and conclusions from you that make absolutely no sense. Please at least give us the fairness to ask our questions."

As we began our questioning, we asked why no reconstruction had been done for our son. I said, "Why did you not bring in a reconstructionist for my son? "I know that the MDSP do reconstructions all day every day when there is an accident or a death involving a vehicle." "Why was this not done for my son?" They just looked at me stupidly with spite and said nothing.

We continued that we knew the MDSP had concealed and withheld information from us and that the medical examiner had changed Joseph's manner of death from accident to undetermined with a strong possibility of homicide. We said we also knew that Joseph was definitely backed up over and asked, "Why do you keep saying Joseph was driven over forward?" "This is impossible." State's Attorney Jeremy Bines denied receiving any letter from Medical Examiner Dr. Ali. We said, "What?" "We know the letter was sent to the MDSP and to you." "My sister and I both spoke with your assistant, David Doggett and he read part of Dr. Ali's letter to us." "He was holding it right in his hands." They all continued to ignore Dr. Ali's letter and so did Carroll County State's Attorney Jeremy Bines. We were stunned by their deceit and overt manipulation.

We then got to the crux of the cover-up of the case and asked Corporal Kitseng, "Where is Detective Bishtall's report?" My brother Damian and I both knew it was crucial to the case from the conversations Damian had with Dr. Ali, the medical examiner who did the autopsy on Joseph and who met face-to-face with Detective Bishtall. These reports we knew proved foul play had occurred and that Joseph was prone and then backed up over.

Corporal Kitseng looked at my brother and me and said, "Who, who, who is he?" He denied even knowing who Senior Detective Rick Bishtall was. At the same time, Lieutenant Colonel Tim Copsinger, who was head of criminal investigations, Homeland Security and Immigration and second in line just under the MDSP superintendent, turned beet red in the face, put his head down toward the table and said, "Just keep going, just keep going."

We could not believe what we were witnessing throughout this meeting. It was atrocious and appalling. Then Sergeant Monroe was going to read a report of Mr. Antoine Ruberra, the driver of the Bobcat. The police report was tucked away at the bottom of Corporal Kitseng's pile of papers. Detective Monroe was sitting right next to Corporal Kitseng but Kitseng kicked him under the table to stop him even though Corporal Dan Kitseng knew for a long time that Joseph was driven over backward and it was impossible that he fell through the two left tires. Corporal Kitseng continued the whole time during the investigation and up to and during this meeting to state that "Joseph was driven over forward." He was revealing such stupidity, lies and corruption that it was inconceivable. We also noticed that State's Attorney Jeremy Bines just doodled on a note tablet, basically said nothing and just stared up at the ceiling on and off for over an hour.

We were not allowed to address most of our forty-one questions and then we asked, "Why are you going against the facts and science of the medical examiner and all thirteen coroners who agreed about what happened to our son?" Then the MDSP reconstructionist, Bryan Perry, who was present at the meeting, just said he was never called to the scene on July 20, 2006, when we asked. At that, Attorney Apestein asked, "Adrienne, do you think the MDSP could be corrupt?" I said, "I feel certain that Outside Unliving is corrupt, but I don't know. I put my faith and trust in these police to do their jobs, but I suppose it is very possible given all that my family and I have witnessed here and continue to witness firsthand."

Then Corporal Kitseng got up to the drawing board and made absolutely no sense in his reconstruction. He tried to draw a diagram of how Joseph fell through the sixteen-inch space between the two left tires and was driven over forward with the tire crushing his head and then the tire either driving backward over Joseph again or sitting on top of Joseph's head and then rolling off of Joseph's head backward. He made absolutely no sense at all; his physics were impossible and these facts had already been told to the MDSP that this was impossible and that Joseph was already flat on the ground when the left rear tire ran over his head and crushed him as the Bobcat was moving in reverse. Dr. Ali's letter also said Joseph was definitely not driven over twice and the tire never just sat on top of Joseph's head. Even Bryan Perry, the MDSP reconstructionist, just put his head down and said nothing. My brother, Damian, then asked to go up to the drawing board and he drew and explained exactly what happened to Joseph. He drew the sixteen-inch space between the two left tires and the undercarriage toolbox that sat only ten inches from the ground and showed that it would be impossible for even a contortionist midget to survive this without suffering any broken bones on his or her feet, ankles, legs, hip and back. Joseph was five feet ten and a half inches tall and he had no broken bones below his neck—none. It was crystal clear that Joseph was already flat on the ground and then backed up over. There were also only backup tread marks and there was no forward motion whatsoever. Damian then returned to his seat.

I then asked again about Dr. Zabiullah Ali's letter and insisted it was sent because my sister, Lisa and I had both talked with David Dogged (Carroll County's SA Jeremy Bines assistant state's attorney). Corporal Kitseng then reluctantly but finally pulled the letter out from the bottom of his pile and would not read it aloud. He actually handed it to us, Joseph's parents and said, "Here. You read it." I cried as I heard Joseph's father read the words that Joseph Miranda was already prone on the ground, the rear left tire backed up over him crushing his head, face and neck and there was undisturbed brain matter that clearly indicated there was never any forward motion. Dr. Ali insisted on further investigation, had changed the manner of death to undetermined with a strong possibility of homicide and until further investigation was completed will we then finalize our conclusions.

Hebrews 11:6 "Without faith it is impossible to please God, because anyone who comes to him must believe that he exists and that he rewards those who earnestly seek him". I know to never put my faith in man. Only God can answer prayer and show his faithful servant how powerful and mighty He is. It is all for His children that He loves and longs for so deeply. "I hear you Father, God; I hear you and trust and believe in only you.

Clearly, from Dr. Ali's letter, Joseph was not driven over twice, there were only backward tire tracks and the spotter's statement did not describe something that was possible and was a complete lie and blamed the victim. After reading Dr. Ali's letter, out loud by Bob, I was in agony and tears and trying to absorb what I had just heard. All of my family was in shock and then State's Attorney Jeremy Bines yelled, "I never saw or received that letter and you'd better not go to the media." Attorney Karl Frinze had his arm around me trying to console me and said to Jeremy Bines in a harsh tone, "Hey, hey, back off." I tried to keep my composure as best as I could and I looked directly at Lieutenant Rickerts, who was seated across from me. I asked, "Who is responsible for all of this and ultimately in charge of what is taking place here?" Lieutenant Rickerts looked directly back at me and said, "Him. He is." He pointed to his left to Lieutenant Colonel Tim Copsinger, the coward and evil man who turned beet red in the face. My brothers and I just looked at one another with disbelief.

We noticed that during the entire meeting Senator John Roaching never opened his mouth, nor did Joe Deemonic, the investigator for State's Attorney Jeremy Bines.

After Lieutenant Rickerts had pointed to Lieutenant Colonel Copsinger, Attorney Karl Frinze said, "I have something very important to say." "We have strong reason to believe that Mr. Miranda was not even killed in Carroll County but in Baltimore County." "Adrienne and her brother have done the research and pulled several parcels and plats that confirm this."

At that, Jeremy Bines turned red and screamed, "I know my county, where I pay my taxes and where the lines are." "I have lived here all of my life." "You are wrong." He then swiftly got out of his seat and ran out of the room. We were told, "This meeting is over". Then Karl Frinze asked Lieutenant Dean Richardson if he would please send all the police reports to him. Lieutenant Richardson said to put it in writing and he would do his best.

As I tried to wipe my tears, gather myself and collect my papers, notes and leather satchel, my brothers helped me walk and move away from the table. They were standing with me when Corporal Kitseng came up to me and said with a mean, harsh and nasty tone, "A Bobcat killed your son." We said, "No, that is untrue," and then we walked away as he walked away.

I did go over to Lieutenant Rickerts and thank him anyway for trying to help. I had remembered during the meeting when we were in such shock and we looked directly across the table at Lieutenant Rickerts and asked, "Who is doing this and allowing this to happen?" He looked directly back at us and pointed to his left, where Lieutenant Colonel Tim Copsinger was sitting. We knew, as agonizing and devastating as it was and despite the living hell we had been put through, that Lieutenant Colonel Tim Copsinger was at the core of all of the lies, hidden reports, deception and cover-up.

Lieutenant Rickerts said he was very sorry about everything and that he was going to be leaving the country and moving to Canada. I wished him well.

Attorney Karl Frinze then walked out with me and as we were leaving the room, Attorney Randy Apestein said to me, "Adrienne, if it ends up that your son was killed in Baltimore County, call me and I will help you." I thanked him and said OK.

As we exited the building and walked down the steps, Attorney Frinze was holding my arm. We knew WBAL channel 11 and their reporter would be there. Karl Frinze talked to Bob, Joseph's father and me and conveyed to us to be very careful about what we say to the reporters. "You cannot use Pete Coldwin's name and you should just be rather brief about the outcome of the meeting and what you believe occurred." We both understood and as we walked, Reporter David Collins approached us with his microphone and camera crew and we answered his questions and said how we felt and that we believed a crime and wrongdoing against our son had taken place.

Later, I tried to call Lieutenant Rickerts to see if he would offer me anything because at first I trusted him. He did not take my call, but another detective got on the phone and said that while they agreed that, yes, they knew there are serious inconsistencies, contradictions and untruths, there were just no explanations for them. They would not further investigate. They agreed that, yes, it would only make sense that my son's legs and feet would have been severely injured, but they were sticking to their story. I felt such a deep hole in my center and God was calling me to His purpose. Father God was my rock and my refuge.

I knew that I had to talk with David Collins again about the jurisdiction of Joseph's death and that we felt certain he was killed in Baltimore County and not Carroll County. Both WBAL and WMAR had reported several newscasts earlier for me with investigative reporters Barry Simms, Rosie Leftwich and Brittany Gordon. I will forever be thankful to them as they revealed the truth of what was happening during the first few years of Joseph's death. The people had a right to hear the news of the tragedy and all that we were up against. We would have never believed that it would take us over seven years to continue our crusade for justice for Joseph and all that lay ahead of us in this ferocious and unconscionable battle.

After the July 11 closing meeting by Carroll County State's Attorney Jeremy Bines and the MDSP, unfortunately, Karl Frinze never followed up on getting the reports that had been held back from us prior to the close of our Joseph's case. I, therefore, did it myself. I found out what I needed to do regarding exercising my Freedom of Information Act rights and submitted my letter to the MDSP Central Records Division. It took seven letters, many phone conversations and over four months for Central Records to disclose all of the MDSP reports to me. I spoke to Denise Scherer, Ida Williams and Greg Foote in Central Records and Ms. Scherer talked with me many times, saying Detective Monroe said there were no reports for Bishtell, Ramarez, Hertzler (forensic investigator) and Trooper Quisset Jr., the Spanish interpreter who had reportedly interviewed Antoine Ruberra the day Joseph was killed. Sergeant Monroe said on the phone and wrote to Ms. Scherer that she had the file in its entirety and there were no more reports and no Detective Bishtall report. I have Ms. Scherer's voice messages recorded that confirm all of this. During the first three months, Ms. Scherer and Ms. Williams said they were trying to locate the reports but they didn't know what to tell me. I was told the case was in Legal with MDSP attorney John Simpson.

I then found myself consumed by even more frustration and decided to call MDSP Internal Affairs. I spoke to an officer by the name of Sergeant Phist and at first he listened to all that I had to say, including that it was imperative that I received Detective Bishtall's investigative report regarding the death of my son, Joseph. I told him I knew that it existed but the police were withholding it from me and I had a right to the MDSP reports now that they had closed my son's case, calling it an accident. I explained that I had been talking for months with Central Records and they could not obtain the report either. I told the sergeant that Corporal Dan Kitseng was the lead investigator on the case and that Detective Bishtall worked right alongside him during the investigation but Corporal Kitseng denied even knowing him at the July 11, 2007, closing meeting. Sergeant Phist said, "I have the information and I will get back to you after I do some checking." I thanked him and waited for his call. Two days later Sergeant Phist with Internal Affairs called me and said that Corporal Kitseng drove Detective Bishtall's report over to our office from Westminster and he had it. He said I should be able to get it now from Central Records. The sergeant said it was stuck in the bottom of a drawer and there would be no further investigation or action taken by Internal Affairs. "We are done with this," he said, "and do not contact us again about the case."

This sergeant was so rude, ignorant and coldhearted that it left me feeling sick to my stomach. I told my family about it and it only reinforced our opinions that the MDSP were corrupt and covering up what happened to our Joseph.

Finally, after my relentless efforts and continued contact, Central Records sent the concealed reports of Bishtall and Trooper Ramarez as well as those of Trooper Quisset Jr., Hertzler and Michael Munn, the last of which I did not request because I did not even know that Detective Munn had been involved or filed a report.

My family and I will never believe that this was just a botched, unfortunate mess of a criminal and homicide investigation—never. There is some reason behind and something sinister at the core of why Corporal Kitseng and Lieutenant Colonel Tim Copsinger in particular covered up reports, used impossible scenarios and withheld factual evidence and science that they knew confirmed how Joseph was harshly knocked from behind into the reversing Bobcat to his death while lying directly to our faces.

During this time, after the MDSP closed our son's criminal investigation case, I also met with ICE, the US Immigration and Customs Enforcement. The supervisor who worked out of Washington, DC, Ryan Smitzger, informed he was going to send a special agent who was responsible for work-site enforcement to my home. The agent, Devin Lartin, came to my home to interview me and to look at the employee names on the personnel lists of Outside Unliving.

We sat at my kitchen table and he asked me some questions regarding illegal immigrants and what I had heard and learned about Outside Unliving's hiring practices. I explained to him what I had heard throughout several communities in Maryland and gathered from statements made by Outside Unliving's employees. He asked to see their lists of employee names and the MDSP reports. I showed him what I had. He took some of the information with him and said that they would be getting back to me once they were finished with their investigation. He thanked me for being cooperative.

After several weeks had passed, the ICE supervisor informed me that they found no illegal immigration issues within the company and no citations would be issued to Outside Unliving. I just listened and said that was interesting and certainly the antithesis of what I had been told. Again, Outside Unliving was left unscathed. It was as if they had some kind of powerful protection that towered above all.

Bob outback on the Ocean City deck with the boys and holding Joseph......
Left to right...Rob, Michael, David and Bob holding Joseph; they just could
not wait to go to the boardwalk, go carts and more fun in the sun.

It is imperative to realize that the MDSP closing meeting along with the multitude of lies, tasks left undone, deceit, absurd diagrams and ignorant, coldhearted, offensive and strange responses, as well as not answering any of our very valid questions to MDSP and the MOSH at their meetings made us extremely beaten down to the ground. We were physically and emotionally sickened and overwhelmingly distraught. We left feeling helpless and I became sick with bleeding intestinal ulcers, stomach and digestive problems and soars, clinical and severe depression and post-traumatic stress disorder. I could not eat a bite of food. At times, I cried so much and just screamed out in agony and torment. The intensity of the pain, suffering and stress was unbearable. Joseph's father suffered serious depression and anxiety; at times he had to start using a cane just to walk and his flare-up of colitis was agonizing. These people treated us so horribly and made us feel like our precious Joseph did not deserve one ounce of truth, fairness, or justice and he was ignored and tossed aside as if his life were nothing—worthless—and his human existence did not even matter. How I longed to hold my baby in my arms and stroke his handsome face, embracing every image of his loving, kind and compassionate heart. Again, I would fall to my knees in prayer to my Lord and Savior. How I needed my Jesus to hold me and hear my prayers.

Psalm 116:1–2 "I love the Lord, for he heard my voice; he heard my cry for mercy, Because he turned His ear to me, I will call on Him as long as I live."

Matthew 6:8 "Your Father knows what you need before you ask Him."

The first two years after Joseph was killed, my mother, Betty Gemma, stayed with me almost every day and night. I needed to be held in the arms of my loving mother and feel and receive her love, compassion and tenderness and share our pain and agony. We watched Pastor's Eugene and Melissa Scott twice a week on television. We could not wait to hear the beautiful word and the good news of their Gospel message. We also regularly watched Pastor Charles Stanley, Pastor John MacArthur and Father George Rutler from New York on EWTN along with Mother Angelica. We love them to this day and their faith and love in Jesus Christ indwelled within us so deeply.

God only knows what Metvet and his "crew" did at and after the horrific death of my baby, but my entire family has lived through it all first-hand and we know in our hearts and in the facts that there was a hateful crime and a cover-up. Evil was at work that day. Through my faith, while I am certain that Father God knows all, He has given me the gift of the Holy Spirit and said, "Follow me, I am the Light and you will come deeper into the light." Almighty God has revealed so much to me and now I know what God wants me to know and what he wants me to do.

John 3:19–21 "This is the verdict: Light has come into the world, but men loved darkness instead of light because their deeds were evil. Everyone who does evil hates the light and will not come into the light for fear that his deeds will be exposed. But whoever lives by the truth comes into the light, so that it may be seen plainly that what he has done has been done through God."

How I love my heavenly Father, creator of all things and master of the universe. I live for Him and will follow Him all the days of my life and will respond to His instruction until I am reborn into His kingdom.

We know all of the facts, science, physics and evidence are there, but no one in the state of Maryland will charge Pete Coldwin with any crime or even question him in order to make an arrest. He remains untouched and unaccountable, living his life with no remorse or responsibility for killing Joseph. Under God's law we must be held accountable and suffer the consequences of our actions. Whether it is in my lifetime or during God's Day of Judgment, we will all kneel down before the Lord Almighty and be judged. I know who my higher power is, but I do not know who the higher power is of these wrongdoers, liars and cruel human beings who disgrace humankind and who lie and kill. They are filled with hate, envy, greed, the love of money and pride. Proverbs 6:16–9: "There are seven things that are detestable to the Lord; He hates haughty eyes, a lying tongue, hands that shed innocent blood, a heart that devises wicked schemes, feet that are quick to rush into evil, a false witness who pours out lies and a man who stirs up dissension among brothers."

These men have committed these acts against our Lord and have no shame or remorse. God knows we have been victimized by these vultures. It is not for us to condemn, yet we are human and are hurting. In our human portion, we weep and cry out for justice. In our spiritual portion, the part of us that supersedes anything else about us, we can only pray for them that they come to Christ and ask for repentance and forgiveness. But only God knows what will be and is in store for them. God tells me the story must be written down. Humankind needs to know the power of our Almighty Father and that he will always prevail in victory over evil. God's children must know they can have a voice and have their voice heard through the Holy Spirit. Trust in only Him and take it to the cross of Jesus, who shed his blood for our salvation. Father God gave his only Son till death for us.

I do know my loving and compassionate Father tells me what is in store for me and what I must do to accomplish His will and His purpose. I do whatever and go wherever and however He guides and instructs me. I humble myself again and again as my Father does speak to me and shows me divine intervention. The miracles He has gifted to me are endless and you will see as you read on how God does, indeed, perform miracles each and every day. "Hallelujah, praise to Jesus, my Lord and Savior."

I remain relentless and have vowed to be the voice of my precious, loving, sweet, kind and beautiful son. I will move forward with truth and conviction for justice for Joseph to prevail and I know that Father God will be victorious in His purpose, plan and path He has given me. I am His vessel and through me God will produce fruit and help people to understand how great thou art and that His plan is always for the good of His people. We all have the ability to serve God and be His instrument when we acknowledge that He is the way, the truth and the life. He is the only way and Jesus Christ, our Lord and Savior, is our deliverer.

When we left that day, July 11, 2007, we really did realize and know what was going on. There was no question in our minds that this was a cover-up. But why? What was at the core of this deeply disturbing and inconceivable deceit?

I knew I had to contact the media. My family and I watched on WBAL the newscast by Reporter David Collins. He did an excellent job and we remain truly grateful for their integrity and responsible reporting.

A few days later, I phoned Senator John Roaching and asked him if he could help us. He sat there, on that day, at the same meeting and witnessed the outrageous actions, demeanor and deceit of the Maryland State Police and State's Attorney Jeremy Bines. Senator Roaching just said, "I am sorry, but there is nothing I can do." I said, "Why? You told me you would help us in any way you could and that you have power, too. I want to sue the Maryland State Police for what they have done in the so-called criminal investigation of my son's killing." He said, "Ms. Miranda, I am telling you, do not sue the Maryland State Police and if you ever say that I told you that, I will deny it." I said, "Really? You will lie about what you just said to me?" He said, "That's right." I then told the senator how disappointed I was in his public service and I would get justice for Joseph with or without him. I then said good-bye.

Throughout August 2007 Attorney Karl Frinze was very busy, but we stayed in touch, mostly through e-mail communications. I told him that I had all of the evidence that proved Joseph was killed in Baltimore County and not Carroll County. I said it looked like Joseph was killed on parcel 254, which was definitely in Baltimore County. I realized that he knew the state's attorney for Baltimore County, Todd Slicenberger and I asked Karl if he could set up a meeting with him so we could show him our evidence that Joseph's case was in his jurisdiction. Attorney Frinze complied and agreed that Mr. Slicenberger should be made aware of this, so he said he would contact Todd Slicenberger. Attorney Frinze was more familiar with and had worked with State's Attorney Albert Webster and thought it would be best to go through him first to get to State's Attorney Todd Slicenberger. Mr. Frinze also knew Assistant SA Albert Webster from working with him in prosecuting vehicular manslaughter cases. Again, during this time, Mr. Frinze's busy schedule left him limited time. He did talk with States Attorney Albert Webster over the phone but not face-to-face. Attorney Frinze felt confident that once we had the correct jurisdiction confirmed and documented that Joseph was killed in Baltimore County, State's Attorney Webster would wantonly take on the case. He wrote to me that State's Attorney Albert Webster was a strong advocate and would not back down from a fight.

For some reason, Mr. Webster did not get involved with the case and in early September Attorney Frinze was able to speak by phone directly with SA Todd Slicenberger, who agreed to meet with us at his office on Bosley Avenue in the Baltimore County courts building. We both—Karl Frinze and I—went together and met with State's Attorney Todd Slicenberger and showed him the pictures that showed exactly where Joseph laid on the ground and the specific and distinctive tree that was parallel with Joseph. We also showed him all of the documents and plats that my brother and I had copied from the Towson Library that clearly recorded parcel 254 in Baltimore County. During our meeting Mr. Slicenberger offered his condolences and said that he would have to meet with the Baltimore County surveyor, Mr. Pat Simmon and he would get back to us. We cordially thanked him for his time and left.

Karl Frinze, my attorney who was assisting, said, "Adrienne, it was good of Mr. Slicenberger to meet with us. Now, let's just give him a couple weeks as he promised and let him get back to us with his findings on the correct jurisdiction." I said, "OK, Karl, that sounds good." Karl Frinze also wrote to me in an e-mail that he was sorry about what the Maryland State Police added to their report after they did decide to meet with my reconstructionist, Roy Gink, in late July. He said, "We know they would not allow him at the July 11 meeting, but for whatever reason, they called Mr. Gink to meet with him so they could simply paper their file with whatever they could to show that they "considered his opinion" but discounted it for who knows what reason. "I guess this is nothing new or unexpected from them—just another CYA."

Weeks went by and I still had not heard anything from State's Attorney Todd Slicenberger. Karl and I were e-mailing often and he kept telling me to be patient. I said, "I understand, but Todd Slicenberger told us about two weeks and it has already been six weeks. After a little more time passed, Karl suggested I give Mr. Slicenberger a call or e-mail him. I agreed and then sent Mr. Slicenberger an e-mail asking that he please give me an update on the correct county and jurisdiction. The next week I received a letter in the mail from State's Attorney Todd Slicenberger saying that he and the Baltimore County surveyor could not determine what county Joseph was killed in and it was inconclusive. He again offered his condolences and wrote that he was sorry but this matter was not something he could assist us with.

CHAPTER 6

No GPS Done to Even Determine the Correct Jurisdiction

I then phoned Mr. Slicenberger and told him that I had received his letter, but it was unacceptable. I said, "Inconclusive" means "unsettled." I continued by saying that my son was killed in either Carroll County or Baltimore County and it had to be resolved. All of the evidence pointed to Baltimore County. He said, "Well, there is nothing more that I can do." I said, "What do you mean? Can't Mr. Pat Simmon, the Baltimore County surveyor, go out and conduct a survey of the property?" He said, "I do not think he has time to do that and I do not know if we can do that." I said, "Well, if you don't, then I will hire my own surveyor and have him do it."

I was on my knees every night praying for God to show me my way—His way and His purpose of what I needed to do and put into action so that justice would be brought for Joseph. I was talking with my brother, Damian, almost daily. He would hear my pleas for mercy and how I cried out to my Lord to bring truth.

One day in September, I was on the phone with my brother from Florida. I regularly kept him updated on everything. I would cry to him and tell him how much I loved him and how much it meant to me that he was by my side. He said to me, "Adrienne, I was driving home from work today and I prayed for Joseph to please give me a sign that he was OK." He asked Father God, "Please show me—show me something." He told Joseph how much he loved and missed him and to please give him a sign. Damian said that right after his prayer request, the most gorgeous rainbow he had ever seen appeared across the sky. He said it had to have at least twenty radiant colors that were so rich and beautiful that it took his breath away. He had to pull off to the side of the road as he wept in gratitude and prayers of thankfulness. How great is our God! He is so awesome!

I cried with Glory to God. I said, "Yes, Damian, this was Father God and Joseph showing you that our precious boy is in heaven and he is just fine." I knew miracles were happening and I got to the place where I knew I could expect them from my Father in heaven. He is our almighty, sovereign Creator and He hears our prayers and knows what we need even before we ask Him.

I knew that Mr. Slicenberger was at first being uncooperative regarding the jurisdiction in which my son was killed, so I contacted the Board of Public Works and talked with a very kind gentleman, Mr. Berman and explained the dilemma that I was in. He was very understanding and said, "Ms. Miranda, this information is public record and I will send you the map of the property and the document that identifies where each stone was laid when the Carroll-Baltimore County line was determined." I thanked him so much and told him how very grateful I was for his willingness to assist me. He said, "Ms. Miranda, I am just doing my job and you have every right to this information."

Within the next few weeks, there was a lot that occurred. I had also contacted an independent surveyor who said he could do the survey and it would cost about $2,000. I also e-mailed both Karl Frinze and Todd Slicenberger and they e-mailed me confidentially. During that time I had received from the Board of Public Works the large map and the document that identified each stone that was laid over 130 years ago designating the line of Baltimore County running through the property where Joseph was killed. This property, at least ninety acres, was owned of course by Jay Metvet, the owner of Outside Unliving.

I was so glad to now have this in my hands and I knew if Chris, the independent consultant, could come by and view the map with the clearly drawn red line, the distinct tree and the stone placement, he would know if Joseph was killed in Baltimore County. From what I saw and all that I had looked at regarding the parcels and the plats, it appeared to be definite that Joseph was killed in Baltimore County.

It was now late October 2007 and as the e-mail communications continued with Attorney Karl Frinze and State's Attorney Todd Slicenberger, things seemed to get even stranger. Todd Slicenberger was still very reluctant to have Mr. Pat Simmon, the Baltimore County surveyor, conduct a survey of the property. He wrote that he thought there would be a problem even getting on the property because the owner would not allow it. I wrote, "How can that be? My son was brutally killed on his property and the medical examiners are saying his manner of death remains undetermined at present, with a strong possibility of homicide."

I wrote, "Mr. Metvet does not own the county lines, nor does he oversee or have any authority in this criminal investigation." Todd Slicenberger wrote back to Karl and me that there may be a back way to get in but he still had to do some checking to see if that would work. He inferred, "There are legal issues and the owner will not allow us on the property and he has retained attorneys for legal counsel."

Meanwhile, the independent surveyor, Chris, came to my home and looked at the large map and the document with the laid stones. I showed him the distinct tree just parallel to where Joseph was killed on the dirt road and he clearly understood what the red line on the map meant regarding the actual line carved out by the laid stones dividing Carroll County and Baltimore County. He looked at me and said, "Adrienne, it is very clear. Your son was killed in Baltimore County and I have no doubt." I thanked him for his time and explained that there was a situation with State's Attorney Todd Slicenberger and the owner of the land stating that he would not legally allow anyone on his property to do a survey. Chris just shook his head and said, "Adrienne, I am so very sorry for you." He continued, "We, I suppose, would then have the same problem legally but I am here if you need me and just keep me updated." Again, I thanked him and was so very appreciative to him for coming out to my home to give me his professional and expert opinion on where my son was killed and what the correct jurisdiction was—Baltimore County, not Carroll County.

The e-mails continued among Karl, Mr. Slicenberger and myself. State's Attorney Todd Slicenberger now informed us that he had found a way to get on the property and have Mr. Simmon conduct a survey but we had to be very secretive about it. I had to maintain a low profile, have no contact with any media and let Mr. Slicenberger do his thing. We were told we had to wait until the third week in November for them to do the survey. It seemed suspicious to us because we knew from the personnel records faxed to police by Mr. Meanton that the second week in November was when the majority of the Mexican workers go back to Mexico until their return in April the next year. Jay Metvet kept some workers still housed in the "red house" he owned on Route 30 and another white house a few blocks away, just minutes from Outside Unliving. You see, Mr. Jay Metvet was the owner of many businesses, such as Westminster Wholesale Nurseries, Sir Sarge, Maryland Winter Services and so on. Metvet and Meanton wanted to keep their business operating all year, so they contracted with companies both private and governmental as well as residents to do snow removal, repair iced-up telephone poles for the gas and electric company and perform some land excavating during the winter months. Metvet also ran a chartered yacht business through Sir Sarge and had purchased two million-dollar yachts. We had heard he paid for both with cash.

Remember, we knew that before Joseph was killed he had been promoted to a foreman and he came home one day telling me that Outside Unliving was doing a job for the White House. This was during the Bush administration, of course. I still, to this day, recall that day just about seven weeks before Joseph was killed; he sat at the kitchen table and said that

"Outside Unliving does bad things," but he would not expound on it to me. I will never forget it.

So now we had to wait until November 2007 for the land survey to be completed. In mid-November the survey was done and Todd Slicenberger asked Attorney Karl Frinze if he could personally give me the results. Mr. Frinze, of course, said yes. I received a telephone call from State's Attorney Todd Slicenberger and he informed me that, yes, my son was indeed killed in Baltimore County. I cried and thanked him for getting this done. I then asked, "Since it is your jurisdiction where my son was killed, would you investigate the case? He said that, yes, he would have the Baltimore County homicide squad conduct an independent investigation and would be contacting the homicide squad in Baltimore County about it. He said that I should wait to hear back from him but the lieutenant of the homicide department would be contacting me. I thanked him and was so very grateful. My family and I felt that now we would get to the truth and that there would be an arrest made, a trial and justice finally brought for Joseph.

I bowed down to my knees and wept to sweet Jesus. I told him how much I loved him and that I knew my Joseph was with him. I told Joseph how much I loved him and that I would be with him soon. I asked for peace and mercy as my tears poured out to the floor. *John 14:27 "Peace I leave with you; my peace I give you. I do not give to you as the world gives. Do not let your hearts be troubled and do not be afraid."*

I prayed for Father God to please bring truth and justice for my Joseph. I told my heavenly Father I would do exactly what His Holy Spirit directed me to do. I said, "I am your servant and I trust and have faith in only you; all glory and honor is yours, in Jesus' name, amen. *John 14:12-14 "I tell you the truth, anyone who has faith in me will do even greater things than these, because I am going to the Father. And I will do whatever you ask in my name, so that the Son may bring glory to the Father. You may ask me for anything in my name and I will do it."*

I called Attorney Randy Apestein to let him know that it was confirmed that Joseph was killed in Baltimore County. I had remembered he said to me as we were leaving the July 11, 2007, closing meeting with the MDSP, "Adrienne, if it ends up that your son was killed in Baltimore County, call me and I will help you." I left a detailed message on his voice mail but never heard back from him.

It was now the season of Thanksgiving. Where was my Joseph? Of course I knew where you were, Joseph: in the arms of Jesus. This holiday was one of our favorites. Rob and Joe would love all the family coming to our home to enjoy this wonderful meal. I would set a lovely table in the dining room with my very best china and Waterford Crystal. Mom-Mom and I would start cleaning and preparing the turkey, removing the giblets for giblet gravy and the neck for turkey soup later on. On Thanksgiving eve, as we would sauté in butter the onions, celery and green pepper for the dressing and add all of our spices, my sons would bask around our home, taking in all of the delicious spices and enjoy the savory, delectable antici-pation of our Thanksgiving dinner. Sometimes—no, every year—they would be the taste testers. They would want to sample the dressing and make sure it was just right. And yes, each year it was. They would smile and tell me, "Yum, Mom, that is soooo good!" The next day, Thanksgiving, when we all gathered round the table, we would say our prayer to the Good Lord for thanks and for all of the blessings he bestowed upon us. We would pray for those in need and ask for God's provision. Oh, how those years were so glorious and how I do cherish them.

But this year there would be an empty seat at my table. I knew that I could not endure a celebration, although I kept in my heart my thank-fulness and my love for Jesus, my Savior. My mom and I spent this Thanksgiving with Aunt Lisa and we all shared with one another and held one another with our reading of scripture. We each said what we were thankful for and we knew the two now-empty chairs, Joseph's and Michael's, were filled with their beautiful spirits and loving hearts. We knew they were feasting at the table of the Lord in heaven with other loved ones. My sister prepared a lovely meal and we spoke with family over the phone and expressed how much we loved one another. My son

Rob spent the morning and afternoon with me and held me as we took flowers to my dad and our angel boys.

On July 20, 2007, one year to the day my Joseph had been killed and went home to the Lord, I woke up with a tearstained face. I brushed my teeth, brushed my hair and threw on some clothes. I prayed to Jesus to get me through this day and for a miracle of justice for Joseph. I went and bought a dozen gorgeous red roses, hibiscus, my love card and another cheerful, colorful bouquet that I knew Joseph would love. As I was driving to the cemetery on Eastridge Road, I actually saw a G873 Bobcat sitting in someone's driveway to the right. I had to pull over and stop; I could not believe my eyes. This was the same exact model that was involved in Joseph's death. I got out of my car and walked up to it and around it. I looked again at the small space between the side tires and the undercarriage that sat only ten inches from the ground. Again, it was just more confirmation that Pete Coldwin was a liar and that my son was intentionally and brutally killed by him.

I got back in my car and noticed that my gas tank was empty, so I tried to quickly think of what I should do. I said to myself, "I don't want to run out of gas on the way back from the cemetery and I may forget about it when I leave from being upset." So as I approached Padonia Road, I quickly made a left-hand turn to go down to York Road to get gas just half a mile away. I pulled into the BP station there on the corner of York and Padonia Roads. I pulled up to a gas pump and stopped. As I put the car in park, I got out, took off my gas cap and began to fuel up. Then I suddenly felt a very strange feeling from just the other side of the pump and I saw two men looking at me. They were getting gas and one was short and dark and had a Mexican accent. The other was about six feet tall, thin with medium-brown hair and greenish eyes and looked to be about twenty years old. I was frozen as I heard the man of Mexican descent say, "Is that her?" and the other younger man say "yes". I hurriedly stopped the gas, put in my credit card, returned the pump to its cradle and closed my gas cap. I remembered the physical description of Pete Coldwin from the police report and Antoine Ruberra's picture was in the MDSP reports because he was here on a visa. These two men matched their appearance identically.

I knew in my heart that I was looking directly at Pete Coldwin and Antoine Ruberra. I pulled my car around to the other side and saw that they were driving a white pickup truck and I jotted down the license plate number. As I did, Pete Coldwin looked at me directly through my windshield with piercing eyes. I also saw that he was wearing a T-shirt that said *Landscape Development LLC*. I quickly pulled out of the gas station and headed up to Dulaney Valley Gardens to take my beloved son his beautiful flowers and my bleeding heart. My heart was pounding inside and I felt like God had just brought a revelation to me. I parked at our family plot and fell down on my knees at Joseph's grave. I cried, prayed and began to arrange my flowers and love gifts. I was still in shock at seeing those two men standing less than three feet away from me and I knew God's Holy Spirit was working.

I saw that other friends and family had taken bouquets of daisies, sunflowers and even more beautiful roses in white and in pink. I also tied a balloon that said *Love You* around his vase. I saw Scott's letter to Joseph and I looked at and kissed the little ceramic turtle I had put on his headstone a few weeks after he was buried. This little guy was so cute and his friendly little face just looked up to Joseph's flowers and to the heavens. Joseph loved all of God's creatures, especially turtles. He also loved everything about the ocean, the bay and the seas. Being near the bay water and crabbing all day was his favorite even as a little guy and I will always love and cherish Mr. Leo, our dear and sweet next-door neighbor in Ocean City. Joseph grew so fond of Mr. Leo and Mr. Leo returned the love to Joseph. He taught Joseph how to crab, showed him how he steamed them and taught him how to clean crabs so they could pick the oh-so-delicious back-fin crabmeat for Miss Irma's crab cakes. Joseph spent many a day sitting, talking, laughing and learning from his buddy, Mr. Leo, since the age of three. He was a good friend and a good and kind man. God rest his soul.

JOSEPH GETTING A BIRTHDAY SMOOCH FROM MOM AND HIS AUNTS ON HIS 14TH BIRTHDAY. HE WAS GETTING READY TO BLOW OUT HIS CANDLES AND SCOTT HIS BEST BUD WAS RIGHT THERE TOO.

I laid out my blanket and while sitting I had all of these wonderful memories of my son's years growing up and the happy times we all shared together, the fun and fantastic summer vacations at the beach in Ocean City, Maryland and the birthday parties my boys always loved.

I wanted and needed to feel some sense of healing and I kept my heart and my eyes fixed on my Lord and my precious son in the paradise of his heavenly home.

My boys, Rob and Joseph, often brought their friends to come for a weekend with us and they had a blast. Oh, how those years ticked by. Scott was always with us and he and Joe were inseparable at the beach. The Andrezejewski's also had a place in Ocean City, so it was great for Joe and Scott. They are a wonderful, kind, loving and compassionate family and it makes me so happy that our families will always remain close.

Scott has grown into such a wonderful, warm-hearted and incredible young man. Over these past seven years, he has never missed remembering me on Mother's Day with a beautiful card and a lovely bouquet of flowers. He is so very dear to me. He will always be Joe's bro and he had made a beautiful gold crab pendant with Joseph's initials, JAM, on it and the dates of his birth and his rebirth. He wears it always around his neck. How the two of them would spend hours and hours out back on the bay crabbing, laughing and feeding their curiosity. Then we would all head up to the beach and the white sand for fun in the sun. Such treasured memories these are.

The sun was shining brightly on this day and I cried tears of sorrow and tears of joy because I knew where Joseph was and that he could see me and hear me. His presence was always with me then and is still with me now and forever. I sang some of my boy's favorite songs and rested under the blue skies of heaven. After about three hours or so, I gathered my things, kissed Joseph's headstone and ran my fingers across the embossed letters and resurrection cross. I then kissed my dad's headstone and my nephew Michael's as well and told them, too, how much I loved them.

I said, "I'll see ya soon and I love you with all of my heart." I got into my car and just looked again at all the beautiful flowers and God's heavenly blue sky with His sun (Son) shining through. I drove back home and worked a little on my angel gardens that I had been creating since the summer of 2007.

CHAPTER 7

THE DESECRATION AND GOD'S RESTORATION

That weekend, my nephew David came down from New York. I knew that he was going to make a special visit to our family plot and also take his love and flowers to the boys and Pop-Pop Joe. My Sister had told him that I had gone yesterday and took beautiful flowers along with many of our family members and Joseph's friends.

David went to the gravesite and called his mom, my sister Lisa, in tears. He told her that all of the flowers were gone—some looked as though their tops had been cut off—and the little turtle was gone and he knew something was very wrong.

My sister called me that evening and told me what David saw. She put David on the phone and he began to explain in detail. I was crying and said, "Who would do such a thing and desecrate Joseph's grave?"

The next morning I drove up to Joseph's gravesite and I saw it with my own eyes; the heads of the roses cut off, the little turtle gone and the other bouquets cut with no flowers on them. Only stems and my breaking heart remained. I pulled out my cell phone and called 911. I told the operator I was at Dulaney Valley Memorial Gardens and I needed to report the desecration of my son's grave. I explained what had happened and exactly where our family plot was. She said to just stay there and an officer would be there soon. About ten minutes later, a Baltimore County officer drove up from the Cockeysville Precinct. His name was Officer Martin. I showed him the cut-off stems of all the flowers; I described the little ceramic turtle that was gone and told him that my son had been killed July 20, 2006 and I happened to see the two men involved in my son's death at the gas station just down the road yesterday morning. I gave him the license plate number of the white truck Pete Coldwin was driving and said that he was wearing a T-shirt that said *Landscape Development LLC*. I told him that I knew it was Antoine Ruberra and Pete Coldwin because I saw a temporary visa picture of Mr. Ruberra and Pete Coldwin's physical description that was in the police reports. I told him that last night I had gone on the Maryland State Assessment and Taxation and looked up this company name. This company was registgered in the Maryland State Taxation records and also who the resident agent was. The officer got in his car and ran the license plate number. I asked, "Are you able to see who owns the white truck Pete Coldwin was driving?" Officer Martin said yes. I asked, "What is his name?" He said, "I can only confirm it if you give me his name." I said, "The resident agent of Landscape Development LLC is William Watkinson." He said, "Yes, he is the owner of the white truck."

I watched Officer Martin write up everything on his report and he said that he was going to go to the house in Phoenix, Maryland and try to reach Mr. Watkinson to ask him some questions. I thanked the officer for his efficiency and he said he would call me in about a week or two to follow up with me. Again I thanked him and said I would be waiting for his call.

About two weeks went by and I had not heard from Officer Martin. So I called the precinct and asked for him. I gave my name and said I was calling regarding an incident report of destruction of property and desecration of my son's grave. They said they would give the message to Officer Martin and he would call me back. Later that day, Officer Martin did call and he told me that he went to the home of Mr. Watkinson and knocked on the door several times. He said no one would answer. He then said he called and left messages several times for Mr. Watkinson to call him but he never returned his calls. Officer Martin said that he went back again and he never saw the white truck in his driveway but still no one would come to the door. I asked, "Isn't there anything more you can do?" Officer Martin just said, "I will go to the house again." I asked, "Could you go to his place of work? We know he is a lawyer in Towson." He said, "I suppose I could try." Officer Martin said, "I will try again and call you back." I said "okay".

Again, another week went by and Officer Martin was not in when I called. I spoke to a Sergeant Honeydwell and an Officer Harting. One of them told me—I can't recall which one—that the report was no longer here at the precinct. I said, "What do you mean?" "Where is it?" The officer said that State's Attorney Todd Slicenberger's office had called and ordered that we send the police report to him. "So he has it." I said thank you and got off the phone feeling very uneasy. I wondered why Baltimore County state's attorney Todd Slicenberger asked for this report before Officer Martin was finished investigating it and, for that matter, why he had asked about it at all or knew about it. I requested a copy of the report and the officers said I would have to pay a fee and go through the Baltimore County courts to get it. So that is what I did. When I finally received the report, it was not the same report written up by Officer Martin with all of the details I had watched him write. His report had been altered for some reason. This was more strangeness and peculiarity that felt very weird. I was actually asking myself why—why were these police reports being altered and distorted?

Attorney Karl Frinze set up a meeting with Bob Miranda, Joseph's dad and me at his office in Towson, Maryland, at eleven in the morning on December 26, 2007. He had told us prior to the meeting that he would have to leave during our meeting for about twenty-five minutes or so to take an important conference call and we could just wait in the conference room for him. He said it would not take long and then we could continue with our meeting. Bob and I arrived at Karl's office on time and he came and greeted us and took us into the large conference room. There was a receptionist at the desk, but the office seemed very quiet. We realized because it was the Christmas week that many employee's were most likely off. I carried in my large box of documents and police reports that I had finally received from Central Records, all of the earlier police reports from MOSH, MDSP tasks and time lines, employee lists and in particular Detective Bishtall's report. I was so anxious to show them to Attorney Karl Frinze and he knew that I was. As we started to converse and I pointed out all of the facts, physics, science and evidence that proved how my son was killed and that the criminal misconduct and cover-up by Maryland State Police needed to be exposed, Karl stopped me. He said, "Adrienne, I see everything that you have, but put all of your documents away." I said, "What"? The Maryland State Police need to be sued for their gross negligence, gross and criminal misconduct, obstruction of justice and perjury. I said, "All of this was done intentionally, Karl. You were at the July 11 closing meeting; you saw it first-hand." He said, "I know, but put your reports away. Put them back in your box." He then said he had to take his conference call and he would be back in about twenty-five minutes.

Bob and I just looked at each other with confusion and bewilderment. We could not believe that Attorney Karl Frinze was telling me to put all of my documents away. We really wondered what in the world was going on. After about thirty minutes, Karl came back into the conference room. He leaned over the conference table and looked at me and said, "Adrienne, you will receive one and a half million dollars—well, two million with Bob—but you cannot sue the Maryland State Police." I was in shock. He looked at me and said, "Adrienne, listen to me." "Todd Slicenberger will most likely try the case himself and he is a good prosecutor, but you absolutely cannot sue the state police." I said, "Karl, what are you talking about?" With that he said, "Put your documents away now." Then he got our coats and hurriedly escorted us to the elevator. I grabbed my box and quickly put my arms in my coat and swiftly Bob and I walked with Karl to the elevator. I had the feeling the meeting was set up by design. Bob and I could tell that when Karl left the conference room for about 25 minutes and had already told us that he would have to excuse himself because he had an important telephone conference call already scheduled for that day and time, it seemed pre-arranged. Then when he came back into the conference room and made this hideous and disgusting financial offer to us and ordered me to put my police reports and documents away, we were in shock. Karl Frinze pressed the down button and when the doors opened, we got in. Karl looked directly into my eyes and said, "Adrienne, do you understand?" I looked back directly in his eyes and said, "Have a good day, Karl, and thank you for your time." This was the last time I ever laid eyes on Attorney Karl Frinze.

Bob and I found our way out the front door of the building and began walking to our cars. I said, "Bob, do you realize what just happened?" He said, "I think I do. "I think we were just offered a bribe to shut up about the police." I said, "That is exactly what just occurred. This is unbelievable and how dare they offer us a payoff to hide the truth about Joseph's killing and the cover-up by these evil people?" They all sickened me and Bob felt the same way.

Bob and I said we would stay in touch; we got into our cars and drove home. When I arrived home, I was completely depleted of my energy and felt helpless. I started to cry and held Joseph's picture next to my heart. I prayed and I told my son that justice would come for sure for my sweet baby boy and Mommy would fight until his voice was heard. Father God would bring it in His way and in His time. They will not do this to you. I said there is no evil or greed that will ever overpower a mother's love. There is no evil, greed, or corruption that will ever overpower our Almighty Father's love. *Matthew 7:24 "No one can serve two masters; Either he will hate the one and love the other, or he will be devoted to the one and despise the other. You cannot serve both God and Money."*

John 16:12–15 "I have much more to say to you, more than you can now bear. But when He, the Spirit of truth, comes, he will guide you into all truth. He will not speak on his own; he will speak only what he hears and he will tell you what is yet to come. He will bring glory to me by taking from what is mine and making it known to you. All that belongs to the Father is mine. That is why I said the Spirit will take from what is mine and make it known to you."

Oh, my Lord and Savior, I do hear and am guided by your Holy Spirit. He lives deeply within me and has guided me without ceasing. All instruction and direction that I have received I have followed and will continue to follow without ceasing. I bow down in humility and my thankfulness for your love and mercy is all-consuming. Praise be to you, my sweet Jesus; you are my everything.

It was now mid-December 2007 and I received a call from Lieutenant Jim Mahoney with the Baltimore County Homicide Squad. He wanted to set up a time for his two investigators to come to my home to talk with me about the case. At first, we set up a day in the last week of December, but then the lieutenant called and said they would have to push it back until early January 2008, to which I agreed.

After I had left Attorney Frinze's office on December 26, 2007, I pulled up all the research I had found about filing a lawsuit against the Maryland State Police. My brother, Damian, had also found information and we both talked about it over the phone. We realized that I had to go through what is called the Maryland Tort Claims Act to file the lawsuit. This is the only recourse in the state of Maryland where immunity is waived for the Maryland State Police as well as other officials. In other words, in order to have your lawsuit even considered legally, you must claim ordinary negligence. If you claim gross negligence, malice, misconduct, or criminal misconduct against the police and officials in Maryland, the law will not allow it and the judiciary stands on their law and position that all police and officials have immunity and cannot be sued. This law and others must be changed in the State of Maryland. No one is above the law; no one.

In our case, they were actually guilty of both ordinary and gross negligence. However, the immunity laws in Maryland give the police a green light and a free pass to do and act in any way they choose and get away with it. There must be serious reformation of these laws now to give the citizens of Maryland a chance to be heard and receive due diligence and justice when confronted with such gross misconduct and very serious criminal behavior by the police and other officials. In addition, the complete autonomy that a state's attorney is given is against our Constitution.

Our Constitution is about equality, not bias and prejudice. The old-age term and analogy of the "boys club" philosophy so very well defines what was going on. In addition, the magnitude of injustice and prejudice for my son and our family here in our state, Maryland, is beyond unconscionable. Especially in certain counties, some more than others, there are historic landmarks and significant archives that give a sense of their origin, land owners and how property and civil rights were protected. For example, it was very peculiar to us when we learned that the Maryland State Police in Westminster (Carroll County) were contracted by the MDSP and independent of the Maryland State Government. We wondered why this would be. We noticed for years on the MDSP organizational chart that the box for Personnel Director always read vacant.

We can hear them scheming and saying, "I got your back this time and next time you'll have mine." "We'll keep it covered up and no way will this one loudmouth mother get even a morsel of justice." They would all benefit in their own way, be it in the form of positions, power, personal and political aspirations, fiduciary or tangible gain and favors, or otherwise. It all just seemed so obvious to all of us.

May God help their souls. The human race has become so self-absorbed and materialistic. They swallow one another up with arrogance and what they believe to be power. They are quick to defend the murderer and the wrongdoers as well as blame the victim. If they believe their case may have a small chance of not being won, they will not exercise due diligence and fight for justice for the innocent victim and his or her family. In our case, they even refused to call in a grand jury. It all comes down to a numbers-and-money game and even with a mountain of evidence, facts, science, physics and a killer's own remarkably telling guilt, they do nothing and just sweep it under the rug. They are really *okay* with this and do not let it affect their core principles or sense of integrity. These people are evil, coldhearted and unjust. "People are their principles," as so eloquently stated by the magnificent Barbra Streisand in the movie *The Way We Were*.

I know there are a "few good men" who show up to do the right thing, do their jobs that they were hired to do and have a conscience and a soul.

111

They are out there but are few and far between. My God will bring them to me. Some have shown up, but others will still come; my God will bring them and of this I am certain. Both good men and women alike will carry out God's will and answer His call even as the storm is passing over. They know who their Highest Power is; they trust only in Him and pray on bended knee to Him, the Alpha and the Omega.

All that is going on in the state of Maryland is reprehensible and people need to be made aware of what is written into law in the state of Maryland and any other state that gives its police complete immunity in our country.

Intentional infliction of emotional distress must also be enacted into Maryland law. There is no doubt that these officers intentionally and knowingly made me physically sick, increased my suffering and agony and prolonged my ability to have any kind of healing. Their cruel and despicable lies and torment put upon a grieving Mother who was just trying to find truth and justice for her beloved son is unfathomable and unconscionable. I have lived it firsthand and have the deep scars, soars, illness and sickness that ravage me with weakness even today. The physical, psychological and emotional torment and exacerbations that have been life altering are devastating. Joseph's father still suffers as well. The loss of enjoyment of life and the residual repercussions inflicted upon this already-heartbroken, grieving mother and father have been sheer torture and intentional cruelty. We were drowning in our tears and feelings of helplessness. I have the police reports, medical reports, agreed tape recordings, voice mails, an army of family support present at meetings and the e-mails to prove it. I have only survived through the sacrifice and mercy of my sweet Savior and the grace and strength of my Almighty Father God. My faith is rock solid and His word is all that matters.

Revelation 7:17 "For the lamb at the center of the throne will be their shepherd; he will lead them to springs of living water and God will wipe away every tear from their eyes."

In my efforts to try to find someone to help me get to the truth and justice for my son, I realized all of my letters sent, my phone calls and my logical questions were only left to be ignored, so I decided to phone the FBI here in Baltimore County, the headquarters for the region. When I called I was first transferred to an agent who took my name and number and said someone would have to get back to me. Later, I received a call from an FBI agent, John Costogian, who told me, "Public corruption is not on our agenda." I said, "What?" "What do you mean"? "You are the Federal Bureau of Investigation." "How can public corruption not be an important part of your work?" He said that their primary work was with terrorism. I said, "I understand that, but that should not mean that you just eliminate very serious crimes such as public corruption." Again he repeated, "Public corruption is not on our agenda; it is at the bottom of the list." I said, "I do not think the taxpayers of Maryland would take too kindly to that." "I need your help." I said, "my son was murdered at work and his death has been covered up by the police, the company, the county state's attorneys, MOSH, ICE and others. There needs to be an investigation into all of this and I have the proof of criminal behavior, felonies, obstruction of justice, aiding and abetting, perjury and more. You must look into this."

He listened and said, "I will have to get back to you after I do some checking." He asked me some of the names of the people and specific agencies involved. I told him and he said, "I will call you in a few weeks."

He later phoned and said he was sending two investigators to my home and they would look at what I had. The two female FBI agents came and sat at my kitchen table with me. I went over as much as I could in the time allowed. They were only with me for about an hour and a half and I was not impressed. They did not ask me if they could take even one document and seemed rather uninterested. Before they left, one of the agents, Ms. Neugine, did ask me if she could take a particular document that proved a name of a person who worked for MOSH, the office in Hagerstown, had been changed on the Maryland State employees website. It was crystal clear that they changed the spelling of the last name. In addition, there were several employees who worked for Outside Unliving with the same last name as this person who was employed with MOSH for many years. This is the same MOSH office they called to the scene of my son's death instead of the MOSH office that was just twenty-five minutes away.

In the end the FBI in Baltimore County did not help me in any way. I was on a mission and I knew there were people out there who would help. I knew that God would bring them to me.

I kept dialing numbers for the FBI and tried to find an office in Washington, DC. I had even written to the executive director of the FBI but got no response. Then on this one miraculous day, a man picked up and said, "How can I help you?" I stated my name and why I was calling and that no one in the Baltimore office would help me. He listened and said, "Tell me, Ms. Miranda, what is happening." I asked his name and he told me and said that he was an FBI agent. I cried but tried to bring clarity to my words so the gentleman could understand me. He listened to me for over five hours as I told him my story and what happened to my son. When I was finished, he said, "Ms. Miranda, I have been with the FBI for over twenty-five years and I have heard a lot of very sad stories but nothing that has brought me to tears like you have." I said, "Thank God!" I knew this good man was going to help me. He gave me his phone number and said I could call and if he did not answer that I should just leave a message on his voice mail and he would get it. He said that if he could contact me, he would, but it would probably be seldom. He encouraged me to just leave any information that I had on his voice mail line and said he would be sure to get it. I did as he said.

Later, I would learn that this incredibly good, honest and compassionate man wrote a six-page report about my conversation with him and my son's death and submitted it internally to the FBI.

We have stayed in touch now for over five years and without him I do not know where I would be. I know that God put him in my path and he has confirmed that everything I researched and found was indeed true. He called one day and told me, "Adrienne, it is all true." "Shout it from the mountaintops." As we got to know each other better and shared with each other, I knew that he was a devout Christian. He is my brother in Christ and I love and respect him completely. I told him one day that I could not leave this earth without giving him a hug. I asked, "Do you think I could ever meet you and give you my hug?" I could see his warm smile through the phone and he said "yes". I said, "Oh that will be wonderful." "Are you sure?" He said, "Uh-huh." I said, "No, you need to promise me; you need to say, I promise, and that way I know for sure it will happen." I could tell he smiled even more broadly before saying, "I promise." I cried and thanked him so very much for all that he had done and was doing. This special man was a lifeline for me and will be always and forever. We are both rooted in the foundation of our faith.

On January 3, 2008, I wrote this poem for my Joseph. I told Joseph, "I hope and pray you like it; each word is on my heart. I love you."

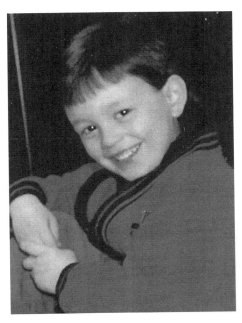

My precious Joseph at age 3. "His smile was so darling and he had that certain twinkle in his eye. He truly did light up a room," How I miss my angle boy.

115

My Joseph, My JAM- My Poem written to my beloved Joseph.

A beautiful morn at 6:07, a precious angel came down from heaven; he quickly encountered the awe of the room; he stole my heart after embracing my womb.

My babe is beautiful, so perfect and sweet; he awaited his family for soon he would meet. That smile on his face so tender and mild; thank you, sweet Jesus, for my darling child.

I will call him Joseph after my dad, a spirited heart and a wonderful lad.

He would love all the earth in all of its glory and take hold of each life that entered his story.

From fish to turtle, to hamster to crab, he filled every nook and with gusto would grab.

My son he lightened the world with his smile, not knowing his time would be but a while.

He traveled here and there and hugged those he met, as I found out the time to go was not yet.

He was to wait till the day of summer, July: I was to learn of tears still to cry.

My Joseph left all and knew we would see how some would not answer and flee from our plea.

But this will not work when all's said and done, 'cause the witness is here, my holy one.

My son had a heart to all he did show; he came to the sky as a colorful rainbow.

Joseph took "up" with Jesus and many and at the same time, he gave me my penny.

The jewel is round and brilliant indeed; it lay on my breast to fulfill my aching need.

The tears do not stop; they seem 24-7, from a hot summer day in the month of seven.

My Joseph who came in the year eighty-seven smiles down on his mom and sends kisses from heaven.

He is always beside me to enlighten my way; he knows what's inside and just what to say.

I love you, my son, with all of my heart; we travel as one and are never apart.

Be still and be calm my dear sweet mother; I'll love you forever for there is no other.

I have been through the valley and am now with the lamb; keep faith, hope and love, your precious JAM.

"Nineteen years my gift," he is now safely home.

On January 4, 2008, I filed my lawsuit against forty-two defendants in the state of Maryland. It had to be filed in the Baltimore County Circuit Courthouse in Towson, Maryland. I recall that there were several county offices, including Baltimore City that needed to be served due to the delegated region that each individual worked out of.

In early January 2008, the two Baltimore County homicide investigators arrived at my home. Homicide detective Carl Bollen and Corporal Lou Geck knocked on my front door and introduced themselves. I thanked them for coming and we walked into the kitchen and sat down at my kitchen table. I had all of the MDSP reports and especially Detective Bishtall's that explained in detail all that had occurred when my son was killed. Detective Bollen pulled out a yellow, lined notepad and was taking notes. They asked me some questions and they said that they are going to do their best to get to the truth of what happened to Joseph.

I said, "We know what happened to Joseph." I explained about the small sixteen-inch space between the two left tires of the Bobcat and the undercarriage that sits just ten inches off the ground. I continued that a contortionist midget could not even possibly fall off the front tire and slip through this small and limited area without breaking his or her feet, ankles, legs, hip, back and more. It was not possible and the medical examiners had already proven it as impossible. I even got up from the table and down on my knees to show them what I meant and that Joseph was already lying flat on his stomach on the ground when the Bobcat reversed over him. I will never forget that Detective Bollen said. "Yes, it is possible." I said, "How? How is it possible?" He still kept inferring that the Bobcat moved forward over Joseph and I asked Detective Bollen and Corporal Geck, "Have you seen the crime scene photographs. There are only backup tread marks; that has already been proven by the medical examiner experts. My son was definitely backed up over. The spotter, Pete Coldwin, pushed my son into the oncoming Bobcat. He actually admits to pushing Joseph. It is in the MDSP police report taken by Trooper Reba Bushly, but she neither says nor asks PeteColdwin anything about the pushing. She never brings it up again in her interview of him. This was a criminal investigation. Does that make any sense to you?"

I was astounded by Detective Bollen's remarks but kept my composure and knew that they had been given orders by Slicenberger to conduct an independent investigation. With this I hoped that there would be fresh eyes examining all of the facts and evidence and they would investigate with integrity and go much further than the MDSP did.

Detective Bollen then started asking me about names of people whom he should talk to and whom I thought should be interviewed. I said, "Oh yes, Detective, there are several." I first said Rod Schwib needed to be interviewed and that he was there on the day Joseph was killed and he was Pete Coldwin's supervisor at the time. I also told them that he was driving another construction vehicle to where Joseph lay underneath the Bobcat and was going to try to move the Bobcat off of Joseph even though they knew Joseph was deceased and the 911 operator emphasized to them that they should not touch or move anything. I said, "Thank God Trooper Hudock stopped him as he was the first one from the Maryland State Police to arrive at the scene." I told them that he lived in Cockeysville off of Cranbrook Road in an apartment complex and I could tell them the address and what he looked like because I had driven by there several times and seen Rodney Schwib walk out and get into his Outside Unliving truck. I said, "I know. I have it written down. Let me go find it." Then Corporal Geck said, "That's OK, Ms. Miranda, we'll find it." I watched Detective Bollen write *Rod Schwib* on his yellow notepad. Then he asked me about the other guy. He said, "Who, who's the man who was on the scene and said he thought he got there first? Uh, I can't think of his name, but—" Then I said, "Oh, Mr. Brodeman." Detective Bollen said, "Yes, that's it." He wrote that name on his yellow notepad as well.

As Detective Bollen wrote down Brodeman's name, I then told them Jim Hovet should also be interviewed. I said, "Mr. Hovet spoke with me on the phone and he was there the day Joseph was killed and spoke to Joseph just about fifteen minutes before Joseph was killed. He described Joseph as being in a happy and good state of mind and said that Joe was just telling him that they would all miss him and he gave him a hug and said he'd better come back and visit. You see, Jim had resigned from Outside Unliving and that happened to be his last day of work, July 20, 2006." I also mentioned that Rich Stauls and Pete Coldwin needed to be interviewed. With that the detective and Corporal Geck said, "We cannot talk with them, they are lawyered up." I said, "What do you mean you cannot talk to them?" The officers said that because they had already retained an attorney, they did not have the right to talk to them or interview them. I said, "Who do you mean, Outside Unliving or Pete Coldwin?" They said, "Outside Unliving and some of their employees. We definitely cannot talk to or interview Pete Coldwin and we are pretty sure that some of the Mexican employees have already gone back to Mexico."

They then gathered their notepad and papers and quickly said that they had to leave. I said, "But I still have so much more to tell you and there are still more names I need to give to you."

They explained that after meeting with me for about two and a half hours, they had a court case that was imperative for them to attend. They said a mother was at risk of losing custody of her child and they needed to be there for her in court. I said, "Oh my, I understand. Will you come back again to my home so I can give you the other information and names you need to follow up with?" They both said, "Yes, we will be back in about two weeks and we will also call you to keep you updated." I walked with the police officers to the door and was so very grateful to them. I gestured to give Detective Bollen a thank-you hug and tell him I felt so relieved that Baltimore County now had the case; with that, Corporal Geck motioned to me and softly said, "No, Miss Miranda." They could see the gratitude that was on my face, so I just said, "I am sorry. I am just so grateful to you both. You will see more of what has been going on as you continue with the case and more unfolds." They both looked at me and said, "What do you mean?" The front door was already opened and I just said, "That's OK. We don't have to discuss it or talk about it now. You will see." They both left and I thanked them again and said I would look forward to hearing from them. I was disappointed inside, but I reminded them to please return to my home because there was still much more I had to explain to them and that I also had to give more names of people who needed to be interviewed. They said OK and got into their vehicle to leave. They did not know at that time that I had filed a lawsuit against the Maryland State Police and other state employees.

I was so relieved that back on January 4, I had at last sued these wrongdoers who were connected with the Maryland State Police investigation and had my case presented before the judiciary. Our lawsuit was recused five times by judges in Baltimore County until Judge Dan Levise finally took the case. It would take some time before we actually received a date for the hearing.

Meanwhile, I waited and waited and wondered why the Baltimore County detectives weren't contacting me about the independent investigation finally ordered by State's Attorney Todd Slicenberger. It had been over a month and they said they would come back to my home to collect the additional information and names of people who needed to be interviewed in two weeks. I called and left a message for Detective Bollen, but he never got back to me. In fact, he never once called or spoke with me again about Joseph's case. I did speak with Lieutenant Jim Mahoney and Corporal Geck a few times. They also e-mailed me. However, the Baltimore County Homicide Squad detectives never did return to my home as promised.

The next thing I knew, Corporal Geck spoke with me on the phone and told me that he did have the feeling that charges would be filed, but he could not tell me for sure. He did feel that the incident was a crime.

However, when I spoke with Lieutenant Mahoney, he was very closed mouthed and just said they were working on it. I asked, "Could I please have the case number assigned to Joseph's case?" He said, "There isn't any case number." I was stunned. I said, "What do you mean there isn't any case number for the homicide investigation into my son's death?" He just said, "It doesn't matter and it doesn't need a case number." I said, "Then how do you document the related hourly costs involved for the accounting records in the Baltimore County Police Department? "You are not making any sense. You are supposed to be conducting an independent investigation of a probable homicide and you are telling me you are not even giving my son's homicide investigation a case number? I have never heard of anything so strange, preposterous and outlandish." He just said he had to go and got off the phone.

I e-mailed State's Attorney Slicenberger about it and he, too, ignored me and he just said it did not matter. I talked to my brother, Damian and my family about it and they could not believe that there was no case number assigned. They, too, were shocked and outraged.

In April, 2008, I learned that the Baltimore County Homicide Squad had completed its so-called investigation. They had the case for four months and when I received their investigative report, it was all of twelve pages it its entirety. It seemed to be a total of about maybe fifteen hours of work over the four-month period. The people whose names I had given them to interview and speak with were never contacted. I was devastated at how they had performed their tasks in this very horrendous and unfair investigation. I, to this day, feel that my civil rights have been violated and we were treated with bias, prejudice and immense injustice and misconduct. The proof is all there, but the officials in Maryland will not recognize it or validate it. They have egg all over their faces, in particular State's Attorney Todd Slicenberger. The source of all of this evil wrongdoing will be exposed. God will reveal it, all of it, in his way and in his time. Yes, indeed, there will be a greater good.

Deuteronomy 31:8: "The Lord himself goes before you and will be with you; he will never leave you or forsake you. Do not be afraid; do not be discouraged." Oh heavenly Father, I am not afraid. I have received your words of victory that you will bring and I am certain that a greater good, "JAM's house, home sweet home," will prevail. This brings me tears of joy and gives me a happy heart.

However, I do thank God that Dr. Zabiullah Ali, the medical examiner who had performed the autopsy on my son and who had met with Detective Bishtall, actually went to Outside Unliving to do a reenactment of what happened to Joseph on July 20, 2006, as he was killed. Dr. Ali was accompanied by Detective Bollen, Corporal Geck, another female and, I believe, a photographer.

Dr. Ali actually sat in a G873 Bobcat and drove it himself after observing another operator driving it. He moved it in forward and reverse motion. He turned and swiveled the earthmover, examined how it was designed and studied the space between the two left tires and the low sitting undercarriage of the Bobcat.

CHAPTER 8

THEIR PHYSICS MADE
NO SENSE

On this day, Dr. Ali was certain and knew without any doubt that Pete Coldwin's story was a lie; it was impossible. We have repeatedly said, "Science doesn't lie."

He knew for sure and with scientific, physical and forensic evidence that Joseph had to be already lying flat on the ground and on his stomach when the rear left wheel of the 7,600-pound steel vehicle drove in reverse over his face, head and neck, crushing him to death. We also knew he was propelled with great force into the Bobcat to his death by Pete Coldwin. Again, to our disbelief, the Baltimore County detectives did not agree with the medical science, facts, physics and forensics. They still kept saying the Bobcat drove forward over our son. This was absolutely absurd and ridiculous and sheer stupidity on their part. They are not scientists or doctors and they have no qualifications whatsoever to refuse and ignore the facts and evidence that were right in front of their eyes. Later, I asked Lieutenant Mahoney, "Did Baltimore County take its reconstructionist along to witness what Dr. Ali did as he reenacted what occurred when Joseph was killed and how the Bobcat maneuvered?" He just said "no".

There were no tire tracks behind the Bobcat, of course, because when the Bobcat was moving backward over Joseph, the driver said he stopped. Then just before he went to go forward, he was stopped by Pete Coldwin when he came to the front and waved his hand across his neck, signaling the driver to stop. The driver said he never drove forward; he then stopped and jumped out, not even turning off the ignition. The driver then saw Joseph crushed underneath and lying in a pool of blood. He screamed, cried, pounded on his chest and begged for a priest.

There were definite reversing tire tracks behind the two front wheels of the Bobcat. You can clearly see them in the photographs and these tire tracks prove the Bobcat was moving in reverse when Joseph was killed. Again, more proof that Pete Coldwin is a blatant liar as he still tried to convince the police and my attorney that the Bobcat drove forward and Joseph jumped up on top of the left front tire and then fell down and in-between a sixteen-by-ten-inch space.

This is absolutely *impossible*. Joseph had no broken bones below his neck and there are only backup tread marks.

I could tell that something was not right with the Baltimore County homicide investigation and I called by brother, Damian. We spoke over the phone and I relayed that we were going to need photographs of the model G873 Bobcat for legal purposes according to the attorneys I had been conversing with recently. I asked if there was any way I could obtain those photographs. Later that day I spoke to my Brother, Damian. He explained to me when he was on his cell phone and in his car that he hung up with me and explained the situation to his wife, Dana. He said that they both kind of looked at each other puzzled. Then he told me in his words that "For some reason we came off of I-75 in Florida and turned down a side street in an industrial area. Something told me to turn left, so I did. I said out loud, "Where am I ever going to find one of those…" and before I got the words out, it was like someone had tapped me on the shoulder and said here it was. I noticed off to the left-hand side a Bobcat and I asked my wife, "What does that say on the side?" She replied, "G873." "I began to get chills and to this day still get chills when I talk about it. The power of God is completely awesome." Damian told me, "God led me right to it and it was out in the open." He said, "We stepped out of the car, walked up to the Bobcat and began taking pictures, first front to back and then side to side and finally underneath. I knew as I stood there next to this machine that there was just no way that what they were saying happened to Joe was even possible." "We went home and e-mailed the photographs to Adrienne as well as printed hard copies to send to her. It was just plain amazing." My brother, Dana and I knew it was a miracle from God.

All we ever asked for was for truth and justice to be served. We are right to expect that the investigators and the judiciary do their job and treat us with equality and fairness in receiving resolution. This person responsible for taking the life of our precious son must be held accountable in a court of law. There is a mountain of evidence, but they have chosen deceit, prejudice and injustice over truth, freedom and justice. They are a disgrace.

I love my Lord with my entire being and know that His Holy Spirit lives in me. He will never leave me and His promises are rock solid. He will bring truth and justice despite the evil wrongdoers. I am certain of it.

John 14:15–17 "If you love me, you will obey what I command. And I will ask the Father and he will give you another Counselor to be with you forever—the Spirit of Truth. You know him, for he lives with you and will be in you."

In summation, Mr. Antoine Ruberra, the driver of Mexican descent, was at first manipulated and Pete Coldwin tried to unintelligibly point the finger at him. We knew, however, after studying specific pictures along with Detective Bishtall's report that Mr. Antoine Ruberra was not at fault. He and Joe liked each other and Mr. Ruberra had no idea at all that Joseph had been pushed and shoved into the Bobcat from behind by Pete Coldwin just prior to being crushed to death.

Through my faith, divine intervention, the Holy Spirit and God's power, after many years, Mr. Ruberra tried to reach out to me. I am so humbled and grateful that I was able to convey to Mr. Ruberra that I knew he did not mean to hurt Joseph. I told his friend to please tell him, since Antoine was in the hospital in Florida and gravely ill, that I knew he did nothing wrong and that I sent my love and prayers to him. His friend phoned me back the next day and said that he did tell Antoine that I sent love and prayers to him and that Antoine said to tell me that he was sending love and prayers back to me. God bless this Christian man, my friend, who I believe is now with the Lord in His paradise. *Matthew 19:19 "Love your neighbor as yourself."*

Matthew 15:11–17 "I have told you this so that my joy may be in you and that your joy may be complete. My command is this: Love each other as I have loved you. Greater love has no one than this, that he lay down his life for his friends. You are my friends if you do what I command. I no longer call you servants, because a servant does not know his master's business. Instead, I have called you friends, for everything that I learned from my Father I have make known to you. You did not choose me, but I chose you and appointed you to go and bear fruit—fruit that will last. Then the Father will give you whatever you ask in my name. This is my command: Love each other."

Throughout the early spring and for many months, I was in contact with CNN. In the early morning, I would call and talk with them. God bless Mary, Brandon, Lisa and so many others for listening and hearing me with such compassion. I will never forget them. MSNBC was also very gracious and compassionate as they listened to my story.

I had spent so much of myself and my heart and soul trying everything I knew to find someone who would help me. I knew that my only help and hope was my faith in my Lord and that in His time He would come through and deliver. I acted on what I heard my Holy Spirit telling me and instructing me to do with each passing day. For some time I had noticed that my mail looked strange. The envelopes were marked with so much ink and the fold-over seal of my mail seemed to have already been opened and then resealed. I looked closely at each envelope and knew something was going on. I was told by a very good and intellectual person that my mail was probably being rifled through by the US Postal Service. Again, I was wide-eyed but I suppose not actually shocked. I called the US Postal Service's main headquarters for Maryland in downtown Baltimore and explained what was going on and how my mail looked. I asked if they could please come look at it. They were the experts and investigators and

I was sure that they could look at my mail and tell if, in fact, it was being rifled through.

The first man I spoke with said he would have to get back to me because they were very busy but he would pass the information on. I did not hear from anyone over the next two weeks, so I called again. This time I spoke with a man who had a very abrupt, nasty tone and said he could not help me and he was moving to a different state. He told me to bring my mail down to them and someone would look at it. I said, "Can you tell me a day and a time that would work best?" He just said, "I have to go," and he hung up. I was getting so frustrated, but I persevered. I decided to leave a message for my friend with the FBI in Bethesda who was there for me and let him know what was happening. He gave me the name of a man who worked at a very high level in the US Postal Service and told me to call him. I wrote down his name and number and said OK. When I spoke with this gentleman, he said, "I do not know why anyone told you that they could not come to your home or help you now. I will send someone out to you and have them take a look at your mail; it does sound like it is being rifled through and this is a federal crime." I thanked him so much and was extremely appreciative. He took down all of my information. Again, weeks went by and I did not get any call back from this man who was a director or top official with the US Postal Service.

I decided to call him again. He picked up the phone and when I told him it was Adrienne Miranda and I had been waiting to hear from him about the inspection of my mail, he said, "Ms. Miranda, we cannot help you; there is nothing we can do. We could get prosecuted." Then he hung up the phone. Now I was in shock. I phoned my friend with the FBI and let him know what had occurred. He said, "Uh-huh, I hear you Adrienne." He said, "Keep doing what you're doing and leave any messages for me". He repeated, "Stay strong, Adrienne. Stay strong."

I say to my son, "My darling Joseph, each step I take moves me further along the path God has designated for me. I am working hard to please and serve my Jesus. I know you are very aware of everything. I am praying always that I hear correctly and my faith in the Holy Spirit assures me that I am." My journey is long and seems unbearable, but I fall to my knees remembering the painful, sorrowful suffering and agony of Jesus's journey. The grief, tears and sorrow of God our Father for His only begotten Son, sweet Jesus, our Christ and our Lord and Savior whom He sent to save us lives on in me and empowers me to die to self and give all of myself to my Almighty God. We are all of the same blue blood that runs through our veins. We are all of the same red blood that releases to the air of the earth. We are all of the same species of race, human. However, while God has given all of us our own individual heart and soul, He has also given us our own free will. Let the will of God's people be heard. Let the "Word", Jesus himself, reach our hearts so that we may live and act in the spirit of love.

I stand strong and convicted to complete my Father's purpose and His plan for me. I will not grow weary but run into his open arms of love.

Isaiah 40:31: "Those who hope in the Lord will renew their strength. They will soar on wings like eagles; they will run and not grow weary, they will walk and not be faint."

It was now April 22, 2008 and Joseph's twenty-first birthday! Oh, how he yearned to turn twenty-one. He was so excited about this day and entering his "manhood." He would talk about it often to me and really enjoyed the big party I held for Rob's twenty-first birthday. He took it all in and was so happy for his brother. I smile when I recall that a few days after Rob's party Joseph stopped me in the hallway in the morning when we were getting ready for work. He smiled and kissed me on the forehead and said, "Mom, I want my twenty-first birthday party." I hugged him and said, "I know, Joseph and you will have a big twenty-first birthday party." He said, "But Mom, I want it now!" I laughed and said, "You can't have it now," and he asked why. I said, "Because you're not twenty-one yet." He said, "I know, Mom, but I want it now!" We laughed and I said, "Oh Joseph, you will have your big party, sweetheart, but you have to wait until you turn twenty-one." We hugged and he laughed and said," I know, Mom."

So here it was, April 22, 2008, Joseph's twenty-first birthday! I had sent out at least a hundred invitations to family and friends. Joseph knew he was going to have his big twenty-first birthday party that I had promised him. I never broke my promises to my sons. I contracted with a local event recording company and they brought in a huge screen to set up on our front lawn with a microphone system. My sister-in-law, Lisa Gemma, went to buy beautiful stationery that had *John 3:16* written on its border and two large boxes of prayer vigil candles. I bought twenty-one pure-white balloons—pure as the love in Joseph's heart—and set up easels with my favorite photographs of Joseph and our family. We wrote a beautiful prayer on the stationery to hand out to everyone as well as a music sheet with the words to "What a Wonderful World" by Mr. Louis Armstrong. Joseph loved that song and the words…He had loved it since he first heard it at the age of thirteen.

We had everything planned and Uncle Damian was going to call in from Florida to pray and sing along with us. The recording company said they could do that and we could hear Damian over the loudspeaker when he phoned in.

When I awoke on this morn, I opened my eyes and sang "Happy Birthday" to my Joseph and prayed. The sun was shining and the blue sky, green grass and blooming flowers were our canvas. I thanked God for such a beautiful day. I knew in my heart how thrilled Joseph was at the anticipation of this "rite of passage" on this twenty-first birthday, the special day we all dream of and yearn for. The two gentlemen from the recording company arrived and started setting up. They were both so very kind and compassionate. I will never forget them. I had given them the CD of the beautiful montage of pictures and songs from throughout Joseph's life that Rob had created. They were going to show it on the big screen out front. I set up our photographs on the easels, put all of the prayer sheets and music sheets in order and put out the candles for each to hold. I knew in my heart I was going to speak to everyone and thank them all for their love and for honoring the celebration of Joseph's life. I knew my heart was full and the Holy Spirit would give me all of the words. Family and friends started arriving in the late afternoon. Dino and Lisa helped me set up and put out some lawn chairs. The day was perfect and I was so overjoyed to give hugs and kisses to all of Joseph's family. Marie and John brought us a beautiful bouquet of flowers, neighbors came by and the front lawn was full of kind, loving and compassionate faces—all of the folk we love. We were ready to get started and I knew Joseph was right there with us and looking down from the heavens with his beautiful, big smile.

I took the microphone and greeted everyone as they stood and sat side by side. I thanked them from the bottom of my heart and on behalf of Joseph's entire family for coming. My son, Rob, was beside me. Joseph's dad, Bob, was greeting everyone as well. I explained how grateful we were that Joseph had such a strong faith in the Lord and we knew he was home in heaven. I told some brief stories about Joseph's life and how he yearned for his twenty-first birthday. I told them about the beautiful montage and music medley that Rob had made for Joseph in celebration of his life. I cued the videographer to start the CD on the big screen. We all watched with love in our hearts, joyful smiles and tear-filled eyes. Everyone could see the heart of Joseph and each had their own cherished memories with him. His brother, Rob, created such a beautiful and amazing piece of work in which song lyrics correspond to each photograph. I will forever cherish this love gift from Rob in honor of his brother. I still marvel at how quickly Rob was able to put all of this together in just two days at the time of Joseph's death.

After the video was finished, we phoned Uncle Damian and connected him on the line. He greeted everyone from Florida and sent his love. We all prayed together the beautiful words to our Lord and Savior after lighting our candles for the vigil. It was now time to sing "Happy Birthday" to Joseph. We all gathered round and sang "Happy Birthday" to dear Joseph and I released the twenty-one pure-white balloons up to the heavens. I cried as I watched them ascend upward and into the clouds as the sky opened and they disappeared into the heavens. It was as if Joseph was saying, "I've got them, Mom. I've got them!" I knew in my heart and soul that Joseph was happy and celebrating. We sang his favorite song, "What a Wonderful World," and after, I tried to wipe my tears and speak. I enlightened everyone on what we had been learning about the tragedy that took

Joseph from us and explained that I vowed to be Joseph's voice. I said, "No greed or evil will ever overpower a mother's love. God will bring truth and justice and there is a purpose in all that He does. Everything happens in God's time. We must all keep faith and trust in our Almighty Father."

Psalm 9: 7-10, 16: "The Lord reigns forever; he has established his throne for judgment. He will judge the world in righteousness; he will govern the peoples with justice. The Lord is a refuge for the oppressed, a stronghold in times of trouble. Those who know your name will trust in you, for you, Lord, have never forsaken those who seek you. The Lord is known by his justice."

The evening was closing and we all gathered in love and worship to our Lord and Savior. Oh, happy day, when Jesus wiped our tears away. How very true this is. When I went to sleep that night, I knelt down and said my prayers. I lay down and held tightly to JAM and my Joseph's T-shirt that encased my pillow. My Bible was right beside me as well as the blessed prayer shawl, my tallit that I received from Jerusalem. I closed my eyes and I was calmed.

Psalm 119: 169–175: "May my cry come before you, O Lord; give me understanding according to your word. May my supplication come before you; deliver me according to your promise, May my lips overflow with praise, for you teach me your decrees, May my tongue sing of your word, for all your commands are righteous, May your hand be ready to help me, for I have chosen your precepts. I long for your salvation, O Lord and your law in my delight, Let me live that I may praise you and may your laws sustain me."

CHAPTER 9

JOSEPH'S TWENTY-FIRST BIRTHDAY; HIS RITE OF PASSAGE

In April for Joseph's twenty-first birthday, I had taken flowers, balloons and cards to his gravesite. So did many of his family members and friends. Once again, a few days later, when I went to the cemetery to pray, Joseph's gravesite was desecrated—the flowers stolen, the blooms cut off and the balloons gone—and I just wept. I remained in prayer and after I went into the offices of Dulaney Valley Memorial Gardens and wanted to speak with the owner or the supervisor. You see, they had known about the first desecration back in July of 2007. I reported it and told them that I had filed a police report and they were very understanding and empathized with me.

They early on told me sometimes deer eat the heads of the flowers, but they realized that you could see the cut stems on our flowers; there were beautiful roses just gone—stolen—and the little ceramic turtle was surely not eaten by a deer.

Now, once again, a supervisor walked down to the gravesite with me to see for herself. I asked if they could put up some kind of motion detector or at least close off the open areas where there were no gates installed.

They were very sorry but said they could not accommodate us in that way. They said they would talk with their ground maintenance crew and ask that they keep a special eye on our gravesite. In 2007 and 2008, they had hired a new landscaping company—a very large corporation that also does all the ground work for a specific, very large religious organization in Maryland. I asked if many of the grounds crew were of Mexican descent. They said they were. I asked, "How are they able to understand what you are asking them if they do not speak English?" I was told that their head groundskeeper is American and she is able to communicate with them. I thanked them and said that I appreciated them looking out for me.

It was now May, my favorite month and I was requesting to the courts that they give me a postponement for the hearing in Baltimore County. My brother, Damian, was getting married to his beautiful bride, Dana. They live in Naples, Florida and I so badly wanted to attend. I had to submit the necessary request in writing and fortunately it was granted.

Before, in March 2008, we had started doing a search to have T-shirts made for our crusade, "Justice for Joseph." My nephew, David, found a great source that was able to make the T-shirt just as I had designed with Joseph's picture on the front and *Justice for Joseph* printed in red letters across the front and the back of the shirt. They came out beautifully. We all knew in our hearts that it would be necessary sometime up ahead to plan a march for justice and truth.

Today was Mother's Day and the sun was gleaming. My mother and I shared the day together and honored each other. My mom gave me a long-stem red rose from Joseph and a written note that read *I love you, Mom and you are the best Mom in the whole world.* The written words made me cry and the *x*'s and *o*'s for kisses and hugs that all of my family put on their cards were so sentimental and sweet. I could feel the kisses and hugs Joseph was sending from heaven and I knew that he knew.

My mom and I put on our *Justice for Joseph* T-shirts and drove to the cemetery to bring flowers, prayer cards and our love to Joseph and Michael, our angel boys. We stayed for a while; the weather was so beautiful. As we were standing with our arms around each other and looking at Joseph's marker, my mom moved her head slightly to the right as she kissed me on my tearstained cheek. She then whispered softly to me, "Adrienne, if you look around to your right, about thirty yards away, there is a man standing under a tree with a camera. He has the camera pointed directly at us." I slowly motioned to look and sure enough there was a man wearing a suit looking through the long lens of a camera that was on a tripod. He definitely had the camera focused on us. I turned my head back around and just kept praying. I said, "I see him, Mom. It is odd." We stayed in prayer to Joseph and kissed his headstone. The photographer was there for a while and after a bit I turned and saw him leave. He got into a silver, gray, or blue sedan and left. My mother and I knew it was unusual, but we had the feeling that it was something positive rather than negative. When we returned home, I made sure to leave a voice message for my friend with the FBI so he would know about it.

I visited Joseph's grave often with prayer and my agony and I rode up to the cemetery on a beautiful May morning after Mother's Day. Now, for the third time, my son's gravesite had been desecrated. Again the flowers my mother and I took were gone, the heart balloon that was securely fastened was gone and just dead stems lay on the ground. I could only believe what was happening had been done with malicious intent; I knew in my heart that it was. I, again, went up to the offices tear filled and a very nice woman, Lisa, talked with me. She was so kind and compassionate. She, too, realized that something despicable was going on. She said that they would put up a small sign in the ground that read in both English and Spanish *Do not touch or remove anything from this gravesite*. I thanked her and hugged her. I knew not to call the Baltimore County Police again because nothing would come of it.

Psalm 59: "Deliver me from my enemies, O God; protect me from those who rise up against me. Deliver me from evildoers and save me from bloodthirsty men. Fierce men conspire against me for no offense or sin of mine, O Lord. But for those who fear you, you have raised a banner to be unfurled against the bow. Save us and help us with your right hand, that those you love may be delivered. With God we will gain the victory and he will trample down our enemies. For you have heard my vows, O God; you have given me the heritage of those who fear your name. May he be enthroned in God's presence forever; appoint your love and faithfulness to protect him. I will forever sing praise to your name and I long to dwell in your tent forever."

I know God gave me the strength and the fortitude to pack my bags and be together with all of my family and Dana's family for their lovely wedding day, June 14, 2008. I also was so happy to see all of their friends. Joseph had spent several of his teen years during the summer months vacationing with Uncle Damian; he worked with him too and loved it. Joseph had a family of love, friendship, fun and joy with all of these blessed friends who knew Joe and his heart. He loved them and they loved him. To this day, their love continues to flow to and from Joseph. I love them all so very much for their compassion, support and remembrance of Joseph.

My family and I packed our bags and headed for Naples, Florida, for the wedding day! I was so happy for my loving brother and his bride, Dana. We stayed a few days at the beautiful hotel where they were to be married. I wore my *Justice for Joseph* T-shirt on the plane and some kind people asked me, "Who is Joseph?" I told them he was my beloved son, who was now home with the Lord.

June 14, 2008, was here and the sun was shining brightly. The guests were arriving and the pastor greeted our family. Dana was still upstairs getting ready to walk down the winding staircase in her beautiful wedding gown and her bridesmaids would come before her. I sat alongside my mother, Betty Gemma, and with my other family members. My brother Damian looked so handsome in his tux and so did my brother Dino, his best man.

Everyone was seated and the beautiful music began. I knew that Joseph and Michael were right there with us and so was our dad, Joseph Vincent Gemma, who had gone home to the Lord at the age of sixty. I held my mother's hand as we all stood up. The bridal party was dressed in a beautiful coral melon color and looked so lovely. Dana was exquisite and stunning. She gracefully came down the staircase in her gorgeous white gown and veil, moving toward her husband to be, my brother Damian. He was gloriously happy and you could see the love in their eyes for each other. The ceremony began, the words of the gospel were spoken and they both exchanged their wedding vows. My mom and I were filled up with tears of joy for them. After the vows were spoken, my brother said a few words about our dad, Michael and Joseph and how they were loved and missed but their presence was always with us. "You are now husband and wife" was spoken and everyone clapped, smiled and hugged. What a splendid display of love and happiness! How our Lord blessed us on this day and showed his favor upon us.

We flowed into the reception line before taking our seats in the ball-room. Dana and Damian were glowing. Each attendee got a chance to extend his or her love, joy and happiness to Dana, Damian and the wedding party. I was so glad to see so many of Damian's close friends and meet more members of Dana's family. Jacqueline looked beautiful and Jesse so handsome. They are Dana's daughter and son, whom we love so very much. Dana's mother, Ms. Janyce, was also so lovely and our families were so exhilarated to be in union through the deep love that Damian and Dana shared.

There was so much love expressed and shared on this day that I will remember and cherish it always. I was also able to meet many of the wonderful people whom Damian worked with. All of them are so very special and their love and support have been so helpful and comforting to me.

The food was outstanding and abundant and the music made you get up to dance. Yes, I actually danced at my brother's wedding! I have always loved singing and dancing and I can't imagine the world without music. Since Joseph's death I had not socialized in any way like I used to. I was a changed person in many ways, still praying to find my way, truth and justice and to listen to my Lord.

Two days after my brother's wedding, we were still in Florida. I was asleep beside my mother. I clearly remember feeling that I was leaving my body and flowing into the light. I felt such a peaceful presence and my Lord calling to me. I was happy and yearned to go with him. I think I sat up and my mom awoke. I heard my mom and family screaming and calling my name, "Adrienne, Adrienne, oh my God. She is blue. Is she gone?" They must have called 911. The next thing I heard was doors opening and I awoke, even though I thought I was already awake. I calmly said, "What is wrong? I was just on the path to heaven."

Suddenly the paramedics hooked me up to all kinds of devices and put an oxygen mask on me and heart monitors. I heard them speaking and asking me questions. They also asked my family members questions. They said the blue color was now leaving me and my color was returning. The paramedics said, "Her heart was racing, but she is now stable and her vitals are good." They asked more about recent occurrences after being told by my mom that my son had been killed. They monitored me for a while and then said they thought I had had a panic attack. They asked how I felt and I told them I felt OK. They asked me about medications and I said I was taking antidepressants and a sleep aid. I told them I take them only as prescribed. I pointed to the bottles on the dresser. They said OK and that if anything else happened and I had chest pains or felt faint, I should go to the nearest emergency room. My family and I thanked them and they left.

CHAPTER 10

BE NOT SHATTERED BY THE EVIL FORCES AND STAND STRONG IN HIS LOVE

My faith was not shattered by the evil forces confronting me and I knew my Lord was with me. My Holy Spirit, the love in my heart and my innate conviction to always try to do the right thing restored me. I will never, never give up despite these evil wrongdoers. God will not overlook the deception and criminal misconduct of these wicked people. Genesis 3:13–14: "The woman said, The serpent deceived me. So the Lord God said to the serpent, 'Because you have done this, Cursed are you above all the livestock and the wild animals! You will crawl on your belly and you will eat dust all the days of your life.'"

Revelations 12:9–11 "The great dragon was hurled down—that ancient serpent called the devil, or Satan, who leads the whole world astray. He was hurled to the earth. Now have come the salvation and the power and the Kingdom of our God and the authority of his Christ. They overcame Satan by the blood of the Lamb and by the work of their testimony; they did not love their lives so much as to shrink from death. Therefore rejoice, you heavens and you who dwell in them! But woe to the earth and the sea because the devil has gone down to you! He is filled with fury, because he knows that his time is short."

Proverbs 6:12–15: "A scoundrel and villain, who goes with a corrupt mouth, who winks with his eye, signals with his feet and motions with his fingers, who plots evil with deceit in his heart—he always stirs up dissension. Therefore disaster will overtake him in an instant; he will suddenly be destroyed—without remedy."

Proverbs 10:16: "The wages of the righteous bring them life, but the income of the wicked brings them punishment."

I sadly remember that on June 13, 2008, Mr. Timothy J. Russert went home to the Lord. I loved Tim and was so impressed by the truthfulness, integrity and uncompromised fairness and kindness he extended to each of his guests on *Meet the Press*. I prayed for his wife, Maureen and his son, Luke. He was loved by so many and admired for his forthrightness spoken and diplomatic speaking and for getting to truth. I told Joseph to give Mr. Russert a big hug in heaven and that his heart was full of love just like yours, Joseph. God wanted him home; it was his plan.

On June 18, 2008, Timothy J. Russert was laid to rest. I watched his memorial and funeral on MSNBC and heard the beautiful words and love expressed to Tim by all of those who loved, respected and honored him. He was an exceptionally good man and an outstanding journalist. I know the agony and pain of Maureen, his beautiful wife and his wonderful handsome son, Luke, but more than this I share their love and faith in Jesus Christ our Savior. I remember I called MSNBC and wanted to express my condolences to the family. These people were so kind that they put me through to Mr. Russert's voice mail and I heard his distinct voice. I was filled with gratitude, tears and the grace of God and left a message on his voice mail to him and to his wife and son. I said my name and that Tim was now in heaven with my son, Joseph. I told them how much I always loved and admired him. To this day, I remember the last words Tim Russert spoke when he closed what would be his last *Meet the Press* airing. He said, "Fasten your seat belts folks and get ready for the ride of your life." How true this was and how it would come to pass throughout our nation and the universe.

When the funeral and memorial service were over in Washington, DC and as people exited, there was a beautiful double rainbow across the sky. I cried and was filled with joy. For in my heart I felt that Tim and Joseph were giving us a sign from heaven. At the same time, the closing song, a beautiful medley, was Joseph's favorite and the first on his iPod, *"Somewhere over the Rainbow"* and *"What a Wonderful World."* It was a splendid musical medley performed and arranged by a Hawaiian artist who played the ukulele, Israel Kamakawiwo'ole. This song is very popular and has been played on television and has been in movies. It truly captures the heart and soul of the love that God wants us to show and have for one another. Tim Russert must have also loved the medley same as Joseph.

It was now July 4, 2008—Independence Day! I depend only on my Jesus for he is my protector, my rescue and my freedom. I took beautiful bouquets of red, white and blue flowers to my loved ones, my father, my son and my nephew. The flowers looked lovely standing next to the American flags. I prayed earnestly and asked God to bring truth and justice for Joseph. I know the integrity of our Almighty Father; He is Truth. He is all-knowing and all-powerful. I told Joseph that I felt how ever present he was and that I delighted in holding him in my arms. I cried to my precious boy, "Hear Momma! Hear Momma!" I told him that my promise and vow to him were grounded in my faith that Father God had given to me and shown to me. It was miraculous and I followed. The Lord is my shepherd and Love is the most powerful possession, faith the most powerful knowledge and hope the most powerful gift. But the greatest of these is *love*!

Again, within the next few days, the patriotic blooms of red, white and blue taken to my beloved father, son and nephew were destroyed. The people at Dulaney Valley offered to put netting over my flowers, but I said no; it would take away from their beauty and nothing was going to keep me from honoring my family and my son. I knew in time God would reveal who was behind these malicious and cruel acts that were intentionally repeated. My love and my prayers are always heard by Father God, His Son, Jesus Christ is always with me and His Holy Spirit lives and thrives inside me.

During these years and still today, there are also several desecrations of my angel gardens at my home: flower blooms deliberately cut off, the rocks that were laid by Luke rearranged so the cross would be broken and not be seen, the wing of an angel statue broken off, my front eucalyptus bush that had grown for years completely stomped on and bent forward, my shed door hammered, smashed and broken into and a gas can stolen and my adorable garden statue of a turtle with a bunny standing on top of the turtle and then a little frog that lit up on top of the bunny destroyed. This was a strong and solid garden statue and Joseph and I loved it. I had it for years and came home one day to find the frog completely yanked off the top with the inside wires just hanging out.

Our neighborhood community is very aware of the problems in our court and so are the Baltimore County Police. I have filed many police reports of destruction of property and trespassing, but there is nothing they can do. I need to have a picture of the person or persons who are committing these crimes. I have been working on that.

July 8, 2008, was soon approaching and my brother Damian had planned to fly in from Florida to attend the circuit court hearing pertaining to my lawsuit against the Maryland State Police, MOSH and other Maryland State employees. In total the number of defendants was forty-two. Damian came in on Monday, July 7th and spent the night at my home. We were very prepared for Tuesday's hearing at nine in the morning before Judge Dan Levise.

I awoke early on July 8 and prayed. I had taken out a good suit to wear and had all of my documents in order and placed in files in my black leather satchel. My penny and my cross were around my neck. I knew Father God would give me the strength to persevere and say the words that needed to be said in a court of law.

My brother, Damian, was also dressed in a very nice business suit and he hugged me before we left my home. All of my family was present as we walked up the steps of the Baltimore County Courthouse in Towson, Maryland. We took the elevator up to the courtroom where our case was going to be heard. As I walked up to the front to take my seat at the plaintiff's table, my brother followed behind and sat to the right of me. Joseph's dad sat in the row of benches behind with our son, his brother and some of his family members as well.

I could see that the courtroom was beginning to fill up. Up front and to the left of me were six state's attorneys from the attorney general's office acting as defendants. There were people seated behind them whom I did not know; there were some other friends, family and newspaper reporters also seated closer to the back.

The court attendees, stenographer and men in uniform were all in readiness. Then the words were spoken for Judge Dan Levise to enter and for all to rise. Just before the judge sat down, I noticed a middle-aged man with slightly salt-and-pepper, brownish hair dressed in a very good suit sit down in the back on the side of the defendants. I did not know his face, nor did my family members.

As Judge Levise proceeded, he first wanted to find out who was present. I, of course, was acting pro se (meaning as my own attorney) and my brother was beside me at the trial table for support and assistance. He looked at my brother, who said, "My name is Damian Gemma; I am the brother of Adrienne Miranda, the plaintiff." The judge said, "Damian what?" My brother said Gemma, G-E-M-M-A. The judge said, "Are you a lawyer, sir?" Damian answered, "No, sir, I am not." Judge Levise asked, "Are you listed as a plaintiff in this case?" Damian said, "I believe I could be considered the et al. It means "and others." The judge said, "Yeah, well, the et al is you have to name the others; "et al" could be anybody in the world." Damian said, "Your Honor, I am just here to help my sister."

Judge Dan Levise continued with a very hostile, nasty and cruel tone. "Well, let me say this to you, sir. Unless you are an attorney licensed to practice law in Maryland, you are forbidden from doing anything that would be acting as an attorney. It's a crime in Maryland. You—you're not allowed to say anything. You are not allowed to participate in this in any way. It is a crime to do that."

My brother said, "Your Honor, am I allowed to hand Ms. Miranda some documents?" The judge said, "I'm happy to have you sit at the trial table and you can talk to your sister, but you are not allowed to say anything, OK?" I said, "That is fine, Your Honor." Then Damian said, "Yes, sir, I understand." The judge said, "And this is just a Maryland law." The judge looked at me and I said again, "That is fine, Your Honor. My name is Adrienne Miranda. I am the plaintiff." Judge Levise said, "Yeah, I figured that out."

"OK, who do we have here?" Judge Levise asked. Then all the assistant attorney generals introduced themselves and explained who they were there on behalf of and representing. It took a while. There were forty-two defendants named and they tried to go by name and number assigned to each defendant. The assistant state's attorney who was representing the attorney general's office of the state of Maryland and some of the MOSH employees had a little difficulty. She said that four of her defendants had not been served yet but she would be representing them also. "Your Honor," she said, "they are on the list, but…" Judge Levise said, "And who are they?" She looked down at her papers and said the four names.

Then another attorney said, "Just one housekeeping measure, Your Honor. The Maryland State Police is also listed as the MDSP, which is defendant number two." Judge Levise said, "OK. Now what I understand that we are here for today is a complaint that was filed pro se by the parents of Joseph Miranda, who died on July the fifteenth, 2006." I said, "No, excuse me, Your Honor; he died on the twentieth of July."

The judge said annoyingly, "Ma'am, I'm just going by the papers that are in the file." I said, "Oh, I'm sorry." Judge Levise said, "It makes absolutely no difference whether it's July the twentieth or July the fifteenth. Let me finish what I am saying." I said OK. The judge said, "Then I am going to let you correct anything that I have said that you think is improper." I said, "Alright, Your Honor. I thought that was an important date, the day of the death of my son."

The judge went on to summarize, "The lawsuit filed is a pro se action by the parents of Joseph Miranda who died in July of 2006 and there are exactly forty-two defendants who have been sued by Ms. Miranda. The lawsuit was filed on January the fourth, 2008 and apparently Mr. Miranda died in an accident that was investigated by the Hampstead Police, the Maryland State Police, the Maryland Department of Labor, Licensing and Regulation, Maryland Occupational Safety and Health and various state's attorneys' offices. The plaintiffs state that the various investigations were inconsistent and incompetent and the investigation was negligently closed, which resulted in overwhelming emotional distress, suffering, inability to work, severe grief and anguish, despair and interference with the victims' civil rights and human rights, leaving them with the inability and denial to obtain justice, resolution and reprieve for their son and their family. This was a direct result of the inept, incompetent, unprofessional and negligent services provided by the state. The plaintiff alleged specifically that there was direct negligence in withholding certain findings and reports and not properly following up, causing the investigation to be closed erroneously on July the eleventh, 2007. The answer filed by the state treasurer states that notice was filed with the State Treasurer's Office on January the third, 2008. We are here because there have been eight separate motions to dismiss filed by various defendants in this case alleging various grounds for dismissal of the action. That's what I understand we are here about. Is that your understanding, counsel?" "Does anybody disagree with why we are here today?" No one disagreed with why we were there. I did just say, "Your Honor, I would like to offer that the Maryland tort claim was submitted on the second of January, not the third."

Judge Levise then said to me, "The problem is, Ms. Miranda, after reading your complaint in Maryland, the state does not recognize any cause of action for what you have alleged. That's the problem. That is the underlying problem. There is no such suit. There is no tort for negligent infliction of emotional distress. There is no tort in Maryland for negligence, incompetence, or inept and unprofessional services. There is none." I said, "There isn't any tort for incompetence?" The judge said, "Absolutely not." I said, "What? Well, what is recognized if the police investigators are unprofessional, incompetent and act with no due diligence and because of their actions I have been damaged, injured severely, have bleeding internal ulcers and am physically and emotionally suffering nonstop?"

The judge said, "I am sure you have—there is no doubt in my mind that you have suffered greatly as a result of the death of your son. But quite frankly, ma'am, you can't sue the state or its agents of the government because you have been emotionally disturbed or emotionally upset. The only way that you could do that and make such a claim is if your suffering was done intentionally—if the state intentionally wanted to hurt you, Adrienne Miranda and/or Adrienne Miranda's family. He continued, "The only thing you can do is just vote them out."

I said, "So the police and investigators do not have to do everything that is required in a competent investigation?" The judge said, "No, they do not. Vote out the executive. That is your only relief—the only relief that a citizen has." I asked, "Who do you mean by "executive?" He answered, "The governor for the state police. The governor appoints the state police. He appoints the superintendent. You can also vote out any county state's attorney."

I said, "What about immunity in the state of Maryland? I have researched state law about government immunity and injury to a person or party in Maryland. I have been injured emotionally, psychologically and physically and so has Mr. Miranda." The judge said, "That is irrelevant and it doesn't matter or make any difference. When you sue, you sue them in what is called a tort. A tort is a wrong. There is no wrongdoing here." I said, "My tort claims negligent and intentional infliction of emotional distress. These police and officials were malicious. They intentionally wanted to hurt me by covering up the facts and truth about the violent killing and murder of my son." Judge Levise said, "Why? Why would they do that?" I said, "Well, we have to get to trial to find out why." He said, "No, ma'am, you need to tell me why for the case to get to trial. You need to be able to put on the facts." I said, "Your Honor, are you asking me for a disclosure at this time?" He said, "I'm asking you to tell me what the alleged intentional acts on the part of the state to harm you are." I said, "Well, the intentional acts include perjury, manipulation, being led down a path of deceit, having very crucial documents and reports withheld from me, a reconstruction never being done at the crime scene of my son's brutal death when a vehicle was involved, sending only one crime scene photograph to the medical examiner when there were ninety-one photographs taken and documenting the crime as an accident to the Medical Examiners when it was already determined to be a criminal investigation."

Judge Levise said, "So they were negligent. They didn't do what they should have done is what you're saying." I said, "No, I'm saying much more than that, Your Honor. I am saying it is malicious and manipulative to mislead me when I am trying to get truth and justice for my child who was violently killed. I have the proof and the evidence of how my son was killed. There is nothing about my son's death that is an accident, "Nothing."

The judge said, "Yes, ma'am. And what I am saying is that may be one hundred percent correct." "Let's assume we have a case where we know—there is no question—that somebody was murdered. We know it. We know it and the murder occurs in Baltimore County. So we know where the murder occurred. We know who murdered the victim," he repeated. "We know it." "The state's attorney's office says, "I'm not prosecuting." The state police say, "I'm not investigating." The department of whatever—name any Department—says, "I'm not going any further with this. I'm just not doing it." "There is still no suit against those government agencies. "None."

I said, "Well, what do those government agencies exist for? Do they exist for getting justice? Do you exist to be the fact finders and the truth seekers? Does somebody in the judicial system and process in the state of Maryland exist for that?" The judge said, "No, my only job is to apply the law that exists." I said, "And I am trying to comply with the law, Your Honor." Judge Dan Levise just kept telling me that I couldn't file a lawsuit against these government agencies in Maryland and that was the bottom line. He said, "Forget about governmental immunity or not governmental immunity or whether you filed within the correct one hundred eighty days and the treasurer did not respond to you in the required time frame—I am not even going to get to that.

I said, "Your Honor, I am asking valid questions." He just said, "I have no idea why they have done what they've done." I said, "These people have treated me with malice, cruelty, meanness. They have acted with no jurisprudence or due diligence. This is not the way these people are supposed to conduct themselves. This is negligence, gross negligence, malice, misconduct—use any word you want; they all apply is what I was so desperately trying to get across." The judge said, "What evidence do you have?" I said, "Well, number one—" The judge stopped me and very harshly said, "Ma'am, you can't move." I said, "I can't move?" He said, "No, ma'am." I said, "I am sorry. I did not know that I could not move. So, I have to stay here. Well, how do I get a document to you?" The judge asked, "What is the document you want to get to me?" I said, "I would have liked to have had an attorney represent me, Your Honor, but I could not find an attorney in the state of Maryland to help me." The judge said, "And do you know why?" I said, "I don't really care why."

Judge Levise said, "You don't have a case you can file. It can't be brought to court." I said, "No, that is not what I have been told. I was told for other reasons, but not what you're saying, Your Honor, with all due respect." He said, "OK, I don't know what you were told."

"Your Honor," I said, "can someone give this document to you?" He asked, "What is the document?" I explained it was a letter from the Maryland Insurance Division's Deputy Director. I said, "Your Honor, I can only go on what I have received from the state of Maryland. I am at the mercy of the people within the state of Maryland. Her letter is asking me for all kinds of documents and she is telling me that she is going to pursue the claim that you say I do not have."

150

The judge said, "I have no idea why this lady sent you this letter and she can't change the law in Maryland. She doesn't have the power." I said, "Well, I made call after call and each time someone gave me a different answer. Then I get her letter. She is higher up in her position, so there has got to be some reason she was trying to manipulate and confuse me. Don't these employees know the parameters and guidelines of their duties and their work?"

"Ms. Miranda," the judge said, "you can't sue based on the death of your son because these agencies of the state of Maryland didn't do their job, or did it poorly, or did it negligently, or did it incompetently, or didn't do it at all."

I said, "Well, does the state of Maryland have a code of conduct? Do they have a standard of policy and procedure that if they break certain laws it is criminal? It is misconduct? It is against the law?"

The judge said, "Well, we are not here to talk about what is criminal and what is not criminal. Let's suppose it were. The only person who can prosecute a crime in the state of Maryland—well there are two. Well, no, there are three." I said, "Uh-huh, the special prosecutor, the state's attorney for that county jurisdiction and the attorney general for the state of Maryland." He tried to remember their names and I tried to help him out with the three names. He said, "OK then. Nobody else can. I can't prosecute somebody for a crime and I can't charge somebody with a crime. And you know what you can do if you don't like what those three people do; you can vote them out of office."

I said, "I understand, Your Honor. I appreciate you telling me that and I am not trying to make anyone prosecute anything." "I am trying to look at my options and increase my understanding of where this will go, what the process is and what I will have to do to get justice." The judge said, "We are here in this court now and we are here because this is a civil suit. This is a claim for damages that you filed against these forty-two defendants." I said, "So their negligent actions, cause and effect resulting in my physical, emotional and psychological disabilities and severe illness as well as Mr. Miranda's, the Maryland Tort Claims Act does not cover?"

"Yes, that is correct." It does not cover for what you are claiming in your suit—that these people didn't do their jobs. And the Maryland Tort Claims Act doesn't cover claims for intentional infliction—excuse me, for negligent infliction of emotional distress. It is not a tort in Maryland. The Maryland Court of Appeals has said Maryland does not cover for negligence. In a negligent action, there are four elements." I said, "Right." He said, "You have to have a duty, a breach of duty, causing and the fourth, damages." I said, "Well, I don't know why I don't meet that test." He said, "Because you don't have number four. There is no such thing in Maryland as negligent infliction of emotional distress." I said, "So you are saying, Your Honor, that along with all of our added suffering due to their breach of duty and them causing us to have exacerbated physical and emotional sickness and that they interfered and denied us our human, civil and constitutional rights that I still have no claim in Maryland." He said, "That is right. You don't." I asked, "Where do I have a claim?" He said, "I have no idea. All I know about is Maryland law."

I said, "Well, maybe the Maryland law needs to be reconsidered. I don't know who wrote the Maryland Tort Claims Act, but it needs to be changed." Judge Levitz said, "Well, I can tell you there have been many attempts to change it and have negligent infliction of emotional distress recognized in Maryland, but it has never happened. There are other states that do recognize negligent infliction of emotional distress, but Maryland does not."

I said, "When you talk about the malice and deliberate injustice—" He stopped me and said, "It is silly to keep going on." I said, "You're not allowing me to keep going on, did you say?" He said, "No, I said, "What is the purpose in going on?" I said, "The purpose is because I want to be heard. I've waited two years to be heard in a courtroom and I have a right to be heard and I am asking to be heard." He said, "You do not have a claim." I then said, "Well, maybe I need to refile it." He said, "No, I don't think you can refile it." I said, "Are you telling me that the Maryland State Police are immune to any type of cause and effect that would leave a person with physical injuries and damages?"

Judge Levise said, "If a state police car hits you in the rear, then that officer is negligent and you can file a claim and most likely be able to recover. It is a recognized tort in Maryland." I said, "OK, so what is the difference between hitting me in the back with the front of their car and taking cruel words, lies, untruths, barefaced manipulation and perjury, as well as, concealing crucial reports, fraudulent cover ups, obstruction of justice and socking me right across the mouth with it and putting a knife right through my heart that is already broken. What is the difference? You tell me, Your Honor. What is the difference? What is worse? Having a fender bender and being hit from behind or being torn down and beaten down, knocked down to the ground over and over again with lies, torment and cruelty that physically sickened me and while I even stated that I was fearful of a particular person and just being ignored by them. How is that not causing damages? I said, "Since when do physical damages only include flesh and bones?" Your heart, your brain, your nervous system, your intestines, your stomach are all part of the human anatomy and all of me has been injured and damaged by the actions of these people." "Help me, Your Honor; help me to understand the difference."

He said, "I don't think you want me to explain it. I don't think you're interested." I said, "Because there isn't any explanation." I went on to convey more about the manipulation and no accountability in the Maryland State Treasurer's Office. I said, "Why are they so anxious to dismiss a claim that you say I don't even have? All of this is outrageous and makes no sense. Does no one know the laws except for you, Your Honor? What is going on in the state of Maryland?" The judge then said, "Ma'am, if you are so emotionally involved." "I don't think you are." He said, "I think you want to make a speech."

I was hurting so deeply inside and with that I started to cry and felt my knees buckle. I said inside, "Oh dear God, please help me." At that moment I literally felt the arms of my Lord, my Joseph, my Michael, my Dad and my Mema (my grandmother) holding me up. I said, through my tears, "Make a speech? This is not a speech. This is about justice for my child. This is about justice for me, for my family, for Joseph's family." The judge said OK. I said, "You refer to it however you want. I don't know, Your Honor, if you have children, but what I have been through is a living, horrifying nightmare."

Judge Levise said, "I don't—I don't dispute that." I said, "I only know the agony with burying my child being duplicated and compounded by horrendous and cruel intentional treatment of these people and their blatant lies and hidden documents and begging for a survey to be done to find out the correct jurisdiction of my son's death. I have been offered a payoff and witnessed perjury and misconduct clearly beyond negligence and obstruction of justice. I did nothing but set out to seek truth and justice for my son and I put my faith in the people who enforce our laws only to find out that they are breaking the laws. These very laws are written and endoctrined for these people to enforce, not to violate. And at the expense of the bloodshed of my beautiful child—this is repulsive." "Why did they leave my baby flat on the ground bleeding out in the burning hot sun underneath 7,500 pounds of steel for four hours? You wouldn't do that do a dead animal lying in the road. "In a catastrophic event, the closest MOSH office is to respond; that is Maryland policy. Yet they called in a MOSH inspector from West Virginia more than three hours away who knew nothing about Bobcats—nothing. There is a MOSH office only twenty-five minutes away from where my Joseph lost his young life and took his last breath. I need answers to these questions, Your Honor."

Judge Levise said, "Unfortunately, ma'am, I am not in a position to give them to you." I said, "Well, I need to know who is." The judge just said, "I have no idea. I have no idea." I said, "Judge Levise, I am sure that you are a respected judge who has served in these chambers for Baltimore County for many, many years. And your answer to me today is you have no idea?"

He said, "I have no idea. I am only here to determine if you can proceed with a civil case in this court for the things you have alleged. That is what my job is and that is my only job. "I certainly, certainly, as a human being, can sympathize with your loss and your family's loss. I don't for one minute think or denigrate it, dismiss it, or think it's not everything you say it is." "I'm sure it is. As a matter of fact, I know it is. I know it is." "My only job here today is to determine if your suit can go forward and under Maryland law it can't."

I said, "My job, then, is to change the Maryland law because it doesn't look out for the citizens of Maryland. I need to ask you this, Your Honor, if you allow me." He said, "Well, I haven't stopped you from saying anything, have I?" I said, "No, you haven't and I am thankful for that and so is my baby. During my research I found a Maryland Tort Claims Act case. It was represented by a state's attorney for the attorney general's office. He talked about the Tort Claims Act being skeletal when citizens are trying their best to seek justice so they established very strict standards under which a claim may be considered. I believe you are trying to explain to me those strict standards. In this disclosure, this 12-101, it talks about the definitions of the personnel of the state of Maryland and it does not disclose that a person needs to wait one hundred eighty days to file a lawsuit." Judge Levise said, "I know, but that is not my ruling. Whether I filed under the Maryland Tort Claims Act or whether I filed my suit against an individual individually, it would not matter. I am simply saying that the things that you say have been done to you are not an action that the state of Maryland recognizes."

"So, in other words, they have the green light to do and act in any way they choose. There is no manual—there is no police ethical manual and policy and procedural manual that they have to live and conduct themselves by. Don't they take an oath of office when they are sworn in as police officers saying they will enforce the law and work to protect, serve and provide upstanding services to the public? After all they are public servants. Our tax dollars pay their salaries."

The judge said he didn't know what they had regarding manuals or procedures. I said, "On the treasurer's website, it says you can file a claim for professional liability and for services not provided." The judge continued, "A police officer, a Maryland State police officer, could be driving down the road and talking on his cell phone and drinking a soda and eating a pie and driving with his knees and he could look the other way and crash into the rear end of you. Certainly, the police officer by any definition would be found to be negligent. You sustained emotional injury strictly. That is what you sustained. There were no broken bones."

Again I said, "I do have physical injuries. I have a bleeding intestinal ulcer, internal bleeding, a stomach X-ray that appears like a cat clawed my insides repeatedly, stomach and abdominal pain. I had to have an endoscopy and colonoscopy, I have PTSD, I tremble and I am on all kinds of medications to try to help subdue the pain. I know that you know these are physical injuries, Your Honor."

He still kept saying the things I am suffering from and complaining about are emotional distress. This wasn't making any sense at all. I still stood convicted that the nervous system, the digestive system, the intestines and the heart are all part of the human, physical anatomy. I said in the tort claim I thought I used both intentional and negligent infliction of emotional distress. I said both apply to what they did to me, Bob and our family.

The judge I am sure felt he was following the laws in Maryland. However, my family and I did not agree with his definitions or his conclusion. Once Judge Levise said again that I had no claim and his interpretations were completed, no one at any time on the side of the defendants said a word. The judge then announced, "The motions for the dismissal are granted and the court dismisses the case with prejudice for the reasons stated on the record here. Maryland does not recognize the tort that the plaintiff has claimed in this case. And that concludes the case. Thank you." I said, "Your Honor, I wanted to say more because I really haven't given you all the detail you asked for yet." Judge Levitz said, "No, ma'am, I don't want all of the detail. I can't." I asked, "Why is this with prejudice? Why is this not without prejudice?" Again, he said, "I am not saying that you have not sustained everything you say you've sustained, but Maryland does not recognize it as a cause of action. Now, if you think I am wrong or misinterpreting the law, you have the right to appeal the decision to the Court of Special Appeals of Maryland. That would be the next step."

As I was still talking to the judge, a Baltimore County officer came beside me, grabbed my arm and told me I had to leave now. I said, "Get off of me. I am still talking with the judge." He gave me a nasty look and backed off a bit. Judge Levise continued as my brother and I were writing down the information. The judge continued, "Be sure you file within thirty days a notice of appeal with the clerk of the circuit court for Baltimore County. It will then require you to file briefs with the court of appeals—the Court of Special Appeals. I'm sorry. That Court will take up my decision. If they determine that I am wrong, then you come back and I will certainly reverse my decision based on what they say. But I honestly don't think I am wrong. I think I am interpreting the law correctly and that is where we go from here."

The AG attorneys representing the defendants started to ask if they could be excused. Judge Dan Levise said, "Thank you. Certainly." I then just repeated, "Your Honor, so everything is dismissed?" Judge Dan Levise said, "It's dismissed."

I hugged my brother and thanked him for being beside me. I quickly gathered my papers and belongings and we headed for the door. My family followed behind me and we dried one another's tears. We went down the elevator and out of the circuit court building. My family was telling me that I did really well and they didn't know how I held up. I said, "It was only through the grace of God and the Holy Spirit within."

Proverbs 21:27–30: "The sacrifice of the wicked is detestable—how much more so when brought with evil intent. There is no wisdom, no insight, no plan that can succeed against the Lord."

Proverbs 24:23–25: "These also are saying of the wise: To show partiality in judging is not good: Whosoever says to the guilty, 'You are innocent'—peoples will curse him and nations denounce him. But it will go well with those who convict the guilty and rich blessing will come upon them."

Proverbs 28:5: "Evil men do not understand justice, but those who seek the Lord understand it fully."

Proverbs 28:9: "If anyone turns a deaf ear to the law, even his prayers are detestable."

Proverbs 28:12, 16–17: "When the righteous triumph, there is great elation; but when the wicked rise to power, men go into hiding. A tyrannical ruler lacks judgment, but he who hates ill-gotten gain will enjoy a long life. A man tormented by the guilt of murder will be a fugitive till death; let no one support him."

Proverbs 28: "When the wicked rise to power, people go into hiding; but when the wicked perish, the righteous thrive."

Proverbs 29:12: "If a ruler listens to lies, all his officials become wicked."

Luke 12:33–34 "Provide purses for yourselves that will not wear out, a treasure in heaven that will not be exhausted, where no thief comes near and no moth destroys. For where your treasure is, there your heart will be also." I know my treasure is in heaven where Father God and Jesus Christ my Savior live. I have found my heart, my treasure and no one will ever take it from me. My heart is filled with the Holy Spirit and I know he continues to instruct and guide me so that His purpose and His plan are fulfilled. May I continue to be his vessel, his instrument for all that is good.

After the hearing, as our family went to our cars and I was getting into the car, Bob's brother, Rick, hugged me and we cried. I said, "Our Joseph was murdered and these people are covering it up." He said, "I know, Adrienne. I know. Just keep fighting." I told him I loved him and God bless him. I thanked everyone for coming and showing their support and told them I would never forget it.

The following day the hearing was reported in at least three papers. I knew exactly what I needed to get working on right away: preparing my brief and record extract for the special court of appeals. I needed to do the research and make some calls to assure I would not miss a beat and have each specification exactly done to its perfection under the law.

That night I wrote in my journal once again to Joseph. I had been writing in my journals since Joseph passed in 2006 and recorded each and every occurrence. Even today, I am still writing in my journals as the cover-up, corruption and injustice continue. I talked to Joseph, prayed to my Almighty Father and thanked my Lord and His Holy Spirit for all of his love, miracles, callings and blessings. I still do and I will always. I told Joseph on this day that the court judge was very unkind, at times cruel and condescending and spoke to me in a tone that was unnecessary and should not be allowed in a court of law given our circumstances and our case. I told him I felt the hand of the Lord and his on my shoulders and I consumed their love and strength. I said thank you to my Almighty Father and my precious son for holding me up against these bad and stupidly acting people and that they should rest assured that I would continue our crusade. I said, "The justice sought will be served and my work is God's will to be done."

CHAPTER 11

OUR CRUSADE FOR JUSTICE FOR JOSEPH

On July 11, 2008, we marched for "Justice for Joseph." There were approximately forty people who wore the "Justice for Joseph" T-shirts that I had made and they carried the "Justice for Joseph" banners that I also made that were large with bold red letters conveying our quest for justice and that the corruption must stop now. Joseph's picture was on the front and the red letters saying *Justice for Joseph* printed across the front and back of the T-shirt.

We marched around the Baltimore County Circuit Courthouse where the state's attorney, Todd Slicenberger, worked. We were right in the heart of Towson, Maryland and many people came out onto the courtyard to watch; some even took pictures with their phones. I was so glad to see Michael Stewart, the brother of James Stewart, who was brutally killed and purposely run over by a driver who was employed at his workplace, join us. They, too, had gotten not an ounce of justice and they never even got a chance to be heard. James's beloved wife joined us, too, and so many felt the passion in our hearts calling out as we demanded truth and justice to be served. I knew Joseph and James were looking down together from heaven. I said in my heart, "I see your beautiful smiles and our message and your voice is being heard loud and clear! I rely only upon my Father, God. He is awesome and amazing and He loves us so much! You know, Joseph! You know!"

On July 18, 2008, I had decided to take a road trip and left my home at quarter past midnight. I wanted to drive north on Reisterstown Road (Route 30) all the way up and past Outside Unliving where my son was killed. I had seen this area during the daylight but was called by God to take the trip to see it by nightfall under the starry sky. My stomach was hurting and I had been feeling a bit nauseous from the ulcerated lining, so I stopped to buy a large bottle of Mylanta to drink as I drove. I knew it would coat my stomach and nothing was going to stop me from taking this journey.

I drove onto the Baltimore Beltway 695 until I reached the Reisterstown Road exit and headed north. I knew my Jesus and Joseph were right with me and I could also feel the presence of my dad, my nephew Michael and my grandmother. My Grandmother, whom we called Mema, was very special and a wonderful lady and we loved her so much. She lived with us in our years growing up and walked with a crutch due to being hit by a tractor trailer when she was in her thirties. Even though she had the crutch, she was as strong as an ox. She would help my mom with household chores, carry us on one hip and go about her day with love, joy and happiness in her heart. She was of Irish descent and had those beautiful, blue, smiling Irish eyes. She would cook, clean, give us baths at times and tell us the most enchanting stories of her years growing up. We would listen with childlike curiosity and smile, laugh and giggle as she wrapped her arms around us with love, warmth and hugs. She would sing her favorite songs to us and always when in the kitchen, we knew she was cooking a delicious, home-cooked, good, wholesome meal with her special brand of love and comfort. She loved her bingo and her favorite desert was ice cream. Yep, we all love ice cream! She taught us many life lessons, had a strong and deep faith in our Lord, prayed daily and stood strong in her beliefs. Our Mema was the best! We all loved her so dearly and she loved us so very much and was always there for us. Her name was Hallie May Albert and her mother was a Bailey. Yes, she was Irish and her father came from Dublin. He had a strong Irish brogue and when she would imitate him, it would make us laugh with delight. She was a one-of-a-kind grandmother; I still make many of her delicious recipes and there are never any leftovers. She has a special place in heaven and I know she is with Joseph, Michael, my dad and all of her loved ones. "I love you, Mem, with all of my heart."

JOSEPH AT AGE SEVEN WHEN HE MADE HIS FIRST HOLY COMMUNION. HE WAS SO DELIGHTED AND KNEW WHAT THIS SPECIAL DAY MEANT IN HIS HEART; HE ALWAYS LOVED THE LORD AND HAD A VERY STRONG FAITH. HE ACCEPTED THE BODY AND BLOOD OF CHRIST WITH A PURE AND OPEN HEART.

As I was driving, I knew there were particular landmarks that I wanted to drive by. For instance, one was a little diner called Elmo's. Joseph had always told me about their breakfast sandwiches made on potato-bread rolls and how good they were. I knew he sometimes stopped in there to pick up a sandwich for breakfast and I wanted to visit there. I also wanted to see the redbrick house where many of the immigrants were housed by Jay Metvet and the Elan Funeral Home owned by Jim Hertzler, who was also the forensic investigator for the Office of the Chief Medical Examiner in Maryland. Mr. Hertzler was there on the day my son was killed and did not submit one piece of forensics throughout the criminal investigation of my son's killing. I had learned after they finally removed my son from underneath the Bobcat by lifting the machine off of him that they took him to the Elan Funeral Home until he was transported to the morgue in Baltimore.

I was driving and saw the redbrick house on the left. I pulled into the driveway and could see in the second-story window a large green neon sign that lit up with the word *Exit* on it. Two white, old pickup trucks were parked in the driveway and someone peered out the window. Then a rather small-framed male who looked to be of Mexican descent slightly opened the side door and I began to back up. I got back on Route 30 and continued heading north. I saw Elmo's Diner on the left and knew I was going to stop in on my way home. I then came upon Outside Unliving's property on the left and saw the large sign. I knew up ahead was the intersection of Bortner Road, which also becomes Saint Paul Road and I turned left there. As I passed Jay Metvet's large stone mansion and drove farther down a bit, I could see the other entrance to Outside Unliving's property and their offices. I drove down farther and saw a few other large homes and then acres of what looked like farmland. I turned around and as I drove back, I stopped at Jay Metvet's mansion and stayed in my car. I could see through the thick-brushed hedge around his mansion the front of a large black Mercedes-Benz parked there. I continued back toward Route 30 again, turned left at the intersection and continued north. I then saw the Arcadia firehouse on the left, which was all of two or three minutes from where my son was killed. I stopped and got out, but as I approached the front door, the lights went out; they were locking up it seemed. I could see a large fire truck parked inside. This was where the emergency EMTs came from when the 911 call was made after Joseph was killed. It took them fourteen minutes to get there and they thought they were on a rescue call, not a recovery call. Yet no shock trauma or any rescue helicopter showed up when my son was killed on July 20, 2006, on the premises of Outside Unliving.

I continued north on Reisterstown Road (Route 30) and I had to stop for gas. I filled up quickly and left. I noticed a man in a pickup truck that pulled out behind me. I had seen him sitting on the parking lot of the gas station and convenience store as I was getting the gas. I don't know why, but he drove behind me for quite a distance and it felt like he was following me. It was now about three in the morning. I still drove north and it felt like I had gone some distance as the road became hilly. I was not sure how far I had gone, but I started to see signs that said *Hanover, PA*. I knew if I kept going I would soon be in Hanover, Pennsylvania and I was not sure when I should turn around. On the right I noticed a new building that looked like a school. The architecture was very streamlined and it looked to be a state-of-the-art design and plan. I started to pray out loud to my Lord, Joseph and my grandmother. I said, "Please give me a sign when I should turn around and not go any farther." I was heading over a portion of Route 30 that was hilly and to the right I saw all of these lights and realized it was a new home construction site. I saw the model home lit up and the sign reading *Starting at $280,000*. I remember thinking, "Wow, these homes look beautiful and large and the price is that low!" So, I turned right to get a better look at the model and drove around the long court, seeing stakes in the ground with *sold* flags on them. I thought, "I am sure these homes will sell and the lots are already being sold quickly." As I headed back to Route 30, I kept praying, "Give me a sign, guys. I don't know whether to turn right and head north or turn left and head back toward home." At that moment, when I came to Route 30, I looked up and to the right and saw the street sign of the court and the sign read *Hallie Ave*. I smiled and said, "Thanks, Mema. I love you." Her name was Hallie. I knew I had gone far enough and it was time to turn back toward my home.

I then turned left and headed back toward home. As I was driving up the road a short distance, suddenly I noticed way up high and to the left huge white lights lit up against the dark starry sky that read *Jesus*! I started to cry and said, "Thank you, sweet Jesus. Thank you!" I told all of my family how much I loved them and that I knew all of them were with Jesus and with me. I knew it was divine, magnificent and heavenly.

I was overjoyed and I tried to find a road that would lead left off of Route 30 so I could find out what church or wherever the lights were coming from. I looked and looked but saw nowhere to make a left turn. I knew it was a miracle from God, either way, and I was in awe. I dried my tears and kept driving. I noticed some signs by old churches and gravesites that were built in the 1600s and 1700s and I realized how old this land was; its historical importance was impressive. I kept driving and came upon Elmo's again, now on my right and I wanted to stop in and get a cup of coffee. I pulled in the small parking lot and parked. I saw folks working at a grill and up at the crack of dawn. I wanted to touch the doorknob of Elmo's that I knew my Joseph had touched many times. I knew he had been right there getting breakfast sandwiches before he went home to the Lord and he had told me how delicious they were. I parked my white Toyota on the gravel lot and got out of the car. As I approached, I tenderly and warmly held the doorknob and said, "I love you so much, Joseph." I entered and I could smell the aroma of the fresh coffee and ham, bacon, eggs and cheese on the grill. The diner was so nostalgic and I loved the way it was set up just like in the old days. There were booths around the border and a breakfast bar close up to the grill and coffeemaker. I noticed a young man sitting at a booth reading a book. I decided to sit at the counter and I ordered a cup of coffee. I started talking with a very kind man who was cooking. His name was Dave and he introduced his wife, Nettie, who was very busy and making the fresh coffee. I said good morning to them and that my name was Adrienne. I told them how much I loved their diner and that my son always told me how delicious their breakfast sandwiches were. I could definitely feel the presence of my son.

Dave asked me what I would like and I said, "Just a cup of coffee for now." He said, "Are you sure you don't want a breakfast sandwich?" I smiled and said, "Oh, yes, I will surely order one because my son had told me how delicious they were, but for now I would just like a cup of coffee." He said OK and asked if I lived nearby. I told him, "No, I live in Baltimore County, but my son, Joseph, had worked for Outside Unliving up the road." Dave said, "Yes, the landscaping company." I told him that Joseph was killed there in July 2006 and his death, we believed, was a homicide. Dave said, "Oh my, I am so sorry." He asked me what happened and I explained that Joseph, who was nineteen years old, was a foreman for the company and that a laborer who was the same age threw him into an oncoming reversing Bobcat to his death. Nettie looked over and said, "We are so very sorry." I said, "Thank you for your compassion." The diner was still empty and no morning customers had come in yet. Dave saw me wipe my tears and gently put his hand on mine and said, "It will be OK." I told him that I have been fighting for justice and truth for my son and everything thus far pointed toward a cover-up. He said, "I think I remember hearing about that on the news or in the newspapers." I said, "Yes, it was on the news several times and also in the papers." I asked if he had Outside Unliving employees come in for breakfast sandwiches. Dave said, "Oh yes, they come in a lot." He continued that he didn't really know the owner and the vice president but they, too, would stop in every once in a while. Dave told me that he had heard they hired a lot of illegal immigrants and that someone had been killed there some years ago. He thought there was a drowning in the pond on the property and he also knew there had been some fires related to their properties. He added that they were not well liked around here.

Then I told him about Joseph and how he wanted to become a landscaping architect. I said that he was very skilled and talented and could transform a swampland into the most beautiful garden you had ever seen. I said, "He had a special gift, loved landscaping and would often tell me how delicious your breakfast sandwiches were and that I should drive up sometime and get one. So here I am!" He smiled and I began to tell Dave that Joseph was a very strong Christian. "He loved the Lord and his favorite verse was John 3:16: "For God so loved the world that he sent his only begotten Son, for those who believe will not perish but have everlasting life." I know my Joseph is in heaven and his presence is always with me." Dave nodded and said, "Yes, your son is in heaven and you will see him again."

At that moment, a young man maybe age thirty, came and sat at the corner breakfast stool. I was seated just two seats away. I looked over and he said, "Do you mind if I sit here?" I said, "Of course not." He said he had overheard our conversation and just had to come up. He had such kind and compassionate eyes and extended his hand and said, "My name is John." I said, "Hi, John. My name is Adrienne and you have such a good name—John from the Bible." He smiled warmly back and said, "I know. I just heard you talking about your son and his strong Christian faith." He then, too, recited John 3:16. I said, "Oh, John, that is so good of you to know your Bible and it warms my heart that you are a believer." He then nodded his head and motioned me to look behind at the booth. I turned and saw and then realized John was the man sitting in the booth reading a book when I came in and the book he was reading was the Bible. It was lying open on his table next to his motorcycle helmet. He told me how very sorry he was to hear what happened to Joseph and he was so encouraged to hear about Joseph's faith and my strong faith.

He started to give me a little background and said that he was at a point in his life during his college years at University of Maryland, College Park, when he was experiencing a great deal of depression. He said he remembered looking around on campus and in class and seeing that almost everyone seemed to be there to party. He felt like he didn't fit in and one day he just opened the Bible and started reading and from that day he has never put it down. He acknowledged that his faith is what got him through those years and he did graduate with his bachelor's degree. I asked what he did and he said he was in management for a flooring company just about fifteen minutes down the road. He said he really did like his job and that things were good for him. I said I was so glad for him

168

and I would pray that he would always be blessed. As I was finishing my second cup of coffee, Dave and Nettie told me that Elmo's had been there for many, many years. Dave said, "It was Nettie's father who started the diner and then he and Nettie took it over." I said, "I can feel the sense of nostalgic significance and the extraordinary value Elmo's must have for their family and the community." Nettie then said, "We have already been in two movies." I said, "Really, that is fascinating, which movies?" Then Dave and Nettie tried to think about it and so did the cashier and the other worker, who were now getting ready for the crowd to start flowing in to order their breakfast sandwiches and coffees to go. Dave said, while all the while cooking his eggs, bacon, ham and melted cheese on the large grill, "I remember that Shirley MacLaine and what's-that-guy's-name…oh yeah, Nicholas Cage were in it and he was a Secret Service agent for the president's wife, the first lady." I said, "Oh yeah, I remember that movie," and he said, "Yes, it was called *Guarding Tess*." I said, "That is really cool; I will have to rent it and look for Elmo's."

The next thing I knew, the diner was filled with men standing in line ordering their sandwiches and coffee. The door was opening and closing as people poured in saying "mornin'" to one another and to me. I smiled and said "mornin'" back. You could see they were all hardworking men getting ready to start their workdays. Most were dressed in jeans and a T-shirt or a workman's uniform. Some ordered up to twenty sandwiches at a time, others eight and others two. Either way, it seemed they had a little breakfast gold mine there. The sun had now fully risen and I figured I'd better be heading for home. John was about to get up and leave for his job and thanked me for talking with him. I said, "Thank you," and I wished him the best. He said, "Keep the faith. You will get justice for your son."

I asked Dave for the check and he said, "There is no check. Aren't you at least going to eat a sandwich? You must be hungry." I said, "Oh, Dave, that is very kind of you, but I insist on paying and yes, I will take a sandwich to go." He said, "What kind do you want? I will make you whatever you want." I said, "How about the egg, ham and cheese?" He said, "You got it," and I watched him pull a fresh pack of ham out of the refrigerator.

Meanwhile, a man was suddenly to the right of me near the cash register and asked, "Is this your shoe?" I looked up at him and said, "Excuse me?" He was wearing a turquoise, collared, three-button shirt and khakis and holding a woman's heeled sandal in his hand. I was bewildered and said, as Dave listened on, "I know that I am very tired and I have been up all night, but I do believe I have my shoes." I looked down at my feet in my flip-flops and held my legs out while wearing my sweats and said, "Yep, I do have my shoes." I looked at the gentleman and said, "Thank you for asking, but that is not my shoe." He then looked at me and said, "Isn't that your white Camry parked outside?" I said, "Yes, it is." He then said, "Well, when I was coming in, I noticed this shoe on the ground by your car and thought perhaps it was yours, so I picked it up." I said, "No, that is not my shoe," again. I believe I heard Dave say good morning to the man when he came in and I thought he said, "Hi, John," but I am not sure.

Either way it seemed very strange to me. Dave was now wrapping up my sandwich and I got up and was ready to leave. I asked how much and again he said no charge. I said, "Dave, please let me pay you. I really appreciate your kindness, but—" He stopped me and said, "No, Adrienne, please take the sandwich on us and enjoy it." I thanked him from the bottom of my heart as he put his hand in mine and I put my hand back over his. I said, "God bless you and Nettie and thank you again. You are very kind." He said back, "God bless you and everything will work out; you will get justice for your son. It will all be OK."

As I left Elmo's and got into my car to head home, the entire journey felt surreal. I knew in my heart and soul I was supposed to go on this path and the Holy Spirit was with me and guiding me. Joseph's presence was astounding and my precious son was right with me. The morning sun was now shining brightly as I drove home and I felt a serenity and peace that was amazing. I was completely in the light and my Lord and Savior was giving me His immense love and mercy.

John 12:46 "I have come into the world as a light, so that no one who believes in me should stay in darkness."

When I returned home and pulled into my driveway, I just sat for a moment. I prayed and thanked God for all of his gifts and for being my refuge. I went into the kitchen and took a few bites of the breakfast sandwich. Oh my gracious, how good it was! I knew that it would be delectable. I went upstairs, took a quick shower and put on my PJs. I held my JAM and my Bible, closed my eyes and went off to sleep.

The next morning when I awoke, I wrote in my journal. I remember thinking for some reason the man who was holding the shoe somehow looked familiar to me, but I had no idea why or how. I later called my brothers and told them what had happened. I asked them both if there was any way they would pick up a woman's shoe sitting on a gravel road outside a diner and go in and ask a woman if it was her shoe. They both said, "What? No way. Not under any circumstances." I, too, felt the same way and that it was so odd and strange that this man did this. We actually laughed about it because it seemed so funny and peculiar to us.

I then said to them, "What is even stranger is I had been sitting in Elmo's for at least two hours before that man ever arrived. How in the world did he know that my car was the white Camry?" They both said, "Adrienne, that is weird—really strange." I remember calling my FBI friend and telling him about my journey and he, too, said, "What?" when I told him about the man carrying the shoe. He, too, was not sure what to make of it. I was glad in my heart that I made the trip, saw the landmarks I set out to see and knew that my Jesus, my Joseph, my Michael, my Father and my Mema were right with me and the grace of God empowered me. This earthly journey is temporal; let us serve our Lord at our best. For soon cometh the eternal journey of making our way into the heavenly kingdom of everlasting life with all of our loved ones...our family, the children of God.

It was now July 20, 2008, two years since my Joseph had been killed. How can it be? I see you, hear you, smell you, hold you, kiss you, talk with you and love you every second of every day. I carry myself to your resting place again only with the arms of my Lord holding me up. I pray to you,

Joseph and tell you, "My angel, hear Momma and tell Jesus that I know He is my shield and my armor. He provides me the ability to thrive, not just survive. All truth and justice will be done in God's time. Tell him how much I love him, Joseph. Tell him. I know he hears me, but you have an even closer ear to him. I must stay on course; I must continue in my purpose so God's will be done."

On July 22, 2008, the Office of the Chief Medical Examiner agreed to meet with me and my family. Dr. David Fowler, Dr. Zabiullah Ali and their assistant discussed Joseph's case with us. They had changed the death certificate at this point from accident to undetermined with a strong possibility of homicide. However, they were still looking for confirmation of the evidence they had and the police were not cooperating with them to further investigate and to interview or polygraph Pete Coldwin. Why would they not polygraph or ask Pete Coldwin the appropriate questions when they knew for certain he was lying? In fact, he lied many times and the police had it all on record, yet they continued to do nothing even after Mr. Coldwin had no legal representation anymore from Jay Metvet's hired attorney. They could not, at that point, change the death certificate to indicate homicide even though we knew and they knew that was exactly the manner in which my son's life was taken. They knew Joseph was already prone, lying flat on his stomach on the ground, prior to the Bobcat reversing over his head and neck, crushing him to death. At one point they said, "Somehow Joseph fell in an awkward position to the ground before being killed." I said, "Why do you say somehow Joseph fell? That is illogical, unfeasible and makes no sense." Throughout all of the police reports and Pete Coldwin's statements not once did Coldwin say Joseph fell. Not once did anyone say Joseph just fell. Joseph's boots were not untied, he did not trip over his shoe lace or his feet and he never just fell—never. To the contrary, Pete Coldwin says, "Joseph ran and jumped up on top of the front left wheel while the Bobcat was moving forward and then slipped off of the tire and fell underneath the Bobcat through the two left wheels." We all know that is a confounded, deliberate lie and what Coldwin said happened is impossible. We are certain of that given the injuries Joseph sustained and more importantly the injuries Joseph did not sustain. You have all of the physics, science, facts and forensics that prove Joseph was shoved and pushed by Pete Coldwin to his death.

My Mother, Betty Gemma, then asked, "Are you gentlemen sworn in under oath in your authority and position as coroners for the state of Maryland?" They both said, "Yes, we certainly are." My mother continued, "From the very beginning, the entire legal system and participants have been full of deception, lies, cover-up and a worthless and phony investigation into the callous murder of my beloved grandson, Joseph. We have received no due diligence nor had our questions answered. They tried to beat and pound my daughter into the ground with their stupid and outrageous remarks, theories and absolute lies and cover-up. They are a disgrace."

I then said, "You know that what these police are saying happened is impossible. You know scientifically and forensically all of the facts add up to only one thing: a crime occurred against my son that ended his life. There is not one thing that is OK about any of this. Nothing about this is OK—nothing. I will continue to be the voice of my son until justice is served." We thanked them for their time and said we would stay in touch. We knew they were good men and would act in good faith, as they are tasked to do. I knew there was still more work to be done and somehow, someway, I would find a lawyer who would depose these wrongdoers and reveal the truth. I knew in my heart that God was going to bring it and it was only a matter of time.

I remained on course and committed to the vow I had made to my precious Joseph to be his voice. I knew my crusade was still going to be a very tough road, but my God is faithful and mighty.

My family members and my dear cousin were so supportive and helpful to me. She listened intently with her warm and compassionate heart and we would often pray together. There are so many family members, family friends, friends and neighbors and folks in my community who have been with me and shown me such love and support. Even all of my doctors and their staff have been so compassionate, kind and supportive; I hope they know how much their love and kindness has meant to me.

On August 13, 2008, I wanted to visit the resting-place of my son. The day was just beautiful and the sun was beaming against the clear, beautiful blue sky. I took my roses and my blanket and knew the Holy Spirit was guiding me, as always. I drove to Dulaney Valley Memorial Gardens and parked beside our family plot. I got out and looked directly up to the heavens. Again, I raised my arms up and said, "This is the day the Lord has made; Let us rejoice and be glad in it." I laid down my blanket and kneeled at the teal blue marker that read my Joseph's name under the resurrection cross shining in the beautiful gold lettering and embossing.

I brought water to fill up the vase and replace it with fresh-cut roses. I ran my fingers across the headstone and then kissed it. I was praying and weeping, but the warmth of the sun brought me such comfort. I then saw a mother duckling and I smiled. I thought, "I want to take a walk on this beautiful afternoon," and I knew the pond would be so soothing to see. I then stood up and started walking across the lawn toward the pond. As I walked I noticed the mother duck was walking right beside me. She was so pretty and I felt like we were somehow in unity.

The Mother was to my left and then I turned and realized all of her baby ducklings were walking with us; there were hundreds waddling right behind us. I knew they, too, were making their way over to the pond. As I was gently walking with the family of ducks toward the lake, I could feel the sun's warmth and soothing inspiration. The whispers of the soft breeze flowed through my face and hair and it felt heavenly. I noticed family names on headstones bordering the pond and some that were quite famous as well as other acquaintances whom I had known during my young-adult years. I did not realize that some of them had passed and I prayed as I took it all in. I could hear the sweet voice of my precious angel, Joseph and I knew he was there with me. I continued strolling and I felt like I was completely enthralled in my spiritual dimension.

I came across a private family mausoleum that was just beautiful with stained glass windows and a private gated entrance. There were many like this that had started being built throughout the cemetery. I then turned and felt I should start to make my way back and as I did I could feel and sense in the distance, probably about sixty to seventy yards away, someone staring at me. I continued walking with my hands folded in prayer and as I got closer, I realized there was a very tall, muscle-bound, dark man standing with his arms folded across his chest and looking directly at me with a very angry, mean face. He was wearing a white muscleman T-shirt and there was a girl in a red shirt standing beside him. Even though I knew he was trying to frighten and intimidate me, I did not feel afraid at all.

I continued walking in prayer and taking in all of God's natural earthly beauty. I got closer and closer to where the big man was standing and I was just going to walk right by him and say, "Isn't it a beautiful day?" As I got closer to him, he started to nervously glance at the girl beside him and then realized I was going to walk up close to him. Before I knew it, he started running away and so did the girl. I was surprised and watched them run over to the driveway and jump into an old, beat-up, grayish sedan. I still kept walking toward them and they hurriedly started up the engine and drove away as fast as they could. I was able to get the license plate number and to this day I have no idea what they were running from. I also wondered why they were at Dulaney Valley Memorial Gardens staring at me with such angry and mean looks and trying to intimidate me.

Genesis 26:24 "Do not be afraid, for I am with you."

I walked back to our family plot and prayed some more to Joseph and to my Lord. I told all of my family how very much I loved them and that I would be united with them soon. I gave hugs and kisses, picked up my blanket and headed home. I remember telling my family members about it and I called my dear friend with the FBI and told him what had happened. He listened and wrote down the license plate number that I gave him. To this day, this man has remained by my side. I thank God for him every day.

Hebrews 13:5–8 "The Lord is my helper; I will not be afraid. What can man do to me?" Jesus Christ is the same yesterday and today and forever. My Lord tells me "Never will I leave you; never will I forsake you."

During July and August, I had been requesting a meeting for my family and me with the Baltimore County state's attorney, Todd Slicenberger, and the investigative detectives regarding his position on the case and the status of the investigation at that time. After several back-and-forth e-mails with State's Attorney Todd Slicenberger, he was finally able to coordinate a meeting date that worked with Baltimore County's homicide detectives. At first, State's Attorney Slicenberger told us the only ones who could be present for this meeting were Bob and I. I asked why. I explained that I and many of Joseph's family members—his aunt, his uncles and his grandmother—would also like to attend.

Slicenberger later agreed and said that they could attend and I also asked if my brother could join in by phone—my brother Damian Gemma, who lives in Florida, had spoken to Todd Slicenberger a few times by phone. Therefore, I requested that they patch him in on conference call. My brother had stayed very close with me in all aspects of Joseph's death investigation and was very familiar with all of the circumstances.

Slicenberger said he would get back to me and let me know.

Also, at the scheduling of this meeting, Slicenberger said the ones who would be present would be him and the lead homicide investigator, Detective Carl Bollen and probably his assistant state's attorney. I then asked, "Why is Corporal Geck [who is Detective Bollen's supervisor] not going to be present?" He had joined Detective Bollen when they came to my home and interviewed me.

I added, "Lieutenant Mahoney is the head of the homicide squad and the one they appointed to correspond with me throughout their investigation. Why will he not be there?" State's Attorney Slicenberger just said, "It is not important that they be there."

I disagreed and said, "I did not want to meet at this time unless at least both Detective Carl Bollen and Corporal Lou Geck were both present at the meeting. It is only fair that they both be there because the two of them led the investigation and I spoke more with Corporal Geck than Detective Bollen." Later, Todd Slicenberger got back to me and said they would "both" be there and that, yes, my brother would be patched in through conference call. I thanked Mr. Slicenberger for his compliance with my requests and we agreed on the date for the meeting. I spoke with Damian over the phone and he was so glad that he could be included and would be able to hear all that took place at this very important meeting.

It is important to realize that up until this meeting I had been in communication with State's Attorney Slicenberger by phone and by e-mail. He was well aware of all of the facts, science, physics and evidence that proved Joseph had been pushed prior to his death and was already prone lying on the ground just before the Bobcat was driven backward over him. He also knew Joseph's manner of death was changed from being considered an accident to undetermined with a strong possibility of homicide. He had Dr. Ali's letters, the autopsy report and all of the facts that added up to a brutal crime against our son. He knew about Dr. Ali's own reconstruction and that he actually sat in the same model Bobcat and drove it, concluding that Pete Coldwin's description of what happened was impossible. I asked him why he did not call or talk with the medical examiner, Dr. Ali and he told me that that was not what prosecutors do. He said there was no reason for him to have to talk to the medical examiner and it was just never done.

I still do not understand this protocol if that is a standard practice; it seems to make no sense. The medical examiner who knew the science, physics, forensics, facts and evidence of the case was not talking with the person who would eventually make the decision regarding prosecution of the case. Todd Slicenberger is not a doctor or in the medical field, but Dr. Ali is and was very competent and specific in his findings of what happened to Joseph that resulted in his death.

State's Attorney Slicenberger knew that everything pointed to foul play and a crime being committed against Joseph by Pete Coldwin. I had sent him all of the information prior to the meeting and he knew what most of our questions were going to be. I stayed in earnest prayer throughout and I knew God understood what was on my heart.

A few weeks passed and State's Attorney Slicenberger finally informed me that the meeting was scheduled for August 27, 2008, at 10:00 a.m. on the fifth floor of the Baltimore County Circuit Court building in Towson, Maryland. That morning we woke up bright and early and I was very well prepared. My family and I wanted our questions finally answered; we wanted resolution and justice and felt we would be able to accomplish our goals and finally get some results.

I took with me my large box filled with all of the evidence, facts, science, physics, MDSP reports, MOSH reports and Dr. Ali's letters and was very prepared to visit with the Baltimore County state prosecutor, Todd Slicenberger and his homicide detectives. When we entered the conference room at the Baltimore County Circuit Court building, my mother, my brother, Bob, I and one of my dearest friends, Rick, were quite surprised. Around the conference table sat State's Attorney Todd Slicenberger, Assistant State's Attorney Len Roan Jr., Baltimore County Police Chief Tim Hannson, Lieutenant Jim Mahoney, Corporal Ray Spice, Corporal K. Hudgeon, Senator John Roaching, Corporal Lou Geck and Detective Carl Bollen. We took our seats and then all went around the room and introduced ourselves.. All of us were wearing our "Justice for Joseph" T-shirts. I reminded Mr. Slicenberger about patching in my brother as he was waiting by the phone from Florida. He said he would have his secretary get him on the phone. I noticed the telephone sitting on the conference table and felt all would go as planned.

Prosecutor Todd Slicenberger began by telling us that even though I thought MDSP trooper Quisset Jr. may not have been the Spanish interpreter at the scene on the day my son was killed, he indeed was. He proceeded to tell me that I was incorrect because he called MDSP trooper Quisset Jr. himself and asked him if he was present on July 20 and Trooper Quisett Jr. told him that he was there.

You see, soon after Joseph was killed, I had asked Corporal Dan Kitseng, with the MDSP, who the Spanish interpreter was on the day Joseph was killed. Corporal Kitseng told me Detective Sergeant Monroe was the Spanish interpreter. So therefore, when we saw much later during the investigation by the Maryland State Police that Trooper Quisset Jr. was actually the Spanish interpreter for Antoine Ruberra, we were perplexed. Also, Trooper Quisset Jr.'s name was not listed on the MDSP time line and task list that I finally received from MDSP Central Records. Remember, as I previously stated, as more time went on and everything including disturbance of the crime scene, serious repeated deception and criminal misconduct were unfolding, nothing was making any sense and we were left in shock, distress and disbelief.

As Mr. Slicenberger said he had confirmed Trooper Quisset Jr. was the Spanish interpreter, everything in my memory recall was activated. I listened and quickly recalled the day that Detective Carl Bollen and Corporal Geck came to my home and spoke with me for about three hours. They had told me Outside Unliving was "lawyered up" and they could not talk to Pete Coldwin at all. I remembered everything, all of it, including Detective Bollen taking notes on his yellow lined tablet and Corporal Geck listening intently as I gave the detective specific names and explained why it was important to interview these people. I knew from the Baltimore County investigative report that certain names I had given were never contacted and I had wondered why.

Anyway, we listened and just said OK. I then asked to speak. I asked Detective Carl Bollen why he never talked to or interviewed Rod Schwib. I said, I had explained it was important to talk with him and I needed to understand why he never attempted to call or meet with him and ask the questions I had talked about with him and Corporal Geck when they came to my home." Detective Carl Bollen kept shaking his head no and saying, "No, you never did. You never gave me his name." I could not believe my ears. I said, "Yes, Detective Bollen, I distinctly gave you his name and where he lived. I watched you write it all down on your yellow note-pad in my kitchen when you came to my home. Corporal Geck, you were there. You saw and heard me give the name of Rod Schwib and say that he needed to be interviewed." Corporal Geck just looked and said nothing. Detective Bollen just kept denying it. I then asked, Detective Bollen, why are you lying?" Detective Bollen then abruptly jumped up from his seat, said, "I am not listening to this," and left the room! With that, State's Attorney Todd Slicenberger told us to leave and the meeting was over!

We were in shock and could not believe what had just occurred and Todd Slicenberger had no interest at all in continuing our meeting. We so badly needed to get some resolution and understand where the investigation stood. We asked, "Can't we please continue?" We were told no and we were dismissed by State's Attorney Slicenberger and basically told to get out. I gathered my papers and stood up. I held back my tears and I said to each man around the table, "I do not know if you are fathers, but if you are, I don't know how you lay your heads on your pillows at night and sleep. All of this is a disgrace." They just looked at me wide-eyed and started to leave. Slicenberger had already left the conference room. My brother and my good friend Rick were in shock. They tried to tell them and plead that the meeting needed to happen and I had to have the chance to speak. I motioned them to come; I knew it was no use. Slicenberger had already told us to leave and the meeting was over.

Again, I felt that neither the life and brutal death of my precious son nor any of the facts of the case mattered to them at all. We were again being ignored and shoved to the side; there was no doubt in our minds that from the beginning they wanted us to go away! Slicenberger literally threw us out just because I asked the detective why he was lying. He was lying. He was being totally and unequivocally untruthful and dishonest and Corporal Geck knew it. He was sitting right there in my kitchen when I gave the names to Detective Bollen and he, too, watched him write them down on his yellow lined notepad.

As I left the courthouse, I recalled all that was so vividly suspicious, incompetent and distrustful about the Baltimore County criminal investigation. The so-called independent investigation ordered by State's Attorney Slicenberger to his homicide detectives. I had wondered why they did not even give my son's homicide investigation a case number, why their report totaled about only eight pages, why they did next to nothing on the case. I wondered why the two investigators never returned to my home again even though they promised me they would and why they refused to interview or talk to Pete Coldwin even when he was no longer represented by an attorney. All of it was unconscionable, more of the same and just like the Maryland State Police had done. Note Todd Slicenberger never did get his secretary to patch my brother, Damian, in on the phone from Florida.

Later, I received an e-mail and a letter from State's Attorney Slicenberger saying that it was wrong of me to suggest the detective was lying and I should not and could not say or make any kind of accusation like that to the very people who were trying to help me. He wrote that he was done with the case and said my son's death was a tragic accident and he was finished. He wrote, *Good luck*. Shame on you, Mr. Slicenberger. My son's horrific death was no accident at all and you know it. Joseph was violently killed and his death was beyond tragic. It is unthinkable, unconscionable and reprehensible. These men were not trying to help me; they were complying with the same cruel and evil tactics and ruthless and callous conduct and repeating the same deception and cover-up as the Maryland State Police had.

State's Attorney Todd Slicenberger would repeatedly tell me there was not enough evidence and we "needed a confession." I said, "What? You need a confession? How often in the judicial system and in a homicide case do the courts get a confession? Isn't that why we have a court of law and a judicial system that bring cases to court? So there is a fair trial and both defendant and plaintiff get the opportunity to have their cases argued and represented for the perpetrator and the victim?" He still said, "Well, that is what we need—a confession."

I was astounded by his stupid and idiotic statement. I then said, "Well, how do you expect to get a confession from Pete Coldwin when you and your detectives will not even bring him in for questioning? You have not spoken with him at all and don't ever intend to. What is the reason for this? You know that he is no longer represented by Jay Metvet's attorney and he has no attorney at this time. You and your police—the Baltimore County detectives know it, yet you refuse to even question him in any way about my son's brutal and violent death."

Pete Coldwin was there on July 20, 2006; he was at the scene, he physically assaulted my son, he repeatedly lied and told three different stories to the Maryland State Police and he created an outrageous and impossible scenario that no one believed. Then the one qualified, proficient and dutiful detective, Detective Bishtell, got it all right and he acted on it with due diligence and did the job he was hired to do.

I cried to myself and my family out loud. For Todd Slicenberger and his homicide squad to dismiss us and ignore all of the science, physics, tread marks and forensics that proved there was a vicious assault upon my son is despicable. Todd Slicenberger has violated my human and civil rights and still, to this day, has more than not done his job.

He has shown prejudice and bias against me and Joseph's family from the beginning and wanted nothing to do with the case for some very anomalous and abnormal reason. All will be revealed when God chooses to expose him and the corruption in this state as God's power will bring a greater good than Mr. Todd Slicenberger could ever even begin to relate to or comprehend. All of this is written in my journal. May God always and forever bless my family, my friends, my neighbors, Joseph's loving and devoted friends and my church, Grace Fellowship Church in Timonium, Maryland.

The truth is that what is so very tragic is the intensity and depth of corruption and deception that are integral to the judicial system in the state of Maryland. These people were looking out to save their butts, their jobs and their career aspirations and thrive in their dirty games and politics.

Yes, they sicken me. Their actions are appalling. But I know where my angel boy is as he looks down from heaven. I know my Lord will make it right. Joseph's home is incredibly wonderful and beautiful as he lives on with Father God, Jesus and all of his loved ones. He lives on with me too and knows exactly all that is taking place on this earth. Thank you, Jesus, for making me patient and giving me perseverance. All things happen in God's time. His timing is perfection and there is a specific purpose and reason for all that he does.

I pray for wisdom and discernment. Daniel 12:3, 10 "Those who are wise will shine like the brightness of the heavens and those who lead many to righteousness, like the stars forever and ever." Verse 10: "Many will be purified, made spotless and refined, but the wicked will continue to be wicked. None of the wicked will understand, but those who are wise will understand."

When I returned home, I felt exhausted and ready to run forward at the same time. I had been working on my brief and record extract and was spending time at Kinko's day and night. All of the folks who worked there were so kind and understanding. The manager was especially kind and compassionate and they got to know what I was working on and why. They were all so very supportive.

MOM-MOM WITH HER GRANDSONS WHO ADORE HER; SHE IS HOLDING
JOSEPH WHEN HE WAS JUST 4 MONTHS OLD AND MICHAEL, ROB,
DAVID AND JOSEPH WERE ALWAYS ELATED IN HER ARMS.

MOM-MOM WITH ALL OF HER GRANDSONS ON HER 81ST BIRTHDAY CELEBRATION.
JOSEPH WAS HOLDING A LITTLE DARLING FRIEND......HE DID LOVE CHILDREN.

September 7, 2008, was Grandparents Day. I made sure to see my mom and tell her she was the best Mom-Mom in the world. I took her a card and flowers from Joseph and told her how very much she was loved and adored. Our visit was so warm and loving. I took her to get shrimp-salad sandwiches and we ate lunch and reminisced. I remember I marveled at all of her Bibles as we studied the origins of certain Greek words that she had written down. She loved all of her grandsons so very much. She drove them in her maroon-colored station wagon everywhere they wanted to go and they brought her so much joy. She wanted to get a license plate that read *MOM-MOM*, but it was already taken at the MVA, so she had *GEMMA*, her last name, put on instead.

The boys would be so excited when they were going on an excursion with her. They would all wait in the family room looking out for what they called the Mom-Mom mobile. Then I would hear them say, "Mom-Mom is here," and they would gather their jackets, give me a hug and kiss and run out to her. They would go to the sports trading card stores and the sports paraphernalia shops; they would go for ice cream and always come home with lots of specialties and treasures. Oh, how I miss those days filled with such love and joy. Children are truly the sweetness of life and we must all enter the kingdom with the heart of a child: a pure, innocent and believing heart. The Lord says, Isaiah 66:12: "As a mother comforts her child, so will I comfort you."

The autumn leaves were turning in their array of beautiful colors: gold, wine, yellow, orange, red and berry. The air felt crisp and fresh. The season of fall was quickly approaching and I wrote, copied, faxed and telephoned each day. After about six months of Joseph's untimely death, I knew I needed some kind of grief therapy. I was so broken and my tears just would not stop. I truly did not know how to control them.

I had found a network of grieving mothers online and we would write to one another and share our experiences. My doctors told me I needed professional help. I first went to bereavement therapy at Stella Maris. The therapist was so compassionate, loving, understanding and easy to talk with. She helped me for several years and allowed me to cry, vent my agony and my frustrations and share my faith. She was very spiritual and we prayed together at every visit. I truly connected with her spiritually and emotionally and our bond was grounded in the faith in our Lord. I read so many books on the loss of a child: *THE WORSE LOSS, JOY IN THE MOURNING, LIFE AFTER DEATH, NEVER STOP DANCING* and on and on. To this day I love and respect her immensely. She was there for me and I will never forget her.

I also attended a GriefShare workshop that was extraordinarily helpful. The two women who led the group were lifelines for me. GriefShare provides a safe, loving, compassionate and understanding atmosphere for anyone who is suffering from the pain of grief. The people joining and sitting around the room truly became my friends in faith and pals in prayer and love.

We all held one another up and shared our stories and our broken hearts. We would watch a faith-based video each week and we would ask and answer questions as well as be involved in trusting and interactive activities. I recommend GriefShare to anyone who is suffering the loss of a loved one. There are workshops throughout the country.

I also learned about Parents of Murdered Children (POMC), a national program that supports parents and family members whose children had been taken from them by a violent and brutal act of another. Their children, these victims, had been tragically murdered and these parents were fighting for justice. While some had at least obtained justice for their beloved, others had not. They were having an anniversary memorial for the "murder wall" that had been built bearing engravings of each name of the beloved children.

On September 25, 2008, I attended the POMC memorial that was held at the National Press Club in Washington, DC. I had called the organization, which is based in Ohio and explained my circumstances and how Joseph was killed. They were most kind and compassionate and gave me the information, details and directions for the National Press Club.

They entered my name into their system and told me how I could become a member, which I did. This event was held in the evening and I kind of knew my way around DC because I had worked for a world bank many years ago.

I got dressed that morning, put on my "Justice for Joseph" T-shirt and jeans, grabbed my umbrella and my MapQuest directions and left in plenty of time for the event. Unfortunately, it was a rather bleak and rainy day. I entered Washington, DC, by New York Avenue. I knew I had to park and start walking. After parking I scurried through the streets of DC and knew I was headed in the right direction.

I saw people walking at a fast pace and alongside me a young man dressed in a very nice suit and tie was walking. I think he had earplugs in, but I thought, "I will ask him; he will know where the National Press Club is." I gently said, "Can you please help me? I am trying to find the National Press Club." He said very kindly back as we still kept walking, "Sure," and he instructed me where to turn and that I would see a large black awning just over the entrance. I thanked him and was so grateful to him. It felt a bit unusual but like he was supposed to be there for me. I also noticed as I continued my pace that a man was taking my picture with his cell phone. He was just standing near the street curb. It seemed odd, but I was certain he was a very well-known politician and I know he saw my "Justice for Joseph" T-shirt.

I finally saw the black awning and turned right to go just a few blocks more. When I got there, I was just in time. It was ten to six in the evening and the event started at six. I walked in the main lobby and was amazed by the large familiar news-media faces I saw all around me. I stopped when I saw Tim Russert. I went over to his picture and looked into his eyes and I felt the warmth and reality of his smile and heart. I said a prayer and then "God Bless you, Big Russ." I made my way up to the thirteenth floor and took a seat with the audience. I sat beside three wonderful women and introduced myself to them. They returned the gesture and Regina, Lochelle and Katie were dear and so very kind. I knew I was among many other brokenhearted and compassionate men and women.

We briefly said the name of our beloved and how they were murdered. There was a POMC pamphlet on each seat and I began to read it. As we were seated, the room began to fill up and I noticed a choir group getting prepared up on stage; to the left was a black drape that hung over a four-foot wall. I felt sure they were the names of the murder victims to be unveiled during the second-anniversary ceremony.

The event was about to begin and Roberta Roper was introduced. She was the founder of POMC and spoke of their mission and her beloved beautiful daughter who had been horrifically murdered. I admired her love, courage, fortitude and conviction in all that she had accomplished over the years. I knew her daughter was proud of her and looked down from heaven, protecting her. The next to speak was Congressman Ted Poe, who is a very strong advocate for murder victims and their families. I was quite humbled by his warm and caring heart and how he was standing up for justice. There were several others who spoke and then came the ceremonial unveiling of the murder wall.

Everyone stood as uniformed guards lowered the black drape of each wall. The room was so dimly lit that we could not actually see the names at first. People got up and went over to the wall, looking for the names of their loved ones. I got up too. There were wet faces, streaming tears, squinted eyes of parents each in search of their child's name, desperate to see it and touch it. I kept hearing, "Where is my child? Where is their name?" My heart was breaking for them as I wept. They all found their beloved and just to feel and see his or her engraved name brought tears of hope and promise.

I thought they must shine the light brighter on them next time so their brilliance comes through. Each name, each child, is a shining star and they are in the light. Let their eternal brilliance shine through. 2 Corinthians 4:6 "For God said 'Let light shine out of darkness, may his light shine in our hearts to give us the light of the knowledge of the glory of God in the face of Christ.'"

CHAPTER 12

THE HOLY SPIRIT EMBRACES THE PARENTS OF MURDERED CHILDREN

The room was filled with the Holy Spirit and people were all embracing one another. Then the choir started to sing such beautiful hymns. We all listened and sang in praise of our God. After, we had the chance to mingle and get to talk to one another and share our stories and our hearts. I met so many wonderful, loving, compassionate and caring hearts. I met Ann and her husband, several other moms, dads and siblings who were from so many states throughout our country and some of the POMC staff.

I exchanged numbers and e-mails with many and to this day we remain sisters and brothers in Christ who share the same journey for truth and justice. As I was talking, a beautiful young woman from the choir came over and we hugged. I commented on how moving and inspiring their hymns were. She thanked me and said she had noticed me and just had to come over. Her name was Joelle and she said she was from New Jersey and was attending college. Somehow I felt a special warmth from her and a feeling that she had known Joseph. I told her about what happened to Joseph and she warmly hugged me and said she knew and she was so very sorry.

MY LOVING JOSEPH FILLED WITH JOY, A LOVING HEART AND A SMILE THAT LIT UP A ROOM. HE WAS EXCITED TO CELEBRATE HIS 18TH BIRTHDAY AS I WAS GETTING PREPARED IN THE KITCHEN. HIS HOLY SPIRIT WITHIN DID ALWAYS SHINE THROUGH.

The ceremony was so joyful while at the same time sad. God was working miracles and I knew it. It was now time to close the ceremony and say our farewells. I made sure to hug each and every person who had spoken with me and I with them and I especially wanted to stay in touch with Ann. She had told me about her fight to seek justice for her beloved son and was in contact with a Maryland state delegate who was assisting her. She offered to help me connect with her and Ann felt confident that the delegate would want to try to help. I thanked her from the bottom of my heart and said that I would be calling her. As we went down the elevator, I was with Regina, Lochelle and Katie. It was now raining even harder and I knew I had a long walk ahead of me.

Regina said, "Adrienne, where are you parked?" I said, "Oh, I am parked several blocks away." God bless her heart, she said, "We don't have far to go; we will drive you to your car." I said, "Are you sure? I don't want to take you out of your way or inconvenience you." She insisted, "Get in. You are not." I then suddenly realized I had forgotten my umbrella. Regina said, "Go ahead. Run back in and see if it is there." I said, "Thank you so much. OK." I ran out and got on the elevator to look in the room and where I was seated, but there was no umbrella. The umbrella was sentimental to me in addition to working to keep me dry. It was a Coach umbrella that my loving nephew had given me for Christmas one year. I stopped at the front desk, left my number and asked if they could call me if they found it. They took my information quickly and I described the umbrella. I then ran out and jumped in Regina's car. We all talked about the event and the different names of the victims on the pamphlet. We shared love, compassion, strength and safety. These women were in union with me and I could feel the presence of the Lord with us. We found the parking lot, though it took a bit of maneuvering because of my sense of direction in DC at the time. We all gave one another hugs and told one another we would remain in prayer. To this day, Regina and I communicate and I know we are all sisters in Christ.

On my drive back home, I realized I needed to stop for gas. It was a wet and rainy night. I stopped at the gas station just before getting on the Baltimore-Washington Parkway. I pulled up to the pump and a very kind gentleman came out and asked me what kind of gas I wanted. I told him and thanked him. While he was filling up my tank, he said, "Ma'am, it looks like your tires need air. Are you going far?" I said, "Yes, I have a bit of a drive back to the Towson area in Baltimore." He then said, "After I fill up your tank, why don't you pull your car up here next to the air pump and I will fill all of your tires with air." I said, "That is so very kind of you. What is your name?" He said, "They call me Lightfoot." I shook his hand, gave him a little love gift and said, "You really are so kind." He smiled at me and said, "Thank you and you'll see me again." I smiled back and said, "I am sure I will, Mr. Lightfoot!" I now felt very safe in my car and it truly felt like God had put angels in my path.

To this day I receive a warm and compassionate card from Parents of Murdered Children every July 20. This is the date my Joseph was ripped away from me by a murderer. I also receive their quarterly newsletter and I am so grateful to have found them. I pray that every parent who has lost his or her child to murder seek out POMC. Know that you are not alone and there is help out there for you. Know that the presence of the Lord is always with you and you will be reunited with your beloved child.

I continued each day to write in my journal. I wrote of my tear soup based on a book that I was given. I wrapped myself up in my prayer shawl and held Jam, my little pup that Joseph gave me on Mother's Day. I thought about all the tear soup that I have made over these years. Who knew that my tear soup would need so many ingredients? The broth thickens and I have felt my blood boil from heartache and torment. I have spilled some on my apron of love but was able to wipe up and be cleansed by His loving grace and mercy. Yes, the mess is a great one, but the Great One, my Almighty God, will make it all right. My tear soup is rather salty, but all in all it is good. Jesus tells us in Matthew 5:13 that you are the salt of the earth. Salt is a preservative and a flavor enhancer. Pure salt cannot lose its effectiveness and I know I must continue my necessary work for his purpose.

During this time I had reviewed the Maryland State Police reports and I knew that my brief and record extract legal claim was due by the end of the year. I knew that I had to appeal the decision made by Judge Levise that my case did not prove negligent or intentional infliction of emotional distress by the MDSP and the Carroll County prosecutors. My family and I knew that it did.

I noticed in a handwritten report by Corporal Dan Kitseng that when he interviewed Pete Coldwin in his police car, he asked him some questions and the corporal told him he could not take back something that he had already said. Pete Coldwin had said there was pushing before Joseph ran up to the Bobcat. When Corporal Kitseng talked with him and Pete Coldwin said that Joseph fell off the left front tire and fell underneath the Bobcat, the corporal asked him, "What did you hear?" Pete Coldwin answered, "It sounded like a watermelon being squished." When I read this, I could not bear it; my tears overflowed and I fell to my knees. I had tried earlier to tell the Baltimore County Homicide Squad about it because they did not have a copy of this report. I also told State's Attorney Todd Slicenberger. He said, "Take the report over to the homicide squad and let them see it." I called Lieutenant Mahoney and he set up a time for me to deliver it and said that an officer would come down to the entrance of the building to pick it up. I took the report over and handed it to the officer; I recall the man whom I handed it to had a hostile look on his face and seemed annoyed. I gave it to him, said thank you and left.

The next day both Lieutenant Mahoney and Todd Slicenberger told me they saw it but it meant nothing and did not change anything about the case. Once again I had received such a vicious, heartless and sadistic comment from the person who killed my son and the law enforcers ignored me.

Lieutenant Mahoney did offer that he did not think Mr. Coldwin heard anything because the machine was very loud, but they still would not question him even though he no longer had legal representation. That was where they stood and they were not going to further investigate anything. I told Todd Slicenberger, "Joseph was brutally killed at the hands of others while at work. Jesus was brutally killed at the hands of others while at work. You cannot give up on me and my son." He just said I needed to stop pressing and there was nothing more they would do.

As the days went on, I felt so sick to my stomach. My ulcer was causing me a great deal of pain and I struggled to conduct research in the law library and on LexisNexis and talk with a business associate and friend of my brother regarding the brief and record extract. I had a huge hole in my center and I was hopeful to fill it up; it hurt so badly. I knew my God was showing me that I had to stay on my journey and persevere. The Holy Spirit was most assuredly guiding me. As the days, weeks and months went by, I worked day and night to prepare the 35-page brief and 250-page record extract. Carol was so helpful with the formatting and I needed to make sure that all that I was compiling followed the letter of the law to a tee. I will never forget the kindness, compassion, time and support she gave me. I love her and she will be my friend forever. I some days felt delirious from lack of sleep and overwhelmed by how many copies I had to make and how many needed to receive them. The folks at Kinko's, as I stated, were absolutely wonderful and knew to expect me at all and any hours of the day and night.

I knew that I needed to make it crystal clear and list all of the facts and occurrences that I endured and the gross negligence, intentional deceit and misconduct executed by the forty-two defendants. Not every defendant was liable, but a few I had to list because their efforts proved the wrongdoing of the others.

The entire process was a labor of love and God gave me the strength and the perseverance to complete it. My brother, Damian, was so helpful and to this day I do not know where I would be without him. I knew in my heart it was God's will for me to carry out this trial and to act. The Holy Spirit guided me and was a constant. He would pick me up when I was about to drop and build me up upon my rock, my Lord and Savior, my foundation. *Luke 6:46–48 "Everyone who comes to me and hears My words and acts on them I will show them whom he is like, he is like a man building a house who dug deep and laid a foundation on the rock. His house could not be shaken because it had been well built."*

I told Joseph I kept seeing his numbers—ones, threes and sevens—all around me. I knew they had great meaning. One is for God Almighty, the only one, creator of heaven and earth, the one most high. Three is for the trinity, Father, Son and Holy Spirit. Sevens are throughout the Bible and the number seven biblically means complete and perfect. I would see these numbers all the time in any sequence, but they were always present.

I always delight in how pure and precious the heart of a child is. All my life I have loved being around children and hearing their laughter, singing, sounds and questions and watching them grow. *Matthew 18:2–5 "And he called a child to Himself and set him before them and said, 'Truly I say to you, unless you are converted and become like children you will not enter the Kingdom of heaven. Whoever than humbles himself as this child, he is the greatest in the kingdom of heaven. And whoever receives one such child in My name receives Me."*

During the summer I had made friends with three delightful little women. Their father, Ricardo, had purchased the house that sat diagonally from mine. He was renovating it and was going to rent it. Sometimes his precious girls would get bored watching television and one day when I was out front working on my angel gardens, they came over. Ricardo and Laura were so dear and kind and their daughters brought me so much joy. I asked them their names and told them how beautiful and sweet they were. They would visit with me often and we would color pretty pictures, read, sing, dance, watch SpongeBob and go to the playground. I loved them and Vivian, Shelby and Kiley will always be my angel girls and special to me. I would tell them they were my three little angels and how happy they made me. In my kitchen hangs a little plaque that says *Angels gather here.* One day Vivian and the girls were in the kitchen having lunch with me and she said, "Ms. A, are we your angels?" and she pointed to the plaque. I gathered them up and hugged them and said, "Oh yes, you are definitely my angels and I love you." They smiled and hugged me back, saying, "We love you too." It was so sweet; some mornings when I was still in my PJs I would hear a knock on the front door. I would go to the door and say, "Who's there?" They would say back, "It's your angels." I would open the door and could not wait for them to run into my arms. We sometimes would talk about heaven and Jesus and how very much He loved us. I will treasure these precious memories forever. God does, indeed, show us love and give us miraculous gifts of tenderness and hope. All of the children whom God has given me to love and embrace, especially during these past eight years, have been so healing for me and have given me great joy. Children light up my day and I love to be surrounded by them. "Thank you, heavenly Father, for your gifts of grace, mercy, faith, hope and love."

Romans 8:28: "And we know that in all things God works for the good of those who love Him."

On December 29, 2008, I went to the Towson Post Office and sent all of my brief and record extract documents out to the special court of appeals in Annapolis, Maryland. I got to know Andrea, a lovely woman and she got to know my story. I went to the post office so many times and was so glad when I would see her and get to give her a hug. She had worked for the post office for many years and everyone loved her; she was very easy to love. After, when I got home, I called my precious baby brother, Damian and sang "Happy Birthday" to him. He was turning forty-three and I could hardly believe it. We are ten years apart and growing up I would often take him with me to visit my friends. He was so adorable and precious. I tell him, "Many a diaper of yours I changed and you were such a darling and beautiful little guy." He really thought he was Batman! I mean he really did! God bless his pure and loving heart; he is an especially good man and a good Christian and I love him so very much. I am truly blessed to have such a beautiful, loving family.

This Christmas season seemed to come and go quickly, but I made sure to put out my manger scene. My family and I attended the evening service at Grace Fellowship Church, my Christian home of praise, worship, love, understanding and fellowship. My Jesus brought me to Grace after I left my church of more than twenty-five years and I know this is where I belong. Here I am loved, accepted, embraced, cared for, prayed for and filled with hope and the word. I am also able to serve in some of the ministries and through Jesus Christ's love and mercy, I am alive, in the light and continually healing. My beloved pastors are such loving, kind, good and godly men and they are there for every one of their flock. How they have listened, prayed and opened their hearts and given kindness, time and compassion to me is distinctly marked on my heart. Jesus is the head of our church and we are all in union with one another and carrying out His will.

"HANDSOME JOE AT AGE 17"

Before Joseph was killed, he attended Grace Fellowship Church with me. He really enjoyed the service and felt the presence of Jesus there. He felt love and comfort there. I remember we spoke about it and he was happy.

Pastors Danny O'Brien, Erich Becker, Ginny Becker, Khori Smith, George Hopkins, Rusty Russey, Ben Abell, Pat Goodman and staff J. P. Kinhert as well as all of the ministry leaders have been there for me from day one. GFC staff, the worship team, the volunteers, the elders, the project and program directors, my sisters and brothers in Christ at Fallsway and all of my beloved brothers and sisters in Christ who I fellowship with, I give my love and sisterhood in Christ to you and a big hug and may you always be blessed in His name.

I pray that through the proceeds of this book the Lord will bring me the initiation and provide the springboard for "Jam's House, Home Sweet Home" to come to fruition. Joseph loved and adored children and knew he wanted to have three. He is now home and welcomes the little ones when they do arrive early in heaven and he continues to love children the same as I do.

The foundation will provide services to children who are oppressed all over the world—children who are sick, poor, orphaned, hungry, debilitated, terminally ill, abused and in need. I also pray to have a Christian education component so the word and love of Jesus Christ may be spread and studied globally, reaching all of humanity.

Joseph Anthony Miranda, my precious JAM, you know I have been told "not yet" by Father God, for there was still much more for me to learn, listen to, follow by His instruction and become the daughter God has made me to be. Yes, all will happen in God's time and He delights in impossibilities. God already knows everything about His children. He knows our hearts and He knows each and every occurrence of this temporal life and the eternal life to come. He already knows the choices we will make and may we all know and realize His unconditional and unending love for us. Give Him and show Him your love and adoration, I profess. God is love!

I hope for Joseph's legacy to live on in the name and the Holy Spirit of His Savior, Jesus Christ. I also hope that the foundation may become a part of Grace Fellowship Church (GFC). My church responds and moves forward in Him, with Him and through Him, living and spreading the word and ways of Jesus Christ in our daily lives. I am so very blessed. Thank you, Father.

I humble myself and I am "all in" heavenly Father. I give to you all of my mind, body, soul and spirit. I die to self. Monica Baldwin writes, "What makes humility so desirable is the marvelous thing it does to us; it creates in us a capacity for the closest possible intimacy with God."

A new year, 2009, was around the corner and I remained in hope, faith and love for my Savior. I prayed and thanked God for His blessings and I prayed especially for my loving son, Rob. I love him with all of my heart and I know these years have been difficult for him. In January of 2009, I would still receive yet another letter from State's Attorney Todd Slicenberger telling me that my son's death was an unfortunate circumstance and he would not accept any more phone calls, e-mails, or communications from me. He wrote that there was no evidence and all of the time that he and his detectives spent on my son's case was done as a courtesy and he did not have to help me at all. He continued that everyone told him not to help me or do anything but he did feel sorry for me. I thought, "How arrogant and cold of him; my son was, in fact, killed in his jurisdiction, Baltimore County."

I informed Mr. Slicenberger he would not hear from me again, but in tears I asked, "If in the future there is more evidence that becomes available and does indicate that a crime was committed against my son, whom should I go to? Who would prosecute?" He said, "The US attorney general." I said, "Do you mean Mr. Rod Rosenstein, at the federal level?" He said, "Yes, but that is not likely." He said he had to go and then hung up.

I was hurting but knew inside I was relieved that I did not have to listen to or deal with State's Attorney Todd Slicenberger anymore. I felt he was an outsider and he was not in the light.

In Numbers 18:4 it says people near to God are one family in the holy sanctuary and attend to their obligation before all of the tent and the testimony, but an outsider may not come near you.

Actually Mr. Slicenberger did not come near me. He was in my physical presence throughout all of this heartache and extended torment maybe a total of fifteen minutes. Praise be to God!

In the end, my interaction with State's Attorney Todd Slicenberger was unthinkable and unconscionable. Baltimore County's judiciary, Mr. Todd Slicenberger, the police and others were patronizing, unresponsive, emotionally abusive, despicable, hateful, lazy, stupid, uncaring, ignorant, arrogant, abrupt, mean, untruthful and belligerent. It is hard to believe that they could have known that I was a grieving mother and what all of the circumstances surrounding my son's horrific death were. I cannot imagine how these people could treat any human being in this way.

Occasionally, there were a few who were kind and compassionate, but it was seldom and they were not directly involved in the case. I hope they know that I am grateful for their kindness and sympathy and I feel sure they know who they are.

On January 20, 2009, I watched along with the world as Barack Obama placed his left hand on the same Bible that President Abraham Lincoln used and was sworn in as the forty-fourth president of the United States of America. I listened to each and every word as I held tightly to Jam and my special penny around my neck. I could feel the outline of President Lincoln's face on my penny and I thought of his honesty and his fight for justice, dignity, fairness and freedom. The Emancipation Proclamation would shine a new light on the American people and penetrate hope, justice and freedom for a new world order. How I pray for justice, truth, peace and love to lead and empower the nations. But for the faith, trust and love of God, we have and are nothing. Let it be, Father. Let it be!

On February 5, 2009, once again I went to the Towson Post Office. I needed to now send my motions, orders and certificates of service to the nine defense attorneys and also to the court of special appeals. Again, I saw sweet Andrea and we hugged. She knew what was going on. She is a woman of great faith and we will always remain sisters in Christ.

To this day, my mother and I have discussed many times how we would have never believed how dirty, corrupt and despicable so many men and women are in the Maryland government and beyond. The network of ill will, greed and evil is unthinkable but so very real. We continue to pray, even as I write, for justice, peace and truth. We know our Lord will bring it.

The winter cold was heavy and we had some snow. I love seeing the children playing in it, building snowmen and igloos and riding sleighs and making snow angels. It was the same as we did as children and as my boys and their friends did.

My mom stayed with me for a while this winter and we always watched Pastor Melissa Scott and listened intently to her message. This week she taught on Psalm 37. I learned and understood that my refuge and my patience is rested upon my Lord, my God. Justice and righteousness is His and I shall lean on him through my faith and love. I love and trust completely in my Lord and Savior. He shall bring it and I shall inherit my kingdom He has promised. Alleluia, amen.

She sings "The Storm Is Passing Over" with such love and devotion in her heart and I feel and know that each of us at times hits the wall, the bottom drops out, the bomb drops and we fall to our knees when the crisis is overbearing. I cry and take it to the cross of my Jesus daily. He took all our pain, wounds, suffering, sins, agony, desperation and torture and died for us by crucifixion on a cross.

He is our Savior. He rose from death and ascended into heaven and breathed the Holy Spirit into his disciples. We are His disciples. Jesus had victory over death; there is no death—only the living Christ. He lives in each of us so that we may be like him and act in His way, pray in His way, humble ourselves in His way, bring kindness in His way, obey in His way and love in His way. Open your heart and listen, receive and act. I pray to be an ambassador for Christ.

I was also reading *Just like Jesus* by Max Lucado; how beautiful and how true it was. I still shed my tears, but I know that it is OK. I know that I am never alone and my God holds me up and builds me up. I want so badly to hold my baby son. What they did to my boy and how they hurt him. I hold my tissue and wipe my eyes, knowing that Jesus and the angels came and took him right up in the blink of an eye.

1 John 5:12 "He who has the Son has life; he who does not have the Son of God does not have life."

Today is February 9, 2009. Today I took roses and "I love you" hearts to Joseph, Michael and my father. Valentine's Day will soon be approaching and you and Rob know you will always be my valentines. I love you both completely and you know I am forever your "best girl"!

I saw on C-SPAN the inquisition to confirm the position of deputy attorney general for the United States. My sense was promising that he could help with all that must be done to hold the wrongdoers accountable for their public corruption, fraud, violent crimes, murder and domestic and constitutional violations of rule of law.

The American people need answers, truth and resolve. I need answers, truth and resolve and what I know as factual to be called to action. I am taking that action and calling on those in my life who will and want to help me. Each day comes and goes and I am never surprised, now, at what reactions, responses and concern of others may or may not be revealed. God will bring the revelation when He is ready.

Those who love me and whom God has put in my path know that the "to date" is beyond dreadful and excruciating. It has now been over two years and I am blessed to receive love, concern, time, kindness, understanding, sensitivity and involvement in my quest for and devotion to justice for Joseph.

I pray that the knees of the court bow down and then I pray they will hopefully look up and serve truth and justice. Again, the judges of the land are obligated to be the fact finders and the truth seekers to bring justice. My brief and record extract show them the truth and the facts; it is undeniable. However, my faith and trust remains in my Lord, Jesus Christ, who is the Ruler over all and the King of Kings.

After another three days straight of finalizing my words on paper at the hand of God, my brief and record extract were now complete. My feet moved heavily as I made my way home again from Kinko's and placed my feet upon each paved stone the Lord had perfected and placed for my path. My neck pained from the constant writing and preparing and the yoke was tight. I do, though, move forward and up and accept the pressure and bearing down on my body. A new day would dawn and I was lifted to and by my Lord, Jesus. The day not be done till my Father's will be done.

I took a welcoming hot shower and tried to massage my aching, pinching and sore neck. The stress accumulated in my neck and shoulder blades and it was difficult to reach the area, but I did the best I could. I remembered how Joseph would sometimes give me a neck-and-shoulder rub to release the knots when I would come home from a long day's work. He knew just where to rub out the areas and in no time the pain would be soothed. I love you, Joseph and I miss every little thing about you. I am so grateful you are my son. I am so very proud of you and I hold all of the talks, words, stories, promises and love we shared in our mother-and-son bond that was and always will be so close to my heart and soul and forever treasured.

During these months I had also spoken many times to Ann Bolduc. She is the woman I met at the Parents of Murdered Children (POMC) event in Washington, DC. She was so kind and supportive and she connected me to Delegate Joseline Pena-Melnyk in Annapolis, Maryland. I spoke to the delegate about Joseph's case and explained that State's Attorney Todd Slicenberger would do nothing and kept saying there was no crime committed and he was finished.

The delegate was also trying to assist Ann in her quest for her beloved son, Greg and his fiancée. Joseline Pena-Melnyk was very kind and listened intently on the phone. She is a very strong and convicted woman and regarded highly in her position. She is bright, conscientious and articulate. She knows the law, understands the process to have new laws and bills passed and enacted into law and always does the right thing. I knew God had sent another blessing into my life.

We planned a day to meet to review and discuss Joseph's death certificate and where the medical examiners were in their findings. I was so very grateful to her and looked forward to the assistance and expertise she could offer.

On February 27, 2009, I did go to the Towson Post Office and officially submitted my completed brief and record extract after receiving the answer and notification from the nine defense attorneys. I felt that I had accomplished my task and it was now up to the three panel court of special appeals judges to review my case. I hoped for a hearing and I knew it would take several months before I would hear anything.

In March I saw my beloved Sharon, who is the best hair stylist on the planet. She is so sweet, kind, compassionate and filled with faith. She would come to my home all the way from Pennsylvania to do my hair when I was up to it. She knew all that had been going on and she and her family kept me in their prayers. I gave Sharon and her wonderful husband, Gary, "Justice for Joseph" T-shirts. They have both stood by me with unwavering support. Sharon would always bring me little treasures, especially angels and we would cry together often and sometimes laugh at our little similarities. On one occasion Sharon presented me with a very special gift of love and remembrance of Joseph. Her friend, Nancy Lucker, an artist and a painter, created a beautiful hand-painted slate of the teal blue ocean with its white froth at the sandy beach, the blue sky of heaven and gorgeous deep coral pink hibiscus, one of Joseph's favorite flowers. It reads *Joseph A. Miranda, April 22, 1987–July 20, 2006*. I have it placed on an easel in my family room and everyone comments on how beautiful and serene it is. Joseph did love everything about the ocean, the beach, the sunshine and God's display of flowering seed. Sharon is my sister and I will always love and adore her. Today I gave her some delightful "gifts of green" in celebration of Saint Patrick's Day and her birthday. We both have Irish heritage and my mema's (grandmother's) Irish blue eyes are always smiling. We are warmed by the luck and love of the Irish. The gifts tickled her and we were laughing like little girls. She is a true and forever friend.

Early this month I went to Annapolis and met with Delegate Joseline Pena-Melnyk. She is a strong advocate and understood completely what Ann and I were trying to accomplish. Our goal was to now speak before the senate and finance committee to let them know the details of what Ann Bolduc and I had endured throughout our attempt to appeal our son's death certificate regarding a person's rights when he or she believes that there exist suspicious and disbelieving circumstances around his or her loved one's death. It is law in Maryland that any family member or interested party may discuss and meet with the medical examiners to review this. However, the majority of Maryland citizens are not aware of this. We sought to pass House Bill 127, whereby all death certificates would now have it written out clearly on the certificate that a person has this right so that all would now be aware of their lawful right to question or discuss a loved one's manner and cause of death. Delegate Joseline Pena-Melnyk had sponsored the bill and gotten it through the House of Delegates, but it now needed to go before the senate committee members for final voting and passing.

On March 25, 2009, my mother and my brother, Dino and his wife, Lisa, accompanied me to Annapolis. Today, Ann and I were going to speak before the senate committee. I had prepared a few notes as to what I was going to say. We also had a bevy of family members, friends, neighbors and others write in to their delegates and their senators regarding their support for House Bill 127. Ann had done the same. Ann and I, along with our family members, met in the small diner for coffee and to briefly discuss our hopes that our words would resonate with the senate committee.

We all sat together and then finally went into the area where Delegate Joseline Pena-Melnyk was. We hugged and we told her we were well prepared and ready to speak. We were then taken into a conference room and all of our family followed. Ann and I took seats at the conference table. We saw notes on the podium where we knew the delegate would open our meeting and explain the purpose of the necessity of House Bill 127 to pass and be enacted into law.

The side doors opened and about twelve to fifteen senate committee members took their seats around the conference table. The microphones were activated and the delegate began to speak. After, she then introduced Ann and I and allowed us to address the committee. I believe Ann and I did well as we spoke the truth from our hearts and emphasized how imperative it was for victims and family members to have the right to appeal and meet with the medical examiners when there were suspicious and illogical circumstances surrounding the death of a loved one. We both gave examples of some of what we endured firsthand and all that was still going on in the investigations into our sons' brutal killings.

The committee members listened intently, there were a few questions and then they agreed that they had heard what they needed to hear. They thanked us for our time and our declarations and right then and there they voted. We looked at Joseline and around the table as the voting process began. They passed House Bill 127 right before our ears and eyes. All of us were so grateful and elated.

We thanked them and they in turn thanked us again. We gathered our papers and the delegate motioned us to head out to the lobby area. We were all so overcome with appreciation for her. Again, we all hugged and Delegate Joseline Pena-Melnyk said to all of us that this was the first time she actually saw the senate committee vote right after the testimonies and in the presence of the family members. She was so happy for us. We knew we had met our goal for this particular hurdle and there would be more to come; God was right there and Joseph was giving me his affirmative nod from heaven.

We all said our good-byes for then and said we would be in touch. We knew that there would be an upcoming signing ceremony before Governor O'Malley and his officials in Annapolis.

I had earlier referenced another issue with the delegate, asking, "Who is it in law enforcement that has the responsibility to notify the family when there is a change in the manner of death by the medical examiner? This had happened in our case when the medical examiners took Joseph's manner of death out of accident and changed it to undetermined with a strong possibility of homicide."

The Maryland State Police knew this prior to their July 11, 2007, closing meeting, yet they never revealed it to us at any time. This is more than disgraceful in a criminal investigation. Why would they hold that back from our family? We had to call the medical examiners ourselves to learn of this change after the fact.

In conclusion, we remain a strong advocate of House Bill 127 as victim and survivor rights in Maryland need to be established and enforced. However, there still remains much work to be done to modify and change some Maryland laws as well as enact new laws that are grossly needed.

I prayed on my knees when I got home and thanked my heavenly Father for his mercy and His goodness. *Matthew 23:23 "Woe to you teachers of the law, you hypocrites! You neglect the more important matters of the law—justice, mercy and faithfulness."*

I knew my Lord was present and though the wheels of justice move slowly, justice will come when God reveals all that He wants seen and all of His purpose and His plan to be completed.

The season of spring was now approaching and I could smell the scent of the flowering blossoms and the fragrance of the heavenly Father.

2 Corinthians 14–17 "Thanks be to God who always leads us in triumphal procession in Christ and through us spreads everywhere the fragrance of the knowledge of Him. For we are to God the aroma of Christ among those who are perishing. To the one we are the smell of death; to the other, the fragrance of life. In Christ, we speak before God in sincerity, like men sent from God."

I speak the letter written on my heart, the letter of Christ as a result of His ministry, not with ink but with the spirit of the living God in me. I know through His Holy Spirit I am competent to bring forth the will and purpose He desires. For great is His glory and I will lean and press into Him for His strength and righteousness. I love you, Father God, with all of my being.

My dear Uncle Salvatore (Moonie) hand painted beautiful triumphant angels and he and my aunt Marion gave them to me as a love gift. The white angles sit atop my two bookcases beside my fireplace. Their trumpets shine in gold and I can hear the victorious power of their resounding beauty as Jesus triumphed over evil through His love for us; I also hear the sounding beauty that will come when justice is served for my beloved Joseph. Yes, it will come.

Easter Sunday was on April 12 this year. The most holy and sacred miracle of all that Jesus accomplished. His resurrection and His ascension into heaven show us that He is the Christ and life everlasting is truth. There is no death for all who believe and follow our One and only Savior, Jesus Christ.

A few days before, my darling little angels Vivian, Shelby and Kiley came to bake a bunny cake and his face was as cute as a button. Laura and other neighbor children joined in the fun and said the cake was yummy. We took lots of pictures and handed out pieces of coconut cake to the neighbors. It was all good and did my heart well.

This week was the first time I was able to listen to music on the radio. I have loved music, singing and dancing all of my life but was unable to even listen to it after Joseph's death.

I was finding myself again, but I was a new self—a daughter of Father God who was being restored and renewed in His image. I cried to Jesus for being my rescue and my rock. I yearned to be with Him and to follow all that He had for me.

On April 14, 2009, I went to Annapolis with my brother, Dino. The lobby was filled with people there to have their photograph taken as house bill they had signed was enacted into law by our governor. I was able to meet Delegate Joseline Pena-Melnyk's incredible staff in person: Mary, Tim and Spencer. I will never forget them and how they stood by me in my time of need and distress. We waited for our turn as the ceremonial room was filling up and saw media reporters and high-capacity lights all around.

They called out House Bill 127 and the delegate, her aids, our family members and Ann and I went up to the signing table for our photo shoot. We stood directly behind Governor Martin O'Malley and I recall he asked me what our bill was for. I told him in his ear and then he asked, "How old was your son?" I answered, "He was nineteen and his name is Joseph."

The photographer had us ready and with a flash the picture was taken. We quickly moved to the left and down a hall to make room for others. Once again, we all hugged and felt the task accomplished was a strong positive for us and the citizens of Maryland and that the people would put into worthwhile use.

The next morning I awoke and said with joy "Happy twenty-ninth birthday, my beloved Michael, my sweet nephew!" He was a beautiful baby boy born on April 15 and he was at home in heaven with Joseph. I knew in my heart they were together and so very happy. They were cousins who were never apart and Michael, seven years older than Joseph, always looked out for him and demonstrated such love, affection and protection for him. Yes, they both went to the Lord at the age of nineteen. They were strong, healthy, loving, kind and handsome young men with the world at their fingertips. You might say they were "just getting out of the gate." We know the gate that God had in store for them was the pearly gate of heaven. That is the gate they passed through and they live on in the eternal kingdom of paradise. They are our angel boys! I had an oil painting done by a very talented artist with Michael and Joseph both at ages three and nineteen. The painting is just beautiful and you can feel the love and warmth in their souls. I requested that the artist please name the portrait and his consultants said he does not do that. When I told them the story of Michael and Joseph and that I hoped they could name the portrait "Angel Boys," the artist complied with no hesitation. God bless him and his staff for their kind and compassionate hearts. The "Angel Boys" portrait is hung in my foyer as you enter my home. Everyone comments on how beautiful and meaningful it is. It is one of my many treasures that I live through and find joy and peace in.

May 10th was Mother's Day. I shared time, love and giving with my family. My mom and I held each other and she gave me one long-stem red rose from Joseph, as she had done for the past two years. My mother is a very special woman and I still love to be held in her arms. She brings me comfort and her faith is great. Joseph and Rob were in my heart all day as they always are and my boys are my life.

I pray for peace and wellness and for the serenity of survival until I make my way home to be with Jesus and all of those I love so deeply.

Every year I have tended to my gardens. I now have special angel gardens as well. I love to dig in the dirt and plant the seeds and watch them grow. It is so healing for me and my white butterfly shows up every year; he never misses. Joseph loved the gardens and his landscaping so much and he was truly given this gift from God. My son is ever present with me.

My precious niece, beautiful Grace, was now almost three years old. I love and adore her and she started coming to my house for "best-girl parties." I would sing a song I made up just for her about how she is my one and only "best girl" in the whole wide world. It made her laugh and she would sing it with me. We started making our best-girl parties a routine and I could not wait to have her come for the weekend. We made up our own special games and she would put on a special show for me and sing and dance. JAM, Mr. Giraffe and I would be her audience and we loved how she knew each and every word and could carry the tune to perfection. She is so bright and beautiful, has very special gifts and will forever be her Aunt Nonnie's "best girl"! I love you so very much, Grace.

On May 22, 2009, I received word from Ms. Bruno that my brief and record extract were accepted by the Court of Special Appeals The good news is present, she relayed and she also said, "Your son was a very handsome young man." I thanked her and said, "Yes, he was. He is." She informed me that I would learn the next course of action from the three-panel Judge probably in late July. Again, I thanked her and said I appreciated her contact.

May 26 was Memorial Day. Thank God for all of our soldiers and heroes. Each of them lay down his or her life for us and our country; the very least I could do is stand up in honor and gratitude to them and for them and that still is not enough. I support all of our armed forces and their families. Our respect, honor and support for them are so well deserved. I also have much in memories and I look forward to my new birth in heaven when God is ready to call me home.

Today is June 4 and my brother, Dino, will turn the big fifty! I, of course, called and sang "Happy Birthday" to him. We spoke and reminisced about times when we were kids and he told me about the special gifts he received, especially the present he loved from his son, Joseph Vincent. Joe, his son, is another fine young man who is full of kindness, compassion and love. He reminds me of my Joseph in many ways. He is protective of me in his own way and I have grown so very close to him. My nephew is strong in heart and character and if I ever need a favor, he is right there for me.

I thought about how we are all getting older as yet another year will come and go. Time waits for no one and sometimes it seems the only thing constant is change. My Lord, my God, does not change. He is the constant in my life that moves me, inspires me and loves me. I love our conversations and thank Him always for His magnificent gift of Jesus, our Lord and our Savior.

My mother came over and spent a few days with me. We love to sit out front on the gliding rocker and talk. I have always loved to rock since I was a toddler and I vividly remember my mother caressing me in her arms, rocking and singing lullabies to me. I did the exact same with my sons. Those precious moments are the riches of motherhood and the flowing of unconditional love that never dies but thrives for always. I can still feel her tenderness, warmth and love and the beat of her heart. My mom likes to watch me garden and the beautiful array of color, fragrance and blooms makes her happy.

This evening after dinner, we read from the Bible to each other. When she stays, she sleeps in Joseph's bedroom and I usually fall asleep beside her. These are often my most comforting hours along with the alone time I spend with my first love, my Lord. This night my mom read "pillow prayers" to me and I just loved having her near me. She soothes me in the way only a mother can. I can often fall asleep when she is with me. To sleep now feels like an escape from the unbearable pain and agony that I feel inside. Like a type of freedom from torture…I sleep.

Every day I spend time in Joseph's room and I recall him saying to me in his latter teen years, "Mom, don't ever change my room." I smiled and hugged him and said, "Sweetheart, I will never change your room. It will always be right here for you." He hugged me back with so much love in his heart.

This summer was going by quickly and there were so many home improvements that I should have been working on. I tried to do some things when I was able, but I knew sometimes things just had to wait.

July 1, 2009…This was the birthday of my father's, Joseph Vincent Gemma. Happy birthday, Daddy! He would have turned eighty-seven this day. I loved and missed him so much and he was the best dad a girl could have ever had. In those years not that many dads easily and openly showed affection and gave out hugs and more hugs. My dad was so loving, affectionate, kind, fun and always laughing. When he would tell a joke, he was his best audience. It would make you laugh just watching and listening to his laughter!

He had such a great disposition and was always upbeat. He would help anyone and everyone and give you the shirt off his back. His heritage was Italian and my grandparents came from Catania, Sicily. They too were such good people with kind and caring hearts. They worked hard and were so happy to come to America. My grandmother was a seamstress and could sew so beautifully and she went to Mass every day. Their faith was strong and in those days neighbors took care of one another. My pop-pop made his entire yard a vegetable garden and on one side also grew beautiful flowers. I remember how good it always smelled when we would visit and something was always cooking. My father had the same work ethic as his parents and worked so hard for all of us. He provided a wonderful life filled with joy, love, happiness and protection. Yes, my siblings and I were and are so richly blessed with loving, caring and giving parents. I am so very grateful and thankful.

It was now just a few weeks before July 20, 2009, marking three years since Joseph was killed. For so long I had been trying to find an attorney to take our case and help us. Finally, just two weeks before the three-year anniversary of Joseph's death, I found that attorney. We knew that we were not going to get any help, assistance, or justice from the criminal justice system in Baltimore County. We thought, "There is a three-year statute of limitations and we must get something done in order to still try to get justice for Joseph."

In early July, we were able to file a wrongful death lawsuit against Pete Coldwin, Joe Metvet, Outside Unliving, Westminster Wholesale Nurseries, Bobcat and Metro Rentals. Thank God we filed in time and our lawsuit was submitted and accepted. Our attorney was very diligent, intelligent and proficient. He, too, believed Joseph's death was no accident. We went through all of the motions and orders that were mandatory for the courts.

After a while, our attorney experienced some severe personal tragedy in addition to what he and his family had already suffered and he was not able to maintain his representation. I, of course, understood and to this day I remain so very grateful to him.

We now at least had our civil wrongful death lawsuit on the books and we were hoping for truth and justice to be revealed.

On July 20, 2009, I awoke in prayer. It had now been three years since my precious Joseph went home to Jesus. This day was unbearable and I wept hard at Joseph's grave. I prayed, "Have mercy on me, Father, as you, your Son and Holy Spirit live within me. Please keep lighting my way and dry the tears from my cheeks. Once again, I laid down my roses for Joseph and gave him my written love message.

On July 24, 2009, my brother, Damian and his family were coming from Naples, Florida, for a welcomed visit. I wanted to see my brother so badly and hug all of them. They were coming for ten days and I could not wait to spend time with them and share the love and joy within our family. We all got together and celebrated our mother's eighty-second birthday on July 30. A wonderful time was had by all.

On August 5, Pop Al, Lisa's grandfather, went home to the Lord. He was a kind, gentle, loving and wonderful man. He missed his beloved wife, Anna, who had passed just three months after Joseph was killed. They were both such kind, caring and wonderful people. I remember when I went to visit Pop at Stella Maris and he was so devastatingly sick; on his dying bed, he looked up at me with his beautiful, blue, blue eyes and asked how I was doing. I stroked his forehead and kissed him as I held his hand and prayed. What a very special man—so sweet—and I knew the angels were there.

On August 16, my son Rob turned twenty-five. "Wow," I thought, "my son is really quite a wonderful, handsome, hardworking and loving young man." He has been through so much watching my pain as he did his best to deal with his own. He very much misses Joe and both my boys know my heart is always and forever with them. Rob has been very supportive and hopes for justice for his brother to come to fruition. He is so smart and he knew that the investigations were more than a mess. I am glad that Rob has so many wonderful and kind friends. They are all good guys and gals and have helped Rob along the way to move forward.

213

I try to be strong for Rob and Joe. I know that is what they hope for and that I must try to recover from the pain and find peace in my heart. My sons have always truly been my heart and if they were ever hurting, I was hurting for them. That is the way it is with a mom. You know you will lay your life down for your children and stand up against anyone who would try to harm or hurt them in any way. I thank you, God, for the blessing of my beautiful sons.

On September 19, I learned my case to the court of special appeals was finally in the hands of the judges. I knew it would still take some time before I learned of their decision and I prayed for a hearing before them. We thought for sure they would want to hold a hearing so I could testify before them and show them all of the misconduct, the despicable treatment, the lies and the torment we suffered due to their actions. Everything was written out and documented in my brief and my record extract that contained more than two hundred exhibits validating all that had happened. I hoped and I continued to pray for justice and truth to be revealed.

The season of fall again was approaching and the leaves changed into their rich and warm autumn colors. The children were all ready to go back to school. I could see them out my front window as they made their way down the court to the bus stop with their backpacks securely fastened. All of them were so sweet as they began another school year.

CHAPTER 13

MY CIVIL RIGHTS CASE DISMISSED BECAUSE OF IMMUNITY LAWS IN MARYLAND

On October 1, 2009, I received the letter from the court of special appeals in Maryland dismissing our case. I was devastated and in disbelief that Judge Wright and the two other judges involved could come to such an outrageous conclusion. The letter read that my case was dismissed because all defendants have *"immunity."* Again, I was shattered and thought, "How can these state officials and police get away with this? This is an utter disgrace and totally wrong. No one is above the law—no one!" I contacted my brother, Damian, the delegate and other family members. Everyone was in dismay. I prayed to God for his mercy and his power to bring light to the truth and justice for my son. I still knew in my heart that God was going to bring revelation in His way and in His time.

I had recalled so many of the attorneys who did at least give me their time and expertise telling me that in their professional opinion my son was murdered and the civil suit would not hold up because even if there was a working backup alarm, Joseph would have never had the time to get out of the way. I still, today, appreciate these men who did allow me their time, review and expert conclusions. They concluded that the thrusting physical force by Pete Coldwin was so severe and powerful it propelled Joseph forward harshly and immediately into the reversing Bobcat to his death. My family and I knew this was true, but the state prosecutor, Todd Slicenberger, didn't care and would not prosecute for any crime. He would not prosecute for murder, second-degree murder, manslaughter, reckless endangerment, or perjury and he would not call in a grand jury. He refused us over and over again and victimized us with prejudice, ill will and bias. He needed to be removed from his position and interrogated.

Halloween, Thanksgiving Day and Christmas were around the corner. Somehow, with the grace of God, I got through these holidays. Rob and Joseph loved them all and I cherished the precious memories we had. We attended Grace Fellowship Church in Timonium, Maryland, for the Christmas service and it was so beautiful. My church illuminated the love of Christ through the Gospel word, the magnificent decorations, the worship songs, the welcoming love toward one another and the taking of sacred Communion. The service was glorious as we celebrated the birth of our sweet, holy, miraculous Savior, Jesus Christ, who came to save the world and be the ransom for our sin.

This year I put up my little tree and my most sentimental ornaments and listened to the Christmas carols throughout my home. We lit a special candle made of two angels with a torch in hand after Christmas dinner. All of our family gathered round in a circle, each saying a prayer to our Lord and for Michael and Joseph as the candles were lit. The precious babe in a manger, our king, was born and the angles came. There were tears of sorrow, pain, joy and hope. Our Almighty Father was with us, holding us up. We exchanged our gifts and expressed our love for each other and hopes for a wonderful new year to come.

My mother stayed with me this Christmas season and we watched the crystal ball descend in Times Square on New Year's Eve. It was now 2010. We watched Pastor Scott and Pastor Stanley on TV. All of our family members phoned one another at midnight to bid a happy new year and say we loved one another; this was our tradition.

I have great difficulty with the meaning the state of Maryland gives to "immunity" under the law. The posture and practice of this "dismissal" or "not responsible" given to law-enforcement personnel and government officials is unjust and at times outrageous. It needs to be modified. I recall speaking with a very kind gentleman who was a sheriff in another county about my son's case and how and what the Maryland State Police investigators did throughout their homicide and criminal "investigation." I will never forget his words to me. He said, "Ms. Miranda, I am so very sorry for your loss. I was with the Maryland State Police for more than twenty years and I had to get out and leave." He continued by saying that what he actually saw and witnessed by some police and officials was criminal. He said they committed crimes all the time and it was known but nothing would be done. I listened to his heartfelt and honest words to me and so appreciated his forthrightness. I thanked him and told him how grateful I was for his integrity and support. He said to me, "Ms. Miranda, you will get justice for your son—you will. And do you know why you will? Because you are a voice to be reckoned with." I became teary and knew this man was a good, decent person and wanted to give me hope. Again, I thanked him for his time and his concern and said, "May God bless you."

The cold and bitter winter seemed so long. I remained in union with the Holy Spirit and prayed constantly. My brother, Damian, remained at my side and his faith was unshakable. He has been a constant source of strength and has stayed committed to getting answers, truth, solace and justice for Joseph. I was still attending my GriefShare workshop and knew God was leading me. My brother never left me throughout this entire journey. I was not alone and I thank God every night for him. Next to me, he is the only one who knows everything and all that has occurred. People tell me, "Adrienne, no one knows this case like you do and your story must be told." I agree but tell them that if something should happen to me, my brother Damian would be able to continue and run with it. He told me that I can be assured that he will fight the good fight and not rest until justice for Joseph is served. He said, "Adrienne, you know and I know that Father God has put this path before you for His purpose and His plan and in my heart I know He will make sure you see it through until His plan has been accomplished." I told Damian, "I know. I believe, too, that God will have me serve and be the person He has transformed me into. I am His loving and faithful daughter and I will go wherever He takes me and do whatever He orders. I know our Joseph smiles down from heaven and knows how very much his Uncle Damian loves him and stands by his mom."

I was anxious for the warmth of the sun to come and to start my gardening. I would pray on bended knee, "Father, please bring me that one good person who is to help and lead us to rightness in our tribulation." The daylight would soon lengthen and I would realize how often now I was watching local and world news. I really like Rachel and Keith on MSNBC and think they are so bright, well-spoken, truthful, intelligent and forthcoming. They make sense and their reasoning is articulate and logical.

Ah, April was finally here. I could smell the fresh, clean air and the scent of my son was everywhere. I started participating in a life group ministry at my church, Grace Fellowship. I felt called at this time to read *Intimate Moments with the Savior* by Ken Gire. The author was most humble and explained to us his former life before his devoted faith and belief in the Lord and how he never anticipated that he would become an author let alone an author who wrote about Jesus's life and the particular people Jesus personally met with while on earth. His book is beautifully written and reveals the heart and kindness of Jesus and how holy and loving this man, our Lord and our Savior, was.

All of us were assigned to a group according to our age, marital status and other characteristics and we studied the first three chapters of the book together with open discussion. The goal was to recognize from your own heart and soul who you would like to lead your home life group. We were instructed to close our eyes and pray and then when prompted open our eyes and point at the person around the table you chose to lead. Surprisingly to me, when we did this, a majority of the participants were pointing at me. I knew who I was pointing at and then our pastor and his assistants said OK.

I was humbled and knew the Lord was working in me. My sister in Christ, Sharon Yaguez, was also chosen as a leader. There were at least twelve groups and all had chosen their two leaders. We were called up to the front and center of the room and all participants laid their hands upon their chosen life group leaders as Pastor Rusty Russey prayed aloud over us. It was so spiritually fulfilling and the Lord's presence was undeniable.

Our life group met each Monday evening from seven to nine in the evening at my home. I loved having Sharon alongside me and my sisters and brothers in Christ together in worship. We would greet with warm hugs, open in prayer, sing a worship song together and then discuss openly our thoughts and answers to our weekly questions. All of us grew together in our faith and understanding of the scripture. We created a bond of trust and safety as we shared our personal stories and our journeys. We would then each ask for a prayer request and it would be written down so we would pray for that particular need during the week until we met again. We closed in prayer, love and gratitude for our Lord. Oh, how these folks are so dear to me and how we have given love, patience and understanding to one another. The goal of life groups is to come together in union as Christians—to do life together in a safe and sacred atmosphere knowing the Lord is leading us and the Holy Spirit is guiding us. I will always and forever love and pray for Sharon, Judy, Skip, Dean, Gregg, Dawn, Linda, Roger, Maria and all who at one time or another joined our life group.

CHAPTER 14

My Church, Grace Fellowship, My Home and Jam's House

Grace Fellowship Church has so many wonderful ministries extended to their congregation and everyone who enters is welcome. Their Rest Day program is a blessing from God. It is so well supervised and organized as parents who have children with disabilities are able to bring them and their siblings to our church for a day of rest—respite that is so very needed for these warm, loving and wonderful parents. I have volunteered several times and the love, care, tenderness, fun, joy and laughter that the children and all who participate are able to give and receive is miraculous. We have heard many of our church members who have disabilities give their testimonies of what their life was like before Grace Fellowship Church. Sadly, most churches are not equipped and adequately staffed to provide for children and adults with disabilities and they were turned away and felt unwelcomed. GFC does just the opposite. We pray that as all churches move forward in their mission and their goals, they may find a means and a way to open their doors and their hearts to all people. It would be such a blessing to replicate the rest day program so no one is left behind or hurting or feels unwelcomed. On rest day, the moms and dads are so overjoyed when they pick up their children and see the happy faces, the self-made crafts, the enthusiasm and the love that permeates throughout by His grace alone. The GFC staff and volunteers also provide the parents with a delicious homemade dinner with all the fixings and dessert. They leave with happy hearts and tired and hungry kids and mom and dad can go home, set the table, eat till they are full and enjoy their family evening time together. The rest day program has grown leaps and bounds since its initiation six years ago. Father God is smiling and says, "Work well done!"

My church truly offers a home and a safe haven for any and every aspect of life that could touch humankind. Their ministries are numerous, faith filled, trustworthy, guided in spirit, far-reaching and led in the love of Jesus Christ. All of us come together in unity for the love and worship of our King and want to be His disciples, spreading the good news always. I am blessed and so very grateful.

On April 22, 2010, I sang, "Happy birthday, my dear Joseph." My son would be twenty-three years old today. I took my roses, prayer cards, balloons and broken heart to his gravesite. I knelt down and prayed over his headstone. I told Joseph that justice would come when God was ready to bring it. I cried, "Joseph, Mommy has tried so very hard to right all the wrong that has been done, but it has not worked." I told my precious son that I would always stay in prayer and never give up. I told him, "You know that I put all of my faith and trust in God and He sees and knows everything." God loves all of his children and I will see you soon, Joseph. When my work is done and our Lord calls me home, I know that your hand will lovingly reach out for me from heaven and pull me through. We will then be together forever in paradise with our Jesus and our family. I love you and miss you with all of my heart; I will see you soon." Jesus is love and love always lives.

Spring was just beautiful and on Mother's Day, May 9, my family and I were together. Scott, Joseph's best bud, came by with flowers and a beautiful card for me as he has always done these last few years. He loves and misses Joe very much and I am sure my son knows how kind, thoughtful and loving Scott has been to me. Joseph looks down on Scott and feels so blessed to have him as his very best friend and sends his love and respect to him.

During May and June, I was desperately trying to find an attorney who would take on Joseph's wrongful death case and continue where we left off. I must have talked to several hundred attorneys by this time. I prayed constantly and spoke often to my now good friend with the FBI. He would always listen with his heart and his soul and try to comfort me in a way that only he could. I knew that he knew all that I had researched and found was true and that the facts of my son's death added up to only one thing: murder. He also realized and knew there was a very disturbing reason why no one would prosecute or question Pete Coldwin. We both knew, but we knew even more that all would be revealed in God's way and in His time.

There is such immense power in prayer. Today was July 20, 2010 and when I awoke, I went outside to my prayer gardens. The white butterfly fluttered before me and I knelt at my cross. Now, four years to the day of the anniversary of my son's death, I went to visit with my angel boy, my Joseph and took red heart balloons that read *I love you*, flowers, one long-stem red rose, my love and prayer card and all of my being. The sun was shining brightly; I kissed the headstone of my son and prayed so hard to my Almighty Father. I talked to God through my heartache and tears and asked Him to bring truth and justice into the light. I prayed, "Please, dear Lord, on this day bring us just one good, caring, honest man to help us; just one. Please let it be now, Father, please. Joseph, ask Jesus to bring our answers to our prayers now. Mommy is so very tired and I have tried and tried but can find no one. Joseph, put a rainbow in the sky for me today and let me know you hear me. You have done it before. Do it today for Mommy—a rainbow across the heavenly sky so I will know you hear me." I prayed and talked for hours to my Lord and my son. I asked Jesus to please meet my needs and allow me to serve him. As I sat, I looked up and saw my Rob drive up. He came over and we hugged and held each other so tight. I cried so hard inside that I could not breathe. Rob tried to console me and then bent down to his brother's headstone and spoke silently. I knew God was right there with us. I felt in my heart that it was time; the Lord was ready to deliver His Father's will. After a while, Rob and I hugged again and he said, "It will be OK, Mom." We said how much we loved each other and I said, "I know Joseph is in a better place than we are." I love my sons with all of my heart; I will never be apart from them. Rob and I parted and I felt a calming peace embrace me. My Holy Spirit was soothing me and empowered me with a comfort I had not known. I raised my arms up to the heavens and once again gave thanks and praise to my Almighty Father, God.

CHAPTER 15

GOD SHOWS ME MIRACLES

I then folded up my blanket, gathered my water bottles and said, "I love you, so long and see you later" to Joseph, Michael and my dad. I got into my car and headed home. The sun was still shining and the sky was blue and beautiful. I was almost home and just before I turned off of Margate Road and into my court, a beautiful, majestic rainbow appeared across the sky! I was in awe looking at it and cried saying, "Oh, thank you, Jesus. Thank you, Joseph. I know, my son, that you hear me and I know that Jesus is living and is with us and in us always." This was again one of the most beautiful miracles of many that God showed me and I knew it was divine intervention. Our God is so awesome and He does, indeed, hear our prayers. I was overwhelmed with joy and hope in my heart and I felt a breakthrough was on the horizon. I just sat and looked at the colors and the beauty of the rainbow and considered its meaning to me. God's promise to me always was, always is and always will be.

GOD GIVES ME A BEAUTIFUL RAINBOW ACROSS THE SKY AND JOSEPH KNOWS IT.

Genesis 9:13–16: "God said, I have sent my rainbow in the clouds and it will be the sign of the covenant between me and the earth. Whenever I bring clouds over the earth and the rainbow appears, I will remember my covenant between me and you and all living creatures of every kind." I said to Joseph, "Somewhere over the rainbow and what a wonderful world" is where you live now, my precious, in God's glorious kingdom of heaven. I will be with you soon and I await and worship in song seeing my Lord and Savior." Just like your favorite medley says, I see friends shaking hands saying "how do you do", their really saying "I love you".

I then walked across my front pathway, unlocked my front door and went into my kitchen to put down my things and I felt exhilarated; Jesus was with me. I went upstairs to my bedroom and wanted to change into something a little cooler. As I walked over to my dresser, I noticed the red light on my telephone blinking. This light signals to me that there is a message on my voice mail. I sat on the edge of my bed and dialed to listen to the message left. On my voice mail was a kind gentleman saying, "Hello, my name is Keith Truffer and I am calling for Adrienne

226

Miranda. I am an attorney in Towson and I have heard about your case and would like to help you. Please call me at…" He gave me his phone number. I dropped to my knees and gave praise and thanks to my Lord. I gathered myself and grabbed a notepad and a pen and telephoned him back. The receptionist picked up and I asked, "Could I please speak with Attorney Keith Truffer? My name is Adrienne Miranda and I am return-ing his call." She said, "One moment please." Then Mr. Truffer picked up and said, "Hello, Adrienne. I am glad you phoned back so promptly." I said, "Oh, Mr. Truffer, thank you so much for contacting me. Do you really think you can help?" I tried to hold back my tears as he said, "Yes, Adrienne, I really do." He explained that a friend and acquaintance of his, another attorney, had talked to him about my case and explained that he had wanted to help me but there was a conflict of interest and he there-fore could not so he contacted me. Mr. Truffer then said, "Adrienne, con-dense for me as best you can where you left the case that is in Baltimore County's circuit court so I know where we are." I said, "Of course," and I explained to him as best I could the facts, occurrences to date, the upcoming summary judgment and the evidence regarding the death of my son. He listened carefully and said, "Adrienne, I am telling you now to try to rest easy. I am going to take over your case and help you." The tears flowed from my eyes with gratitude and I told Mr. Truffer that he was heaven-sent. The words *thank you* were just not enough. He told me how sorry he was for the crisis and tragedy of Joseph's death and that we needed to move quickly on a few things. He tried to calm me and he was so soothing and comforting. I knew in my heart he was the one good, honest and caring man whom God sent to me…I knew it for certain. We set up a time to meet in his office after I e-mailed some things to Keith that he needed that day. He told me that when we met I should just bring with me everything I had. I said, "Mr. Truffer—" He said, "Adrienne, call me Keith, please." I said, "Keith, please know how grateful and miraculous you are to Joseph, me and all of our family." He calmly said, "Adrienne, I can't even begin to imagine all that you have been through, but we are going to move ahead." I asked him about depositions and he said, "Yes, all of that will happen in time, but I need to bring myself up to speed with everything first." I said, "I know, Keith, and I will be sure to provide for you all that you will need."

First on Keith's agenda was to contact the court and enter himself as my new representing attorney and then look further into preparation for the upcoming summary judgment hearing or having it postponed to give us more time for witness depositions, discovery and other concerns. Keith and I exchanged e-mails daily and I contacted Bob, Joseph's father, to give him the good news and let him know that Attorney Keith Truffer was going to now represent us and take on our case. He said that was great and he was excited to meet with Keith.

I was so relieved to know that I finally had someone who wanted to know all of the facts and get to the truth of how Joseph was so brutally killed. Attorney Keith Truffer kept me informed and current with all of the correspondence he was having with the attorneys representing Clark, Bobcat (Ingersoll Rand), Outside Unliving, Jay Metvet, Westminster Wholesale Nurseries, Metro Rentals, MOSH and Pete Coldwin's attorney, who came in at a later date since Mr. Coldwin thought everything was finished and done with and he was in the clear after Joe Metvet conveyed that to him months ago. Well, Mr. Coldwin was either very misinformed, or he just knew that Metvet would have his back. Either way you look at it, he was completely and utterly mistaken and certainly unaware of whom he was dealing with.

It was upsetting to see that the attorneys wanted to get our case over and done with and that they had more important cases to represent. Then, as Keith communicated back and forth with them to get witness depositions scheduled and further discovery brought in prior to summary judgment, they quickly changed their tune. We knew that more affidavits would be coming, in addition to the ones we already had that were blatant lies by Jay Metvet and others. Keith also had to schedule the depositions for both Bob and I, which I, of course, was very eager and ready to give. Bob and I were both eager and prepared to be questioned and give our depositions under oath.

When I met with Keith in person, I liked him right away. I could see that he was very professional, very intelligent about matters of the law and honest, kind and compassionate. He genuinely and sincerely wanted to help us and bring resolution to us. His work ethic was impeccable and he cared about doing the right thing. I knew he was a man of faith in my own heart and he knew our financial capacity was very limited. That did not matter to Keith Truffer.

He worked with us as we went along and gave to us so many hours of his time, attention, concern and outstanding legal representation. At times, I would fill up with tears and he would always get me a glass of water and a tissue and be a strong shoulder to cry on. Keith had children and he was a father. He was a wonderful family man and as I grew to know him more, he would often remark about how his mother did so very much for him. He knew that burying your child was unthinkable and that the way in which Joseph died was more than tragic. As time went on, Keith became not only my confidant and counsel but my friend. He is one of a kind and his connection to Joseph and our case remains spiritually profound. I knew that God brought him to me and that there was a reason and a purpose for everything that our Almighty Father does. I would tell Keith often, "Please tell your dear, sweet mother that she gave birth to an angel." He would humbly and softly smile and say, "Adrienne, I don't know about all that, but I know she will smile and she will agree." God bless Keith Truffer and may he always be richly blessed with our Lord's favor upon him.

Weeks were passing as Keith dissected, reviewed and examined all the documents, reports, e-mail communications, my research findings, the mechanical engineers' findings and the entire case. He became extremely well versed and was able to represent the facts and evidence we had thus far. He was quite comfortable with his knowledge and understanding of what had occurred and what was still necessary to be accomplished. Bob and I were very confident and certain we were in extremely capable hands. I do recall there was a brief problem with transferring the e-mails on disc from my computer because of the sheer number that existed. There were over five thousand e-mail communications related to the death of my son. Keith told me a good friend of his from high school was very capable of performing the transfer and that was the business he was in. Keith asked if it would be OK if he gave me a call and we set up a time for him to come to my home and perform the transfer task. I said that would be fine. I asked Keith his name and he told me it was Mark Parr. I smiled and said, "You're kidding. Really? "Mark Parr?" Keith said, "Yes, do you know him?" I said, "I sure do; Mark is a great guy and we worked together for years at Citicorp right in the same office." Keith and I both smiled and marveled at what a small world it was. Mark and I spoke on the phone after Keith and he had spoken and we discussed old times, friends, coworkers and more. Mark conveyed how very sorry he was for the loss of my son. He remembered when I was pregnant with Joseph and still working at Citicorp. Mark came over, we hugged and it was good to see him. He had read some of the stories in the paper and had seen Joseph's story on the news years before. I took Mark to my computer; he had special technical equipment with him and I could see he knew exactly what he was doing. He was able to retrieve what he needed and then go back to his office and complete the process for Keith. To this day, I am forever grateful for Mark and his kindness. He did not even charge me any fee for the work that he did. Yes, there are good, caring and kind people who want to help and who know when a friend is hurting and is justified in his or her journey.

CHAPTER 16

SUITED UP WITH THE ARMOR OF GOD

In early August I received an e-mail from my contact and my friend with the FBI. I had talked with him on the phone about my visit to Joseph's gravesite on July 20 and how hard I prayed and talked to my God and my son. I told him about the miracle rainbow and about God sending one good man to me, one honest and upstanding attorney who would take on our case and help us. My friend was so very pleased and he, too, knew God was at work and how powerful prayer is. The next morning, when I went to my office downstairs, I looked at my e-mails. I saw that my friend with the FBI had sent me an e-mail. He wrote to me the story of David and Goliath. Within the body of his text, along with the well-known story of young David defeating the monstrous giant with a stone and his slingshot, he said, "Adrienne, use the God-given unique gifts the Lord has given you. You are up against a giant, but God has gifted you with your own skills and talents and you will make miracles happen through Him." He wrote that David stayed the course and so would I. God and His Holy Spirit have already placed these skills and gifts in my hands. I knew that, yes, the giant would be defeated. There would be justice and there would be victory. Everything and all that matters are what God wants and what he already knows; I am His child—His daughter—and I will obey my Father's will.

I wept and wrote back to him telling how much I valued his support, compassion and faith in our Lord. I wrote that I knew God was in relationship with me and I with Him and that I would do everything and all that He and His Holy Spirit instructed. Again, I thanked him for being there for me and staying the course until all was done in His will. I knew that this man even delayed his retirement and in my soul it was because of the will of God.

1 Corinthians 14:1 "Follow the way of love and eagerly desire spiritual gifts."

Proverbs 10:17, 20, 23: "He who heeds discipline shows the way of life, but whoever ignores correction leads others astray. The tongue of the righteous is choice silver, but the heart of the wicked is of little value. A fool finds pleasure in evil conduct, but a man of understanding delights in wisdom."

Yes, both Keith Truffer and my friend with the FBI are men of wisdom and men of good and right judgment. My confidence in them is immeasurable because they are built up by the character of God Almighty and they know and live in His wisdom that is supreme.

On August 16, 2010, my son Rob turned twenty-six years old. I called and sang "Happy Birthday" to him and he was coming by after work for dinner and cake and ice cream to celebrate with Mom-Mom and me. I could not wait to see him and was overflowing with joy. When he arrived he looked so handsome in his tailored suit and crisp white shirt and tie. We hugged each other close and gave each other big hugs and kisses. It felt so good to hold my firstborn and realize how much God had blessed me with two incredible and wonderful sons. He was very warm and loving to Mom-Mom and we sat at the table and shared in good, loving and warm conversation. We also spoke about Rob's work and how well he was doing. I thought about how very proud I was of all that Rob had accomplished and how he had really proved himself in the field of technology.

Rob had really come into his own manhood and was richly blessed with so many skills and talents and his ability to make wise and good choices. We lit his candles and I said, "Make it a really good wish," and after we sang, he blew out his candles. Rob was smiling broadly and Mom-Mom and I were so happy for him. He opened his gifts and then he walked Mom-Mom and me out front to take a look at his new Passat. His car was really sharp and Rob looked great in it. I knew the VWs were safe and I was happy with his choice. Mom-Mom loved the car too and then she went inside. Rob wanted to take me for a little spin and said, "Mom, I want you to see what I have that is hanging from my rearview window that is so special." I lovingly smiled at him and said, "Rob, Mommy already knows what it is." He hugged me and smiled back. I got in the car and sure enough the shell hemp necklace that Joseph's handsome friend from work, Adam, lovingly handed me at Joseph's wake was hanging from Rob's mirror. I cried and put my hands out to touch it and feel it. Rob said, "Mom, it keeps me safe." I said, "I know it does, Rob."

The car drove beautifully and Rob was very comfortable in it. He had always wanted a Passat and now he owned one. I was elated for him. I knew he was getting ready to soon take a trip with some of his friends to Brazil. We parked in the driveway and Rob came in to say his good-byes and gather up his gifts and some more hugs. I had put together a little "treat bag" of Hershey's chocolate and some Twizzlers red licorice for him and his buddies just in case while in Brazil they had an American urge—a tasty one! I hugged my son tightly and close to my heart and sent him off on his adventure. I told him again how deeply I loved him and to have fun and to be safe.

Mom-Mom and I watched from my front foyer window and waved good-bye and blew kisses as I always did with my boys all of their lives. Rob would wave and blow kisses back and so would Joseph. It had been a wonderful, heavenly evening and one that I would cherish forever.

During the week, I spoke with Keith Truffer and he was informing me that they were getting ready to schedule the date for Bob and I to be deposed. He and the other attorneys were finally in agreement on schedules for the depositions to be taken and in what order.

I was in constant contact with Keith and he told us that August 31 looked like the date for Bob and I to be deposed as it seemed to work with everyone's schedule. I let him know that was fine and he told me the depositions would take place in the large conference room at his office. He said, "Adrienne, I believe that you are well prepared and I know that some of this will be difficult for you and Bob, but just answer their questions as honestly and as best you can." I said, "Thank you, Keith and I will." He communicated the same to Bob.

On August 31, 2010, I arrived at Keith's office and I felt well prepared. I had never been deposed before, but Keith explained the process and I understood. I took with me my shoulder satchel just in case there was some document or something asked for that might not be expected. Keith had everything that I had kept up until now, including the over five thousand e-mails relating to Joseph's death. Keith met with Bob and I briefly before we entered the conference room. Seated around the table were three attorneys, a legal representative from Bobcat and the court reporter. Keith Truffer pulled out the two chairs for Bob and I and then took his seat directly to my left. We went around the table as all the people introduced themselves and explained their affiliations with the case. The court clerk documented and recorded the swearing in of Bob and I and then Keith began with his opening statements. He explained that I would be deposed first and then Bob. The first attorney, before questioning me, outlined the routine and specifications of a deposition and also offered his condolences. I thanked him and told him that I understood.

So the questions started first from the one attorney and then came from the next attorney and continued from the third attorney. I was deposed for more than five hours. They called for a few breaks at intervals to get water and coffee and stretch their legs. Keith told me I was doing fine.

It felt at times like an interrogation of my life and like my person was being exposed. However, I was fine and answered each and every question with honesty and clarity. At one point, one of the attorneys said, "Ms. Miranda, how is it that you are able to remember names, dates, facts, statements and occurrences with such accuracy and precision?" I was puzzled by his question and I said, "Mr…How could I not? This is my life, my heart and my child. I remember and recall everything and each aspect of what they did to Joseph." I wept and Keith handed me a tissue. I continued that I have also kept detailed journals for the past four years and continue to do so. This attorney then said to Keith and the others, "I think we need to see her journals; maybe there is more in them that we should see." Keith first objected and said, "These are her personal and emotional feelings and—" I then said, "Keith, it is fine. If these men think they have a right to read my personal journals, there is nothing in them that I have to hide or hold back. I am a grieving, heartbroken mother and I know my journals are truth, facts and evidence. I am fighting for justice for my son and I will never stop."

At that, Keith asked if I would bring in a journal for him to first take a look at the next day and said that then he would decide if they should be brought in as discovery. I said, "Of course I will." They all agreed. As they continued with my deposition, they wanted to know more about the specific details of Joseph's death. Keith presented the large map of Outside Unliving's property and the exact location where Joseph was killed. The company's offices were right there as well as a pond and the specific treelined road where Joseph was killed. There were also fields of growing trees and shrubs and areas where they parked trailers, trucks and equipment.

In the back of the front office two-story building, there are garage bays. This is where they repair trucks, equipment, machinery and tools. You can also see the three piles of topsoil, crush and run and dirt at the corner where the two access roads meet. This is where the two men involved in the incident were filling up the bucket. It is on record that Joseph was told by his supervisor to get the Bobcat because they needed it to load twenty trees for the next day's commercial job and the two laborers were just loading dirt. He told Joseph, "Go and get it now because we need to get these twenty trees into the truck for tomorrow morning's job at Windsor Mill Middle School."

As Keith laid the map in the center of the conference table, all of the attorneys rose to their feet saying, "We have never seen this before." Keith identified it as an exhibit for discovery and said, "Yes, yes, you will all see it and ask anything you like." The exact spot where Joseph laid deceased was marked as well as other landmarks that were very pertinent to the case. The attorneys kept asking me questions and I had conveyed that I believed Joseph's death was a cover-up. I explained that through my research I had found many local, state and federal contractors who had hired Outside Unliving for their landscaping and irrigation needs. As we continued, the attorneys questioned how I knew that there were federal employees working for Outside Unliving at the time of Joseph's death. I looked at Keith and whispered in his ear. He said, "Excuse us a moment," and motioned for me to go out of the conference room with him. I asked Keith if it was OK for me to talk about the FBI report and my contact there. Keith said, "Oh yes, Adrienne, you can talk about it; it is fine." We went back in and I explained about the FBI agent who had been working with me for three years. I said, "There is a six-page report that was written up by him and entered into the FBI database. He has stayed close to the case with me and has confirmed much of my research that I was able to pass on to him." All of the attorneys wanted to see the FBI report. Keith said, I will present it but let's please continue with the deposition.

I explained to the attorneys that I had contacted the FBI in Baltimore County, the Department of Justice in DC, the governor's office and numerous other governmental agencies and they would not help me. Finally, one day I was just dialing numbers and I asked the operator for the FBI office for the Washington, DC, area where the director was. She gave me a phone number and I dialed it. A gentleman picked up and said, "FBI. How can I help you?" That was the beginning of my relationship with the honest, decent, compassionate and very diligent federal employee who gave me a helping hand and cared and believed in me. He has never left my side while others scattered and intentionally avoided me.

I had already told Keith about my experiences with the Department of Justice and how I was constantly left on hold, hung up on and transferred to people who knew nothing about my letters to the director and others within the department. I had asked every official I could think of, "Who is the person who oversees the Maryland State Police?" They all said they did not know and only that there was an internal affairs department. Well, internal affairs did nothing and they were extremely rude. I finally spoke with an attorney, Mack Keppel, and he said that he would look into it but did not know where my letter to the director was. I asked him, "Who is it who oversees the MDSP?" He said, "Shaunta Cutley." I said, "Please give me her number or extension so I may speak with her." He was hesitant at first, but he complied. I called and left several detailed messages for Ms. Cutley, but she never returned any of my phone calls or responded to my letters. The Department of Justice transferred me from the civil rights department to the special litigation department to the white-collar crime department and so on. Later, I would receive a letter again from Mr. Keppel and his assistant, Jean Grives, stating that they could not help me and I needed to speak with Ms. Cutley. I explained she would not respond to my many attempts to contact her. Later, I received another letter from Anthony Saxtor with the Department of Justice saying there was nothing they could do and that my case did not meet the requirements for further investigation of the Maryland State Police or the company. Then Mr. Keppel contacted me again and said that they did look into it and that after further review they believed the authority for handling this matter rested with the criminal section. I thanked him and felt encouraged that finally someone would listen, pay attention and do the right thing, but to this day I have never heard any more from the Department of Justice.

Now back to my deposition. I also told them about my son's cell phone record and that I was able to match up the phone numbers with certain employees for Outside Unliving even though their names did not appear on Outside Unliving's employee list subpoenaed by the Maryland State Police. I dialed every number on my son's cell phone record that I did not recognize and there was one name, Jerry Farare, that especially stood out for me. This man was one of the men who worked for Outside Unliving and also worked for the federal government's Department of Reclamation (water systems) at the same time. I knew this from the Internet research I did. I was able to find his name on the US federal government's website as well as the name of another employee, Marc Zeno, who was not on Outside Unliving's personnel list either. Mr. Zeno was also listed on the US irrigation certification website as an employee of Outside Unliving and was also connected with Aberdeen Proving Ground, a federal agency. After I saw the unknown cell phone number on Joseph's record, I called it and the voice mail activated; the message said, "Hi, you've reached Jerry Farare with Outside Unliving; I can't take your call right now, so please leave a message." The date that was on Joseph's cell phone record from this man was July 20, 2006, the same date that my son was killed. I first blocked my call as not to reveal my number on Mr. Farare's cell phone and then dialed the phone number again a few days later and Jerry Farare picked up. This time he said, "Hello, hello." I just said nothing and he said, "Shit, I knew this was going to happen," and hung up. I told the attorneys that we knew Joseph's death was no accident. I informed them that the company was involved in criminal misconduct, deceit and a cover-up and the Bobcat vehicle involved in my son's death did not have a functioning backup alarm at the time Joseph was killed. I watched some of the attorneys take notes and then they finally got to the end of my deposition after more than five hours of questioning.

After my deposition was finished, Bob, Joseph's dad, was deposed. They asked him very similar questions and he answered with honest and direct answers. He also added that Outside Unliving was guilty of collusion, a felony and he remained completely perplexed as to why no one in law enforcement did anything about it. He said, "It is stated right in the police reports by more than one employee and all they did was ignore it." The attorneys asked him what he meant and Bob said that Outside Unliving had several sister companies and they would submit contract bids from at least two or three of Metvet's companies. Metvet would underbid himself. That way he would know the other amounts and be sure to win the bid because his other company had submitted the lowest bid to win the job. He also talked about Bobcats and that he was familiar with them and how they moved and turned. He repeated that what Pete Coldwin said happened on July 20 was impossible. They questioned Bob for about an hour and forty-five minutes and then finished. The day was finally over and Bob and I were emotionally and physically exhausted. We had to relive the horror and pain of how Joseph was killed. While we knew the case was nowhere near finished, we were anxious to know when Metvet and Pete Coldwin would be deposed.

After everyone left, Keith took Bob and I into his office and said we did an excellent job. He said that he knew how hard it was to relive the details of that day, but we knew it was necessary. We thanked him again from the bottom of our hearts and said we would see him the next morning for the continuation of discovery.

That evening I got on my knees and thanked God for His grace, His strength and His Holy Spirit who resided in me. I prayed for healing and relief from such tormented pain and agony. I thanked my precious Joseph for letting me know he was with the Lord and I continued to pray that he went swiftly and was not afraid or felt immense suffering. He was with his Jesus now and that was everything. My life was still tearful and my heartache extreme, but I felt certain justice for Joseph would prevail. I know my God has assigned to me this journey and there will be a greater good. 1 Thessalonians 21–24 "Examine everything carefully; hold fast to that which is good; abstain from every form of evil. Now may the God of peace, Himself sanctify you entirely; and may your spirit and soul and body be preserved complete. Faithful is He who calls you and He also will bring it to pass."

The next morning we met with Keith at his office. I took my two journals with me for his review. Keith opened the meeting and attorneys listened and asked questions. Keith addressed my journals and told them there wasn't anything in my journals that would be indicative of having to present them for discovery. He told them, "These are Adrienne's personal memoirs to her son and her intimate feelings written down for her and her family." One attorney asked if I would just open my journal and read a sentence or two and I did. He was satisfied with my response and we moved on. On this day there were many discussions about the Bobcat and the existence of a backup alarm on the involved vehicle and, if it was present and if whether it was functioning at the time of Joseph's death. Photographs were closely looked at and Metro Rentals invoice was also closely reviewed. The Metro Rentals invoice stated in writing that a backup alarm was to be "installed at a later date." Their invoice was sent to Westminster Wholesale Nurseries, a sister company of Outside Unliving and also owned by Jay Metvet. The photograph that Metro Rentals and Bobcat were using to justify the presence of a backup alarm was merely a hole with diagonal openings on the rear door of the Bobcat. We felt that in no way did this photo confirm that an alarm was in fact functioning let alone even present. They needed to open the back door of the Bobcat to see what was inside and if any and all wiring was connected and functioning. This photograph told us nothing; therefore, Keith knew he had to make a trip out to Outside Unliving and actually have them open the rear door and see what was installed on that yard Bobcat. Keith also knew he was going to take a mechanical engineer with him to assure all details were checked during their examination and also to make sure the serial number of the Bobcat matched the earth-mover involved. Unfortunately, neither the MDSP nor MOSH ever considered even looking or testing for the backup alarm on the day Joseph was backed up over and killed. The MOSH investigator and inspector who came all the way from West Virginia never even as much as touched Outside Unliving's Bobcat that crushed our son to death while traveling in a reverse motion. He walked around it but never touched it in any way. He then went and spoke with the owner, Jay Metvet, briefly. We were relieved to know that the MOSH inspector was on Keith's list of persons to be deposed.

A few more days went by and we knew we needed more to prove that the involved Bobcat did not have a functioning backup alarm at the time Joseph was killed. Keith spoke with Bobcat's attorney and they exchanged letters as well. Bob and I were waiting to learn when Pete Coldwin and Jay Metvet would be deposed. Keith informed us that Jay Metvet, the company owner, would be deposed on September 27 and Pete Coldwin on September 28 at his office.

CHAPTER 17

DEPOSITIONS FINALLY SCHEDULED

We were glad they were served and we finally had scheduled dates for their depositions. It was now only a matter of a few weeks. I knew Keith was very well prepared to take their depositions and had everything in order. I prayed daily and asked God to guide Keith so he would be able to get to the truth of how my Joseph was so brutally killed. Our Almighty Father is a God of truth and justice and I knew his plan and purpose would be revealed to me.

My entire family surrounded me during the next weeks with love and support and so did my church and my brothers and sisters in Christ. I was still attending GriefShare and I also signed up to attend BSF (Bible Study Fellowship) courses. I yearned to study the Bible and gain a deeper understanding of His gospel and the truth of God in the Holy Bible. My first-year study began in the book of Isaiah. My group leader was wonderful and so very kind and compassionate. The study of the book of Isaiah was so relevant and inspired me immensely. I often refer back to Isaiah and verse 53 that prophesizes all that Jesus will come to do and all that He will suffer for our iniquities. The Lamb of God will be slaughtered like a sheep, beaten and tortured for our iniquities as He poured out Himself to death on a cross. Our Jesus died for us, the sinners of the world, so that we may procure our peace with God.

BSF conducts Bible study courses around the world. They desire to bring a rich and authentic teaching of learning and comprehending God's word. Through BSF children, youth and adults from many cultures around the globe come to know the Jesus of the Bible and learn the hope that He alone offers. They embrace the urgency to reach us and the next generation with the truth of Jesus Christ. Their structure, methods, attention to detail and lessons are powerful and insightful. Our BSF site teaching leader who explained the overall message and principles for each week's study was truly gifted and guided by the Holy Spirit. We all broke out into groups of ten to fifteen and discussed and shared our weekly lesson questions and answers with one another and our trained group leader. After, we went back into the sanctuary and took notes from our teaching leader for clarification and a deeper understanding of God's word. Bible Study Fellowship is Christ centered and Christ exalting. I have been transformed into recognizing what it is to be Christlike and boldly proclaim the truth and salvation of Jesus Christ. At BSF we are able to learn God's word, live God's word and share God's word. God is indeed all-loving and all-knowing and He does have a specific purpose and plan for each of His children. I pray to be an ambassador for Christ and go wherever my Lord leads me. I have now been a student of BSF for four years and I cherish every moment in it and every step the Lord has given me in my journey and my crusade. All of my group leaders are truly faith filled and are committed to serve. All of us love, cherish and support one another as we grow in our faith and belief that God is our Almighty Creator and His promises have and will come to pass. BSF has been a miraculous blessing in my life and opening my Bible daily in intimate relationship with my Father, God, is the greatest gift and accomplishment I will ever know. I am so grateful and humbled to participate with my Christian family and to know my Lord walks hand in hand with me now and forever. I also adore the little ones who attend BSF and can't wait to see their happy, sweet faces and share hugs and the love of the Lord with them every week. I encourage anyone who has a BSF study in his or her community or region to attend a welcome seminar. You can locate a study in your area online and I guarantee you it will be a life-changing gift that you will desire and yearn for. As you go deep into the Bible and the messages from God that will speak to you like never before, your faith, trust, knowledge and loving relationship with our Lord will empower you and consecrate you.

Psalm 46:1–5: "God is our refuge and strength, a very present help in trouble. Therefore, we will not fear, though the earth should change and though the mountains slip into the heart of the sea; Though its waters roar and foam, Though the mountains quake at its swelling pride. There is a river whose streams make glad the city of God, The holy dwelling places of the Most High. God is in the midst of her, she will not be moved; God will help her when morning dawns. The Lord of hosts is with us; The God of Jacob is our stronghold."

Finally, the long-awaited days came: September 27 and 28, 2010. On the twenty-seventh I awoke, prayed, dressed and made my way to Attorney Keith Truffer's office to witness the deposition of Outside Unliving's owner, Jay Metvet. Everyone was seated around the conference table and when Mr. Metvet walked in, I did not recognize his face. I vividly remember the man who leaned out from the crowd at Joseph's gravesite on the day my son was buried and looked directly in my weeping eyes. I knew that man was Jay Metvet, but his hair was darker and shorter and he just appeared different than the man who entered the conference room. Jay Metvet took his seat. His hair was almost whitish blond and longish and his eyes looked lighter. The court reporter asked him to raise his right hand and proceeded to swear him in for deposition. Keith Truffer began and asked him many very important and pertinent questions about the day Joseph was killed on his premises. I listened and watched as he answered with blatant lies and untruths. Bob did as well. At one point Keith asked him about coming over to Bob and I at the funeral home and handing us the MOSH inspector's card, saying that all of his employees have their green cards and it was all just an accident. He told Keith that he did not do that. Bob and I could not help ourselves and we looked at each other, knowing how he was such a liar. We didn't say anything, but our natural instinct just presented and I suppose the looks on our faces and in our eyes was disturbing to Mr. Metvet's attorney. At that moment, Metvet's attorney stopped Keith and asked to talk with him for a moment and they left the room. The door then soon opened again and Keith called Bob and I out to speak with him. Keith told us that he realized that we knew Jay Metvet was not being truthful but we had to refrain from even looking at each other and that was why Mr. Metvet's attorney had interrupted the meeting. Bob and I both told Keith we were sorry and didn't realize it was that distracting. We said we would be sure not to do it again. Keith said, OK.

The deposition continued and Jay Metvet sounded as if he didn't really have a handle on the daily operation of his business. Jay Metvet was asked about specific people whose names he gave to police on the day Joseph was killed who were standing with him when he was given the news about Joseph. In his response, he denied knowing the person or being familiar with the name at all. It was all so strange and weird and a pack of continual lies. When Keith asked Mr. Metvet about Mick Meanton, his VP, Jay Metvet said he fired him. Keith asked why? Jay Metvet said he was a thief and that he stole from him. Keith asked, "What is he doing now?" Jay Metvet said, "He opened up his own landscaping company called Lifegreen or Leafgreen—whatever—the name of the business doesn't make any sense to me." Keith asked him some personal questions about his wives and divorces and his most recent divorce, which took place about a year after Joseph was killed. Jay Metvet also lied about his many businesses and said he was unsure about the Bobcat having a backup alarm but said all of the Bobcats that go out on jobs have backup alarms.

I thought to myself, "Sure you are going to make sure that any industrial vehicles on your jobs are safe so your company is well represented. Also there are other people who could be in the area other than your own employees and you are going to be sure to follow the rules and not put anyone in imminent danger." My heart was breaking inside because I could sense that Jay Metvet couldn't have cared less about the safety of his own employees who worked on his property and in the yard daily and all he was concerned about was making money at any cost. The sight of him sickened me and Bob as well.

Mr. Metvet had told the Maryland State Police on the day Joseph was killed, when he was questioned, that he was out in the field when someone came running saying someone had been decapitated. He later told a different Maryland State officer that he was standing by his office doorway when someone yelled to call 911. I thought, "How could someone not know where he was when he received such horrific news about a young man who was his employee?" Jay Metvet was a compulsive liar throughout his deposition. When Keith was going to ask him about more vivid details and his account of what he saw and did after learning of Joseph's death, he asked Bob and I to step out of the conference room. Keith gently explained to us that if we could just sit awhile or if we wanted to go get lunch or a coffee while he questioned Jay Metvet about specifics, it would be best. Keith did not want to put us through what Metvet's vivid account of seeing Joseph crushed to death and lying on his dirt road bleeding out under the Bobcat was going to be. We thanked Keith and understood. We decided to go to the sushi bar a block away and Keith told us it should only be about forty-five minutes or so. Then when we got back, we could finish up with Jay Metvet's deposition.

Bob and I walked out of the building and went to get a little lunch. I was not really hungry at all, but at least we had a chance to talk and confirm with each other all of the lies and convoluted distortions given by Metvet. We knew he was covering up and had strong connections with MOSH, the MDSP and other local, state and federal contractors. We both had the MOSH inspector's business card with us and had shown Keith early on and told him what Metvet said at our son's funeral visitation as he handed us both the card. My brother and other family members had even overheard him and could not believe the gall and coldheartedness he approached us with as we were in such severe pain, grief and agony. Bob and I waited about an hour and went back to Keith's office. When we walked in, Keith motioned for us to come into the conference room. We could see that Jay Metvet had already left. Keith then excused everyone for the day and said we would resume tomorrow with Pete Coldwin's deposition and that his attorney would also be present.

After everyone left we went back into Keith's office. He first told us that Jay Metvet was a compulsive liar and he knew that he lied throughout his deposition but it was not anything he did not expect. I asked, "Keith, when you lie under oath, isn't that perjury?" He said, "Well, yes, but we are not in a court of law. We are not in trial yet. This is civil." I heard what Keith was saying, but I didn't understand the purpose of being sworn in under oath in a deposition and why if you lied, it only mattered if a trial took place. I supposed that was how the judicial system worked and I thought, "Well, we will surely get to trial and then if they lie, they will be charged with perjury and maybe they can use the depositions as discovery and evidence at the hearing." I just knew that if we got into trial, the truth about the horrible crime committed against our precious son would be revealed. Then truth and justice for Joseph would finally prevail.

CHAPTER 18

THE TRUTH EXPOSED

On September 28, 2010, the next day, Pete Coldwin would finally be deposed and Bob and I would see him face-to-face for the first time and hear his sworn-in deposition. I knew the day would be extremely difficult and painful. Mr. Coldwin entered the conference room with his attorney and the court reporter began swearing him in. As our attorney, Keith Truffer, began his questioning, Bob and I listened carefully. Mr. Coldwin was now about to turn twenty-three years old, he was dressed in a blue button-down polo and khaki pants, his hair was now short and he had grown a stubbled close beard on his chin just like the one Joseph had before he was killed.

Keith began to ask him some personal questions—where he went to high school, where he lived, if he was married and so on. Mr. Coldwin said that he had attended Franklin High School, he now owned a home in Hampstead (we knew it was a $250,000 home that he signed the contract for on September 20, exactly two months to the day that Joseph was killed and only five minutes away from Outside Unliving) and at the time he earned about nine dollars an hour as a laborer for Outside Unliving. He said that he was living with his mother and his stepfather in Sparks, Maryland, at the time of the incident. He proceeded to answer that he was now married and he no longer was employed with Outside Unliving.

Mr. Coldwin said that after the incident, they had transferred him into the garage and made him an assistant mechanic. When he referred to Mr. Jay Metvet, the owner of the company, he would just call him Jay. He also repeated that they would stay in touch frequently by cell phone and when seeing each other in the office. Mr. Metvet did engage an attorney for him right away after Joseph was killed, but later the criminal defense attorney that they contracted with no longer represented Pete Coldwin and he was on his own. Jay Metvet and Pete Coldwin at that time thought they were cleared from any wrongdoing because the Maryland State Police had closed Joseph's death investigation and homicide investigation on a blatant lie, calling it an accident. That was the July 11, 2007, meeting that I referred to earlier. A sachet of deliberate lies, distortions of the truth and answers that absolutely made no sense and were impossible was their unbearable response to us. The hidden police reports and their resistance to the medical examiner urging for further investigation as well as his letter stating Joseph was already prone on the ground, driven over backward and crushed to death were completely ignored by them. The medical examiner's letter also stated there was a "strong possibility of homicide and probable foul play." However, you will recall that the Carroll County state's attorney and the MDSP investigators continued to lie directly to our faces when we knew we had the proof of their untruths and false and impossible scenarios.

As I sat across from Mr. Coldwin and watched and studied his demeanor, his answers and his display of no remorse whatsoever as he talked about the incident of Joseph's death, I was sickened and in great despair. Keith placed the large map that he had been using throughout the case that showed the exact location where Joseph was killed and the surrounding area and landmarks in the center of the conference table. Keith began to ask Mr. Coldwin what actually occurred with the so-called pushing he'd mentioned on the day Joe was killed. Pete Coldwin replied, "What do you mean "pushing"?"

There was no pushing." Keith said, "Mr. Coldwin, you told the police on July 20, the day Mr. Miranda was killed, that there was pushing. It is right here in the police report." Keith then put the actual police report and Mr. Coldwin's statement in front of him. Mr. Coldwin said, "Oh, that. The police got it wrong." Keith again said, "Obviously there was some kind of physical action. What was it then?" Mr. Coldwin said, "I gave Joe the one-two when he came up to ask to use the Bobcat. It was like a, you know, like "Hey, bud," and I gave him the one-two." Keith said, "You are putting your fists up like in a boxing motion—is that correct?" Pete Coldwin said, "Yes, that's correct—you know, the one-two."

Keith then began to lean forward into the map and asked Mr. Coldwin to show him the exact location where the incident took place. Mr. Coldwin pointed to it and said, "Here." Keith said, "Tell me what you and Antoine Ruberra, the driver, were doing as you loaded dirt from the pile and then into the dump truck." Pete Coldwin stood up and with a pen given to him by Keith drew how the Bobcat went forward to load the bucket and then swiveled to go the right side of the dump truck parked just a few feet in front of the dirt piles. Mr. Coldwin then drew and showed that Mr. Ruberra would drive the Bobcat up to the side of the dump truck as he lifted the filled bucket up and then would empty the dirt from the bucket into the truck. After, the driver, Mr. Ruberra, would back up while bringing the emptied bucket down and then continue backing up for several feet to straighten out his next motion to drive forward again to pick up another load of dirt. Keith repeated the motion again while reviewing with Mr. Coldwin what he had drawn. He asked, "Mr. Coldwin, do I have it correct?" Mr. Coldwin said, "yes". Keith then asked, "How many times did you and Mr. Ruberra load and unload the bucket before Joe Miranda came up to ask to use the Bobcat?" Mr. Coldwin said, "About eight or nine times." Keith then asked Mr. Coldwin to describe to him as best as he could what then happened when Joe Miranda approached the area and asked to use the Bobcat. Mr. Coldwin said that Joe first came up and flagged Ruberra to stop. Pete Coldwin continued that he saw Joe yelling and screaming at Mr. Ruberra that he needed the Bobcat right then and that Joe jumped into the bucket and tried to pull Mr. Ruberra out of his seat so he could take control of the Bobcat. Coldwin continued that he pulled Joe's shirt from behind and got irritated, telling Joe, "No, you have to wait." "We are not finished." Keith asked, "What did Joe do when you pulled him by the shirt?" Coldwin responded, "He didn't do anything; he just went and stood away from the Bobcat."

Keith said, "What happened next?" Pete Coldwin said, "Joe was very impatient and when the Bobcat was moving forward to go and pick up another load, Joe Miranda ran up to the moving Bobcat and jumped onto the top of the left tire." Keith asked, "Then what happened?" Pete Coldwin said, "Joe Miranda's foot slipped off the tire as the Bobcat was moving forward and he fell off and underneath the Bobcat; he said, I think, his foot got stuck under the tire and he went completely underneath." Keith asked, "What foot did Joseph jump up with and what did he do with his hands?" Pete Coldwin said, "Joe jumped up with his right foot on top of the left front tire—" Keith interceded and said, "If the tire were a clock and you had to say what time was comparable to where Joe's foot was on the tire, what would you say...like twelve o'clock or one o'clock?" Pete Coldwin answered, "Twelve o'clock." Keith continued, "And where were Joe's hands?" Mr. Coldwin said, "I think he grabbed the rebar with his right hand to jump up and then his foot slipped off and he fell underneath and the tire of the Bobcat crushed him as it drove forward."

Keith said, "Then what did you do?" Pete Coldwin said that he quickly ran to the front to see if what he thought had happened really did and he saw Joe crushed. He said, "I quickly ran to the front left of the Bobcat and put my hand across my neck to motion Antoine Ruberra to stop. Then Antoine jumped out of the Bobcat and I ran up to the office and said, "Joe Miranda's dead."

While trying to keep my composure and listening to lie after lie and how Pete Coldwin kept blaming the victim, my son, Joseph, I broke down. I was in so much agony and I could not control my tears; Bob was crying too. At that, Keith asked for a recess and everyone else left the conference room. I was trembling and Keith held me and got me a glass of water; his assistants brought in tissues. Keith said, "Adrienne, it is OK. You are doing fine and I know how painful this is to hear." Keith helped me hold the glass of water as I was trembling and allowed me to put my head on his shoulder and I kept saying, "Keith, he is lying. He is lying. He killed Joseph brutally and we know it and so does he." Keith said, "I know, Adrienne, but we have to get through this so we can try to get to the truth." I reached for my purse and took a mild antianxiety pill that I had been prescribed. I told Keith how sorry I was and he said, "Adrienne, you have nothing to be sorry for. It is OK and I can't imagine what this must feel like for you and Bob." I knew we had to continue and that the magnitude of what we would get from Keith's expert questioning and understanding of the facts of the case was vital. I excused myself and told Keith I would be right back and I just needed to go to the ladies' room for a moment. He said OK. The girls, Keith's assistants, accompanied me. I just had to release my tears that kept coming and be still for a moment. The girls hugged me, tried to comfort me and brought me more tissues. They were so kind, compassionate and understanding. To this day, I love and respect Keith Truffer and every one of his staff. They are exceptional human beings and truly showed me support and heartfelt understanding.

I gathered my composure and then went back to Keith's office. I told him I was ready to resume the meeting. He looked up at me and said, "Adrienne, are you sure? Are you OK?" I assured him that I was and I needed to get through this for my son and for truth and justice to be revealed. I said, "Pete Coldwin must be held accountable for brutally taking the life of my boy. He is guilty, has no remorse and believes he is getting away with this." Bob had gone to another room and was also calmed down by now. Everyone re-entered the conference room and Keith picked up where he left off.

Keith asked Pete Coldwin again about the motion of the Bobcat and said, "Are you sure the Bobcat was moving forward when Joe was run over?" Pete Coldwin said yes. Keith then got to the Bobcat yard machine itself and asked Pete Coldwin if the Bobcat had a working backup alarm on July 20, 2006, at the time the incident took place. Pete Coldwin said, "All of the cats had backup alarms and sometimes there might be a wire stuck in the rear door or a mechanical failure, but ninety-five percent of the time, they worked." Keith continued, "Well, surely there was a backup motion in the maneuvering of the Bobcat during the incident. Do you remember the Bobcat beeping—the alarm sounding as the Bobcat reversed?" Pete Coldwin answered, "I don't recall it." Keith said, "You do not remember if the alarm was beeping or not?" Again, Pete Coldwin simply stated, "I don't remember it."

Keith then got back to the incident and asked Pete Coldwin if he remembered who was there and on the premises when the incident occurred. Pete Coldwin said, "Jay Metvet, Mick Meanton, a supervisor—um, I can't remember his name." Keith asked, "Do you mean Mr. Brodeman?" Pete Coldwin laughed and said, "Oh yeah, that bald guy with the hair—yeah, I think that's his name." Keith said, "Well, what happened after you went into the office to tell them Joe had been killed"? Pete Coldwin said that he thought someone called 911 and he went out and sat near a small hill with Antoine Ruberra. He continued by saying that police cars came with other unmarked police cars. He said that all of the other employees drove the big Outside Unliving trucks around the scene so no one could see. He said that Rod Schwib, his supervisor, tried to move the Bobcat off of Joe but the one police officer stopped him. Coldwin continued that he just told Antoine, "This—no good, no good," because he knew he did not speak much English. Then he said that the fire engine came and the police asked him some questions apart from Antoine Ruberra. Keith asked, "Where were you questioned?" Pete Coldwin said, "We were questioned right there near one of the trailers; we were outside and one officer questioned me while another questioned Antoine."

Bob and I, of course, realized that Keith was not going to reveal what we already knew about the facts, science, physics and forensics of Joseph's death. We had the medical examiner's report that Joseph was already lying prone—flat on the ground—and was then backed up over and crushed by the rear left wheel and there were only backup tread marks. There was no way that Joseph or any human being could have fallen in the small space (sixteen inches) between the two left tires of the Bobcat and the undercarriage without having sustained severe ankle, leg, hip and back injuries.

Joseph had none of these injuries; he had no injuries below his neck and what Coldwin was saying was impossible.

We had the truthful documented report of the driver, Mr. Antoine Ruberra's police report, which was in complete contradiction with all that Pete Coldwin said happened. Mr. Ruberra said for certain the Bobcat was backing up when Joseph was run over. He said that Joseph never jumped in the Bobcat and yelled at him and that Joseph simply flagged him down and leaned in slightly to ask him about using the Bobcat for a commercial job they had to do and that Antoine just asked Joe (Jose) if he could just load one more dump. Antoine Ruberra continued to tell the detective that Joe said OK and agreed and that Antoine then saw Joe walk away from the Bobcat and walk past the left-hand side of the open cage to the area where Pete Coldwin was standing. Antoine Ruberra said that he waited a minute and then began to back up, turning the wheels slightly left to straighten out the machine before he proceeded to go forward. Just before he went to move forward was when Pete Coldwin came running up to the left front of the Bobcat signaling Antoine to turn off the Bobcat. Antoine was so shook up when he looked to the left and saw a pool of blood that he jumped out without ever turning the Bobcat off.

As Keith continued his deposition of Pete Coldwin, he went back to the "one-two" physical contact and asked Pete Coldwin again about it. Pete Coldwin remarked, "I don't like that you are asking me about this and trying to make it—" Keith stopped Mr. Coldwin and said, "Mr. Coldwin, I am not trying to do anything; I am just asking you questions and that is my job—to ask you these questions." Pete Coldwin was actually removed, cold, cocky and heartless. Keith repeated, "Again, you motioned that the one-two was that of a friendly boxing motion, so what did Joe do when you gave him the "one-two"?" Pete Coldwin replied, <u>"It wasn't really violent; it wasn't extreme—just a little bit."</u>

With that I wanted to scream out from my seat, "Just a little bit? A little bit enough to take the very life of my son and brutally kill him!" I somehow remained composed and noticed that throughout the entirety of Pete Coldwin's deposition, never once did he look at me or Bob or make any eye contact with us. He acted as if we were not even in the room. That is what it felt like. In our opinion, he seemed overconfident and self-assured that he was going to get away with the wrongful death and heinous murder of Joseph.

Keith asked if anyone had any more questions that they wanted to ask of Mr. Coldwin and all attorneys said, "no". Keith, upon his closing of Pete Coldwin's deposition, asked, "Mr. Coldwin, would you say, from knowing and working with Antoine Ruberra, that he is a truthful and honest man and do you think he would be able to understand the questioning about what happened the day of the incident?" Pete Coldwin responded, "Yes, definitely. I think Antoine Ruberra is a truthful and honest man and would understand the questioning about the accident." Keith Truffer then thanked Mr. Coldwin for his time and compliance and said this deposition was now concluded.

I do want to mention that during this deposition Pete Coldwin did say that he left Outside Unliving about two years ago and he decided to get another job. He said that he was now working for Constellation Energy repairing electrical lines on telephone poles. I would note that Outside Unliving, Jay Metvet's company, had a strong business relationship with Constellation Energy and frequently cut down and removed trees after a thunderstorm or hurricane. It was all so connected and overtly fraudulent and corrupt.

I knew God was showing me that revelation would be coming. God was speaking to me loud and clear. He would keep showing me the next steps and knew that I would follow His direction and be His faithful servant. I leaned into Him and trusted Him with all of my heart and all of my being.

CHAPTER 19

WE MUST WANT FORGIVENESS AND REPENTANCE

I pray that someday these wrongdoers would want repentance from God, but they first had to want forgiveness. I forgive because it is our Father's will to forgive, but I will never forget. Forgiveness sets us free and we cannot allow the evil spirit of Satan to eat at us and destroy our lives. God wants us to trust in Him and to know that He is the Righteous One and will make all things just and true in His name and in His time. In this I am certain and I pray for these people to come out of darkness and wickedness and realize that it is never too late to open their hearts to our Lord and Savior. Without Him, they are nothing and will remain nothing.

So I say to you again, *Matthew 10:26–27 "Therefore do not fear them, for there is nothing concealed that will not be revealed or hidden that will not be known. What I tell you in the darkness speak in the light and what you hear whispered in your ear proclaim upon the housetops."*

In October, my son Rob came home for a visit. It was so good to see him and we sat and talked for a long while. He showed me all of the beautiful pictures of his trip to Brazil. He had taken some great shots and had a spectacular time. He had really ventured out with his friends and learned about the country, its culture and traditions and the people. The photographs of the *Christ the Redeemer* statue were magnificent. It warmed my heart to know that Rob visited this holy ground and could express to me just how beautiful the statue of Christ was. Rob also shared with me several pictures of two adjacent mountains called the Two Brothers Mountains. I wanted to cry. One mountain was higher than the other, but they were joined. It was the essence of a big brother and a younger brother. I felt sure that this mountain had touched Rob so that he felt the love between him and his younger brother, Joseph. This was truly holy ground where the peaks of the Two Brothers Mountains soared up into the heavens. I could feel the love of my two sons and the closeness my boys shared with me and their family all of their years growing up.

ROB AND JOE, BROTHERS TOGETHER ALWAYS LOVING EACH OTHER AND MOM. I AM WEARING MY TREASURED MOTHER PIN THAT MY SONS GAVE ME WHEN THEY WERE 12 AND 9 YEARS OF AGE, I LOVE THEM SO.

Rob and I sat down for dinner and shared in more conversation about his trip, his job and his career aspirations. For dessert we ate some of the delicious Brazilian peanut brittle Rob brought me from his trip. Later, we talked a bit about Joe's case and the progress we were making. Rob was so glad that we were finally accomplishing what we so desperately needed. I cried and Rob came over and comforted me, showing love, concern and support. I was so thankful to have my Rob at my side. I thought how much Rob had grown and how he so skillfully used and applied his intellect and expertise in the technology field. He was always like a sponge wanting to soak up all that he could with his technical aptitude. I was so glad to see him happy and busy with life. Rob was moving forward and I prayed for him to know great joy, love and happiness in his life. I loved him with all of my heart and I always will.

The next few months went by and I visited often with my mother and stayed in contact with Keith Truffer on a weekly and sometimes daily basis. I knew that he was planning on making a trip to Outside Unliving with an industrial engineer to examine the Bobcat and to identify if a backup alarm was present. Keith had told us that if there was an alarm present, he was going to confirm the make, model and year of its manufacturing. I knew Keith Truffer would not miss a beat and would be unequivocally prudent and complete in this investigation of the subject.

In mid-October 2010, Keith Truffer went along with an industrial engineer to Outside Unliving and located the exact Bobcat involved in Joseph's death. When he returned he reported to Bob and I. He told us that he checked the serial number on the yard Bobcat model G873 and he and the engineer were able to examine it. Along with him were the attorneys representing Bobcat and Clark and Westminster Wholesale Nurseries. Keith Truffer continued to explain that there was an alarm present when they opened the rear door. He and the engineer looked at the make and year of the backup alarm now present on this Bobcat; it read *Made in China* and the year was 2007. This information was very telling. Joseph, our son, was killed in 2006. Therefore, this alarm that they had examined was not on the yard Bobcat at the time of Joseph's death. This alarm, made in China, had not even been manufactured yet.

All of this information confirmed that there was no functioning backup alarm on the day our son was backed up over and killed. This also adds up to the fact that Jay Metvet, Mick Meanton and other employees tried to cover up the truth of what happened to our Joseph on that horrific day when he was brutally murdered by Pete Coldwin. I repeat that many attorneys whom I spoke with over the years have told me that even if there was a backup alarm beeping, Joseph would not have had any time to get out of the way. They said that Joseph was forcefully pushed from behind right into the reversing Bobcat to his death. They said, "Ms. Miranda, it is no different than throwing someone in front of a moving train to his or her death." All of Joseph's family and friends felt sure that the facts would speak for themselves and that once we got into a court of law on April 4, 2011, the truth would come to light.

Keith explained that while this evidence was more than interesting, it still did not guarantee that we would survive summary judgment, which was the next hurdle for us legally in our civil wrongful death case. I asked Keith if he was still thinking of using spoliation of evidence and he said he was not sure yet. We would have to prove that there was no functioning backup alarm on the Bobcat the day that Joseph was killed. Bobcat's attorneys were looking for some kind of documentation that could prove that the Bobcat left their manufacturing plant with an alarm already installed. However, Metro Rentals, the third party that sold the Bobcat to Westminster Wholesale Nurseries (a sister company to Outside Unliving), disputed this theory. Remember, their invoice stated—in hand-written words on the actual invoice—"(backup alarm and control kit to be installed at a later date)." These words have an initial beside them: *MP*. We know who he is. MP stands for the owner or salesperson who sold this Bobcat to Mick Meanton with Outside Unliving.

The autumn leaves were already in their rich jewel tone colors and sweater weather was here. I knew Keith Truffer, our attorney, now had many aspects of our case through discovery and the facts of the depositions to follow up on. Meanwhile, I was still communicating with the US Department of Justice at this time and trying to understand why they were so unresponsive and did not care if Ms. Shaunta Cutley ever returned my calls or replied to me in any way. Again, I was told by the DOJ that she was head of the Maryland State Police and all police as well as the director of the Special Litigation Division. The DOJ attorneys informed me that this is the division that should and would follow up with me regarding my complaint of misconduct, malfeasance and cover-up throughout the criminal and homicide investigation of Joseph's death. As iterated, I never heard anything from her. I did hear her voice mail recording and left many messages, but she never called me back, wrote, or responded—never.

Thanksgiving was upon us and my family and I gathered round the dinner table and gave thanks for all of our blessings. Each of us said what we were especially thankful for and sent loving thoughts and prayers to the boys, Michael and Joseph and all of our beloved who are in God's kingdom. The holy Christmas season came and once again our family gathered at Grace Fellowship Church for the celebration service of the birth of our Lord. Rob presented me with a gift of love that I will forever treasure. He knew how much Joseph always loved turtles and he bought me beautiful post earrings that were emerald green baby turtles with golden heads and feet. I put them on right away and I loved them and the sentiment in my Rob's heart.

A week earlier, I had taken my angel wreath, my poinsettias, the little Christmas tree and my prayer card of undying love and desperation to hold my son in my arms. I knelt down in prayer and sang Christmas carols to our beloved three: my father and his grandsons Michael and Joseph. I tried to wipe my tears, but I knew my Lord and Savior would dry every tear from my eyes. In our human portion, we feel such immense grief, sorrow, deep longing and painful absence. How I longed to hold my Joseph—even if I would have only been able to hold him and see him to kiss him and say, "So long for now," and tell him how very much I loved him. But I was never allowed to do that because my boy was injured so severely and no one called us for more than eight hours after he lay deceased. In our spiritual portion, the most real and vivid part of who we are as God's children, I knew my son was reborn into our Father's heavenly kingdom and lives on in eternity. Joseph is in the warm, loving and embracing arms of our Jesus, our Christ and our Savior. My Lord has shown me this and He has given me His will to spread the Gospel truth. When God speaks we must listen, pray and act. Ask, seek and knock and our Lord will answer. He will bring you deeper into the light where there is no darkness and He will be with you and never leave you.

It was now January 2011 and the beginning of a new year. We had still been waiting to learn when our attorney would be able to depose Brent Timber, the inspector with MOSH. I was feeling so strongly about the ignorance and blindness of Bobcat and their ability to manufacture such a dangerous, hazardous piece of equipment (a weapon) and the stupidity of the OSHA rules and regulations that were the antithesis of providing a safe work environment. I stand strong and convicted in having the OSHA laws changed. They must put into practice rules and regulations that protect all hardworking Americans and all people on the job in any kind of industrial or construction environment. Safety in the workplace needs to be enforced and needs to matter.

Where is the accountability as such illogical and idiotic senseless laws continue to exist and cause severe injury, disability and death to humankind? There is an easy remedy to assure that these tragedies are avoided once and for all.

CHAPTER 20

A CALL TO ACTION; INSTALL REARVIEW CAMERAS NOW

I propose that all obstructed rearview industrial vehicles should no longer be in use. They are no different than weapons that cause imminent danger and can and do maim, debilitate and kill our hardworking Americans. This is a tragic oversight by OSHA and any manufacturer that delivers such a product. Look at the statistics: people are severely injured, debilitated, or killed every day due to this hideous failure to rectify the immense and certain danger caused by these ill-equipped vehicles. A call to action is necessary!

I implore that the modification of this kind of vehicle and construction equipment be made mandatory. It may be done easily by installing rearview cameras in the cabins and motion sensors that brake if a person is too close or near the rear of the vehicle. This way the severe danger, probable injury and unacceptable deaths would be stopped. It is scary that our nation has sat back and done nothing to prohibit these unsafe and horrific occurrences from continuing in the workplace. I stand strong in my convictions and do not believe there is one person on the face of this earth who would not agree with this remedy.

We must act now and tell our government we insist on these corrective changes and nothing less will be tolerated. We should collectively join together and shout to save lives in all social and common workplaces across our country—even across the globe. Rearview cameras are now an ordinary option and often already installed in most SUVs and automobiles. This technology is already available. Why, then, is this not a common practice for producing construction vehicles that we know have very limited and obstructed rear views? It makes no sense and has been ignored and disregarded for far too long! A demand for action and rectification is in order!

On Monday, February 14, 2011, Brent Timber, the MOSH (Maryland Occupation of Safety and Health) inspector, was deposed. Bob and I entered the conference room at Attorney Keith Truffer's law offices in Towson. Around the table were seated Mr. Timber, his attorney from the attorney general's office in Maryland, Metvet's attorney, the court official, Keith Truffer and Bob and I.

Mr. Brent Timber was sworn in and the deposition began. First he was asked questions by Outside Unliving's and Jay Metvet's attorney now representing Westminster Wholesale Nurseries. This is a sister company of Outside Unliving that held the title to the Bobcat that ran over Joseph and that was also owned by Jay Metvet. Attorney Hitherong began by explaining the process of the deposition and that if Mr. Timber did not understand a question, he should just say so so he could rephrase it. He continued that he needed to say yes or no and not just use a head or nodding motion so that the recorder would be able to audibly pick up his answers. Attorney Keith Truffer continued, "Just answer the question that you are asked." Mr. Timber said, "He understood." Throughout the deposition by Attorney Hitherong, Mr. Timber, at times, did not fully understand the exact question being asked. For example, when asked if he knew about Bobcats, he said that he never had any specific training on them but he used one a very long time ago when he was repairing some fencing and

264

worked as a laborer. Mr. Timber also said that he was the senior inspector for the Hagerstown MOSH office and that was why he thought they called him to investigate the accident in Carroll County. He first said that their MOSH office covered the region from the western Hagerstown area to as far east as Frederick County. That did not make any sense because Carroll County is much farther east than Frederick County. Of course, we later learned that Joseph was not even killed in Carroll County but actually killed in Baltimore County, as I have previously mentioned. Also in the aforementioned, the MOSH policy and procedure that was and is mandatory is that "In a catastrophic event, the closest MOSH office is to respond and conduct the investigation." Joseph's death was certainly a catastrophic event and there is a MOSH office 25 minutes away from where my son was killed. I researched it, read it, copied it and showed it to many of my family members and my attorney. This policy was most definitely in place at the time and before Joseph was killed on July 20, 2006, on the premises of Outside Unliving. Well, why did they not contact this MOSH office just 25 minutes away? Why? We knew that the investigators did not do so many standard and necessary procedures for our son, but why? Why did they not follow their policies and regulations for Joseph's catastrophic death? What follows is only one piece of the unspeakable and obvious depth of the cover-up and corruption that permeated throughout the heinous criminal act committed against my precious son. The employer's connection to local, state and federal agencies and contractors that endorsed the cover-up and upheld the acts of conspiracy was and remains grotesquely immoral and criminal.

Mr. Timber was asked who called him to tell him to go to the scene and conduct the investigation at Outside Unliving. He answered, "My Supervisor, Rod Chimpall. Mr. Chimpall was the chief supervisor for MOSH in Maryland and he called me to notify me of the fatality." Brent Timber continued that he was the only one in the office who investigated deaths. He was then asked how many other MOSH personnel work there regarding MOSH safety and inspections. He answered, "About four or five." He was asked how long he had been employed by MOSH and he said it was since 2001. Mr. Timber also stated that when he received the call, he was at home. He was asked, "Where is home?" He answered, "West Virginia." He was asked what he did when he got the call. He said that he had been playing with his son but he got dressed and left to drive to Outside Unliving. He was asked about how long it took him to get to Outside Unliving. He said, "About two hours and forty-five minutes." As his deposition continued, Brent Timber conveyed that he had never been to Outside Unliving before, had never heard anything about Westminster Wholesale Nurseries and had never heard of Jay Metvet. He said that while he was en route, a Maryland state trooper, Kitseng, called him and said, "It is so hot and muggy. What do you want us to do with the body?" Mr. Timber said it didn't matter to him and that as long as they had photographs they could remove the body. Detective Kitseng told him the paramedics would lift the Bobcat up and off the victim with airbags and then after removing the body they would lower it back down to its original position.

Mr. Timber was then asked who was present when he finally arrived at Outside Unliving. He answered, "Two troopers and one female trooper." He added that he thought the main detective was Kitseng and the other Hudock. Mr. Timber was then asked, "Where was the owner, Jay Metvet?" Brent Timber said he was not sure if Mr. Metvet came down from his house or if he was in the shrubs because there were very thick, dense shrubs and bushes around his home. He continued that Mr. Metvet then came out to the scene and Mr. Timber explained everything to him. He introduced himself as the MOSH inspector who was there to check out the safety and compliance factors and to see if there were any violations and explained that if there were, the company would be issued citations. He said that Jay Metvet understood and that he advised Mr. Metvet of all of the documents and paperwork MOSH would need to collect and review.

Mr. Timber was asked, "Was the Bobcat still present at the scene?" He answered, "Yes, it was sitting right there." The attorney asked, "Did you inspect, start up, or touch the Bobcat in any way?" Mr. Timber answered "no". He was asked, "Why not?" Mr. Timber said that he was told there was a spotter present and because a spotter was present, there was no reason to turn on the Bobcat or check its functioning. The attorney asked, "Are you aware of the backup alarms on this industrial piece of equipment?" Mr. Timber said, "Yes, but there was still no reason to check for a backup alarm because Outside Unliving had already met the safety regulations by having a spotter present. It is in the Maryland Licensing and Regulations Federal Code." His attorney, Ms. Balling from the AG's office, said it was code twenty-nine, the 1926 code of federal regulations and there was also a COMAR training for forklifts. Well, it was quite evident that Outside Unliving did not require all of their forklift operators to attend this training. Furthermore, just because Jay Metvet, the company owner, referred to Pete Coldwin as a spotter to Mr. Timber did not make it true. In fact, Jay Metvet said at the funeral home, "well, he wasn't really a spotter". Mr. Timber was extremely incompetent and did not do his job at any time during his entire so called MOSH investigation into Joseph's death. Again, we were told by his Supervisor and co-workers at the MOSH meeting that Mr. Timber did not even know what a Bobcat was or how it operated.

Mr. Timber was asked about how long he met with Jay Metvet. He said, "About thirty to forty minutes." He then said that he was going to return the next day and it was policy that he had to interview the witnesses involved, the driver and the spotter. Mr. Timber then said he left the scene and followed detective Kitseng back to the barrack to collect the photographs and the police reports from the two witnesses. He added that MOSH tries to work hand in hand with the police in these fatalities but all they are authorized to do is to check that all safety rules and policies were followed by the employer and that they are in compliance. He repeated that he told Metvet exactly what documents he would need for MOSH's investigation. When asked when he went back to conduct the follow-up interview of both witnesses and collect the documents, Mr. Timber first said, "The next day." The attorneys looked at the MOSH report and said the date it showed was July 24, 2006. They said, "Mr. Miranda was killed on a Thursday, July 20, 2006." Mr. Timber was a bit flushed and said he could not recall exactly. The attorneys showed him the report and the date of Monday, July 24. Mr. Timber then said, "Oh yeah. I took Friday off." He was asked why. He said that when he has several days accumulated to take off, he likes to use his days so he doesn't lose them and that that was why he did not return to Outside Unliving until the following Monday around nine in the morning to conduct the interviews with both witnesses.

Attorney Hitherong next asked Mr. Timber about his meeting and his interviews held on July 24 at Outside Unliving. He asked, "Who was present?" Mr. Timber responded that he first spoke with Jay Metvet and another man. He could not quite remember his name, but Attorney Keith Truffer asked, "Does the name Mick Meanton sound familiar to you?" Mr. Timber said, "Yes, that is the name." Mr. Timber continued that they had shown him all of the documents they compiled for him and everything looked to be in order.

He then interviewed Mr. Antoine Ruberra first. They all knew he was the driver and was of Spanish descent. The attorney asked, "Did they offer a Spanish interpreter for you as you were about to interview Mr. Ruberra?" Mr. Timber said yes, but he did not accept the offer because MOSH liked to try to speak with the witness alone to get the clearest description of what they witnessed. Mr. Timber went on to say that Mr. Ruberra seemed to understand his questions as he spoke slowly and pointed to the words on the interview questioning sheet. He added that it was difficult at times to understand Mr. Ruberra because he would break down crying. Mr. Timber added that Mr. Ruberra would have to take breaks due to how upset he was and his outbursts of cries. The attorney asked, "Were you able to understand enough to accept his answers as sufficient?" Mr. Timber said, "Yes, pretty much."

The attorney asked, "What happened next?" Mr. Timber said they brought in Pete Coldwin. He said that he asked questions of Mr. Coldwin and he was able to answer them. The attorney asked, "Did he acknowledge himself as the spotter on the day of the incident?" Mr. Timber said, "Yes, Pete Coldwin said he was the spotter and Joe Miranda became impatient and jumped up on the Bobcat as it was moving forward and then fell off and underneath the Bobcat. Pete Coldwin tried to stop Antoine, but it was too late." The attorney asked if Mr. Timber was satisfied with his interview with Pete Coldwin and he said yes. Again the attorney wanted to confirm that the MOSH compliance and regulation was that a spotter just had to be a person, any person in the vicinity of an operating piece of industrial equipment, who could assure the roadway was safe and clear and that this person had to be able to communicate it to the operator of the industrial vehicle. Mr. Timber said, "Yes, that is correct." Attorney Hitherong was finished with his deposition of Mr. Brent Timber at this time.

Our attorney, Keith Truffer, then took over. He introduced himself to Mr. Timber and said that he represented Bob and I, the parents of Joseph Miranda. He began by explaining that he wanted to fill in some blanks and that if at any time Mr. Timber did not understand his question, he would gladly rephrase it to assure that he understood what he was being asked. Mr. Timber said OK. Attorney Keith Truffer asked Mr. Timber again why he did not think it was important to inspect the Bobcat on the day Mr. Miranda was killed. Mr. Timber again answered, "Because the company was in compliance because they had a spotter." Our attorney said, "You said earlier that after you and your supervisor, Mr. Chimpall, sat down and looked closely at the scene photographs, you both agreed that clearly the tread marks showed a backward motion of the movement of the Bobcat, correct?" Mr. Timber said, "It didn't matter that the Bobcat was backing up; they had a spotter and that was all they needed. They were following the law." Keith said, "Did anyone else other than Jay Metvet and Pete Coldwin tell you that Mr. Coldwin acted as the spotter on the day Joseph was killed?" Mr. Timber said no. Keith Truffer asked, "Do you know how far Pete Coldwin was from Joseph Miranda at the time of the incident?" Mr. Timber said, "No, I do not." He then asked Mr. Timber, "Do you know what Pete Coldwin was doing at the time of the incident?" Mr. Timber said, "No, I do not." Attorney Keith Truffer was even a bit taken aback and asked, "Why would you not check for the safety of a backup alarm functioning on that Bobcat when you knew that a young man was killed by this Bobcat traveling in a reverse motion?" Again, Mr. Timber said that it was not his responsibility and that he only had to inspect that the company was in compliance. Bob and I felt so pained and were in disbelief of the words coming out of the mouth of this MOSH investigator and inspector.

Keith Truffer continued asking Mr. Timber if he had any conversations or communications with Detective Kitseng after his interviews and up until the time he completed his MOSH investigation. Mr. Timber first responded, "I don't think so, but I can't remember." Attorney Truffer pointed out to him his closing report and referenced the date of August 14, 2006. He put the report in front of Mr. Timber to see. He did say, "Oh yes, I did have one communication with him regarding the confidentiality of the interviews and that MOSH had completed their investigation and no citations were given."

If you will recall, earlier I mentioned that when my family and I were at the meeting in early August 2006 with corporal and detective Kitseng at the Westminster Barrack, he told us that he had not yet talked with MOSH and just put their report up on a shelf. He added that the MOSH inspector, Brent Timber, had left a message on his voice mail that was kind of strange and he did not fully understand it. We asked the corporal, "Could we please hear it and try to understand what his message is?" Corporal Kitseng said OK. He then got up from the conference table and put his phone right there for us while he dialed into his voice messages. We all listened as Brent Timber said he (MOSH) was done with their investigation and had closed the case. He continued saying that he knew the family wanted the names of the two people involved and stated that he didn't care what Corporal Kitseng did but that they were done. Mr. Timber also said that he would not release some Outside Unliving employee names for fear that they could lose their jobs. We feel that this communication speaks volumes about Outside Unliving's failure to implement safety policy in its workplace. The owner, vice president, some of their upper management employees and the employees of MOSH upheld the deceitful cover-up of the tragic death of our son.

Getting back to Keith Truffer's deposition of Brent Timber, he proceeded to ask him what he did after the July 24 meeting and once the interviews were over. Mr. Timber said he gathered all of the paperwork and documents that Outside Unliving had prepared for him and said he would be in touch with them once everything was finished and that they would be fully aware of everything as their investigation took place. He then said good-bye and walked out of the office to the front porch. Attorney Truffer asked if he saw or heard any Bobcats at that time. Mr. Timber said, "Yes, I heard a Bobcat that was in motion about seventy feet away from me." Keith Truffer said, "Did you notice if it was the same Bobcat or a similar Bobcat to the one that ran over Joseph Miranda?" Mr. Timber said he saw that it had some kind of number on it but that he didn't know what the number meant. Mr. Timber offered that it was beeping as it backed up so he knew it had a backup alarm on it. Attorney Keith Truffer asked, "Why did you not go to the Bobcat and check out the serial number to see if it was the same one that backed up over Joseph Miranda?" Mr. Brent Timber said he did not have any reason to do that and repeated that the company had a spotter. Keith Truffer said, "Weren't you even curious to know if it was the same Bobcat?" Mr. Timber just said, "Well, I saw that it said *yard* on it, so I assumed it was the same one."

Keith Truffer said he thought the number he was referring to was the model number, G873. Our attorney asked, "Did you ever once consider that the company would have had time to repair or install a backup alarm on this Bobcat during those three days that passed before you returned for the interviews of the two witnesses and picked up Outside Unliving's safety documents?" Mr. Timber just said, "No, I did not think of that; they had a spotter." Our attorney asked, "What happens after you close a case?" Mr. Timber offered that they keep the documents for a few weeks before just discarding them.

Attorney Keith Truffer asked Mr. Timber, "Were you ever made aware of the supplemental police reports that were later turned over and the letters written by the medical examiners to Baltimore County State's Attorney Todd Slicenberger?" Mr. Timber said no. Keith continued that the medical examiner wrote two letters—first in 2007 to the Carroll County state's attorney and the MDSP and again in 2008 to the Baltimore County state's attorney. The medical examiner and coroner who performed the autopsy on Joseph Miranda said that at first they found no foul play but then when further facts and information came forth and crime scene photographs had been turned over to them that had been withheld; they knew there was a strong possibility of homicide. The medical examiners also met with Detective Bishtall and even more was revealed to them about the criminal act against the victim, Joseph Miranda. The letter continued that the victim was already prone, flat on the ground on his stomach, before the rear left tire crushed his head, face and neck while backing up. The letter from the medical examiner to State's Attorney Todd Slicenberger said that what Mr. Pete Coldwin said happened on the day Joseph was killed was "impossible" and that there was physical pushing of the victim. Joseph Miranda's death certificate had been taken out of accidental and changed to undetermined with a strong possibility of homicide. Mr. Timber just acted unaffected and when asked he said he had heard nothing about a supplemental police report and that he had never asked the police about any supplemental reports. Attorney Hitherong chimed in, "Keith, can I get a copy for the record?" and Attorney Keith Truffer said, "Sure, Bob, I'll give you twelve." Mr. Timber said he did not follow up on anything with police because that was the job of the police investigators and not MOSH.

Throughout the deposition of Brent Timber, the fact that Outside Unliving submitted to MOSH safety sign-in sheets with a multitude of Hispanic names whited out was never brought up. We realized that this was not the purpose of the deposition of the MOSH inspector, but it sure went hand in hand with the knowledge and facts that we learned about Outside Unliving's hiring of illegal immigrants and paying them miniscule wages despite how hard they worked. These company owners and dirty politicians are greedy monsters and care nothing about human life, human rights, or human dignity and they have no conscience. What goes around comes around and God is the Righteous One who will bring truth and justice.

All of these people know what they did and are well aware of their wrongs and malfeasance. Even still, our God will bring a greater good and we will thrive in His truth and deliverance.

1 Timothy 6:11–12 "But flee from these things you man of God and pursue righteousness, godliness, faith, love, perseverance and gentleness. Fight the good fight of faith, take hold of the eternal life to which you were called and you made the good confession in the presence of many witnesses."

John 1:14 "And the Word became flesh and dwelt among us and we saw His glory, glory as of the only begotten from the Father, full of grace and truth."

Yes, God will surely bring a greater good and I pray for the foundation "Jam's House, Home Sweet Home" to start anew and to flourish.

We learned at the very end of March 2011 that Pete Coldwin filed for bankruptcy. Out of the blue, this slimy and sleazy approach to try to get out of the court trial scheduled for April 4 was in our face. Their scheming tactic by Pete Coldwin and his attorney automatically stayed (stopped) our case from moving forward and all legal motions and the process were halted.

We knew that Pete Coldwin was already guilty of the wrongful death of Joseph but he was going to be sure the case never went to trial or that he would never have to stand trial, face a jury and face us. All the facts were racked up against him and proof of his brutal assault on and murder of Joseph was evident beyond any doubt.

We were communicating with our civil attorney, Keith Truffer and he informed us that Pete Coldwin wanted to make us a settlement offer and in this way be released from the case. Bob and I were both extremely upset because we cared nothing about money. All we wanted was justice for Joseph and accountability to be rendered. Keith talked with me and told me that the case could be stayed for a very long time and that he advised that Bob and I accept a settlement offer. I was so troubled by doing this and told Keith I really needed to think about it. I asked Keith, "Does this in any way impact the criminal case that we believed would surely come once our case got into the right hands?" He said, "No, Adrienne, it does not." "There is no statute of limitation on a criminal homicide case and this settlement will not affect your continuation of seeking justice for Joseph."

We knew that Keith would in no way give us unwise advice. I looked over the settlement agreement drafted by Pete Coldwin's attorney and I expressed to Keith that there were some specific terms and wording that I would never sign contained in their agreement. I explained to Keith what they were and why I would never sign this wording—never. I was really disgusted and repulsed that Coldwin and his mother thought they could buy their way out of the violent killing of my son. Pete Coldwin wanted to be released of all liability when his lack of liability couldn't have been further from the truth. I will not give up my son's life or my life for a lie. Keith told me he would let Pete Coldwin's attorney know and see what they came back with. The next day Keith contacted me and e-mailed me the copy of the settlement agreement with the wording removed from the agreement. To this day, I am still sickened inside that they were pulling such a rank and disturbing tactic; however, they agreed to the changes and both Bob and I trusted Keith Truffer completely. We both signed the amended agreement and Pete Coldwin, again, had to be thinking, "I am released from this case and they cannot touch me in any way. I am getting away with murder."

I knew in my heart and soul if I knew that I did nothing wrong and was not guilty in any way, I would not offer anyone a dime. So here we were with the unfair, unjust and unreasonable judicial system in our face, but we knew God would make everything right.

To put a negligible—or any—amount of money on the life of my precious son was heartbreaking and wounding. There is no amount of money that would ever suffice or bring back my boy—no amount of money we ever wanted or spoke of. We just wanted and needed truth and justice. Justice and truth were the very least my precious son deserved and I vowed to be his voice until I took my last breath and beyond. Nothing was going to change that—nothing—and it never will. On April 11, the amended civil settlement agreement was finalized. I still intended to use the deposition statements made by Pete Coldwin and other discovery that would confirm Pete Coldwin intentionally killed Joseph and how and why he did it.

On April 15, 2011, I took birthday balloons, flowers and one red rose and sang "Happy Birthday" to my angel nephew, Michael. He would have turned thirty-one years of age on this day. Exactly one week later, on April 22, I took birthday balloons, flowers, one red rose and my prayer card to my precious angel son, Joseph. Joseph would have turned twenty-four years of age on this day. I knelt in prayer for God's justice, mercy and compassion and thanked Him for all that He was showing me and revealing to me. I sang "Happy Birthday" to Joseph and sat for a while talking with him. I had placed two easels in the ground, one with a lovely Easter cross and the other with an Easter wreath I had made with white lilies and doves around it. I knelt down before my dad's headstone and again told him how very much I loved him. During this month of April, we also celebrated Earth Day, Good Friday and the most holy day of Easter, Christ's resurrection on April 24, the day that Michael went home to the Lord. We know our angel boys live on in the paradise of God's heavenly kingdom and live vibrant, beautiful, joyful, glorious and everlasting lives together with all of their loved ones and God's children. Some of Joseph's closest childhood friends and friends for life came: John, Scott, Brandon, Sam and others. These young men are very special to me and will never forget Joe. I love them and always will. Joe is alive in their hearts and will be remembered always.

I had been staying in contact with Delegate Joseline Pena-Melnyk and keeping her updated. Both of her aids, Spencer and Tim, were outstanding and so very supportive of my goal to achieve justice for Joseph.

On May 10, 2011, I spoke with the delegate and explained that it was very important that I meet with Dr. David Fowler, the chief medical examiner for the state of Maryland and his assistant, Dr. Zabiullah Ali, who performed the autopsy on Joseph. I said I had new information and crucial testimony that they had to be made aware of in Joseph's case. She understood and supported my efforts.

In mid-May I spoke with Dr. Fowler on the phone and he agreed to meet with me and also have Dr. Ali present for the meeting. I explained to him the additional and new information I had and that I would bring all documentation with me. He was very receptive and we scheduled to meet at the OCME's office in Baltimore on May 24, 2011, at one in the afternoon.

Prior to this meeting, I went to my pastor at Grace Fellowship Church and we prayed together. Pastor Danny O'Brien was aware that I was going to be attending a very important meeting about obtaining justice for my son, Joseph. He prayed earnestly for me as I hugged him and listened with all of my heart and I could feel the Holy Spirit. I thanked him and the last words he said to me that day were "Adrienne, put all of your trust in the Lord!" I said to him, "Yes, I will do this and I know my Lord is with me always."

CHAPTER 21

MEETING WITH THE MEDICAL EXAMINERS

On May 24, 2011, I woke up and went to my knees in prayer. I knew my Lord was listening and would be right there for me. My loving, kind, beautiful, intelligent and compassionate sister-in-law, Lisa Gemma, was going to accompany me to the meeting with Dr. Fowler, the chief medical examiner and Dr. Ali, his assistant. My goal was to show the coroners all of the new information and documentation I now had and fully explain it. I felt confident that my son's death certificate would be changed from undetermined to homicide.

Lisa drove over to pick me up and she brought a dolly for us to load up the boxes containing all of the proof and evidence that the medical examiners needed to see. I had been to the Office of the Chief Medical Examiner twice before, so we knew how to get there. Lisa and I hugged tightly and she said, "Adrienne, just explain and tell them all that you now know and show them the proof. You will do fine, I am sure." I hugged her again and said, "Thanks, Lis. I know that God is with us and He will give me the ability to convey to them what they must hear and see."

We drove down and parked and then loaded up the boxes containing the police reports (most importantly Detective Bishtall's and Trooper

Ramarez's reports) that would show both doctors that Joseph was murdered at the hands of Pete Coldwin. All the evidence showed that the Bobcat was definitely being driven backward as Pete Coldwin forcefully knocked, pushed and shoved Joseph from behind right into the reversing Bobcat to his death. I knew in my heart these very qualified, skilled and scientific professionals would see it all very clearly.

Lisa and I entered the lobby area and walked over to the receptionist. I introduced myself and Lisa and said we were there for a meeting with Dr. Fowler and Dr. Ali. She kindly said OK and gave us name tags to wear. There was an armed guard in the lobby and Lisa and I went and sat down in the chairs to wait. It was only a few minutes before the chief medical examiners, Dr. Fowler and Dr. Ali (who had performed Joseph's autopsy), appeared. They greeted us in the lobby as we shook their hands and then they said, "We are ready." We followed them as we walked into a small conference room and sat down at a round table with four chairs.

At approximately five after one, I began to present in a sequenced, orderly and organized fashion the events, facts, science, physics, photographs, MDSP police reports and depositions of both Mr. Jay Metvet, the company owner and Mr. Pete Coldwin. "He is the employee who intentionally killed my son in a very violent and extreme way." I knew as both doctors listened intently that they would see, without a doubt, that Joseph was murdered on that hot summer day, July 20, 2006, by Pete Coldwin, the so-called spotter.

Both doctors listened and reviewed the large map that identified the exact spot where Joseph was killed as well as the crime scene that was disturbed by other employees and the owner. They asked questions at times and intently focused on what I was showing them. I proceeded with reading specific testimony that Pete Coldwin had given during his sworn deposition and the repeated lies and manipulation that added up to guilt with no remorse. I was reading the deposition and at the same time, I had handed a copy of Pete Coldwin's deposition to the doctors so they could follow along. It was all there showing and confirming that Pete Coldwin's explanation of what occurred on that dreadful day was nothing but a deviant and impossible scenario that never happened and his attempt again to blame the victim.

I continued reading and pointing out significant deposition responses from Pete Coldwin. I read aloud and told them the page to turn to where Pete Coldwin admitted to physical contact with Joseph, saying he gave him the "one-two," and where my attorney asked him if he was describing a boxing motion? Mr. Coldwin said, "Yes, that's right—a boxing motion." Mr. Pete Coldwin later said in his deposition when the boxing motion was brought up again that "it wasn't really violent; it wasn't extreme—just a little bit." Again, my heart sunk and I felt and said inside, "It wasn't really extreme or violent—just enough to take the very life of my precious Joseph." I remained composed and both doctors stopped and looked closely at Coldwin's response. Dr. Fowler asked me to hand him the deposition I had been reading from as Dr. Ali had his copy in his hands. With that, they both looked at each other and said, "There it is." Four hours of presenting and discussing had passed and both Dr. Fowler and Dr. Ali looked at me and said, "We both agree that Joseph's death is a homicide and his manner of death will be changed to homicide by assault".

I thanked the Lord and held my face in my hands as the tears filled up in my eyes. I praised my God and my Savior from my heart and soul as Lisa consoled me. I thanked both Dr. Fowler and Dr. Ali and reached out to hug them. I said, "I have waited so very long, almost five years. All I ever wanted and needed was truth and justice for my son." They both returned the gesture and said, "We understand and we realize the battle that you have been put through and we, too, hope that you finally get the truth and justice that your son, Joseph and you and your family deserve." Lisa and I started to gather and pack up the documents. Dr. Ali did ask if he could have a copy of Detective Bishtall's report as well as keep the deposition of Pete Coldwin. I said, "Of course," knowing that I had more copies at home.

Colossians 1:9–12 "We have never stopped praying for you and asking God to fill you with the knowledge of his will through all spiritual wisdom and understanding. And we pray this in order that you may live a life worthy of the Lord and may please him in every way; bearing fruit in every good work, growing in the knowledge of God, being strengthened with all power according to his glorious might so that you may have great endurance and patience and joyfully giving thanks to the Father."

Let us be an extension of the life of Christ and make our lives count. Our lives will make a difference if we are fruitful in God's works. God made us alive in Christ and He gives us the ability to be true servants by accepting and depending on God's grace. Jesus wants our hearts and we must depend only on His grace and follow His will for His good purpose. In this I am humbled and so very thankful to my Lord.

Dr. Fowler proceeded to explain the next procedures that he would have to follow to have Joseph's death certificate officially changed from undetermined to homicide. He said, "Adrienne, it may take up to six months, but I assure you it will be done." Dr. Fowler promised to keep me updated and informed along the way. He gave me both Dr. Ali's and his e-mail addresses. He also explained that they would be informing their legal counsel with the State of Maryland attorney general office. . Dr. Fowler said that this attorney was the legal supervisor and director of the Office of the Chief Medical Examiner and the Department of Health and Mental Hygiene in Maryland. I said, "OK, I understand." Both gentlemen were so very kind, compassionate and certain of their decision. We thanked them again and told them how grateful we were for their undivided time and attention. They said, "You will be hearing from us very soon."

Lisa and I took our boxes and began to walk out of the building. We stood hugging each other in tears and we knew that this was huge. We knew that finally truth and justice for Joseph would come to pass. I knew that God had brought us victory this day. Our God is a God of truth and justice and is against injustice. He is such a loving and understanding God. His love for us is unfailing and He will always provide for our needs. He loves us so very, very much and He has guided me from day one in my journey. He placed before me each footprint that I was to walk in to follow along His purposeful path. He is my Almighty Father and powerful creator and I will carry out the purpose, plan and path that He has chosen for me. I give all of myself to you, Father and you are the lead of my life. Your Holy Spirit lives in me and He is constantly directing and instructing me by your will. "Joseph, Mommy will see you soon, my angel boy. I love you with all of my heart and know we are never apart—never!"

Lisa and I were overjoyed to know that it was now only a matter of time before justice for Joseph would come to fruition. When we got home, she helped me in with the boxes of documents and again we held each other with a peace we had not known. I waved good-bye to her from my front window and we said we would talk tomorrow. I could not wait to call all of my family members and tell them the good news. Each of my loving family members cried with me tears of joy and expressed to me, "Adrienne, I knew God would bring it and you would get the accurate truth of homicide committed against our Joseph achieved." We now knew there was still a journey up ahead administratively, but we were certain both doctors stood confirmed in their conclusion and findings of homicide by assault. We would soon find out that the journey up ahead would be more outrageous and unbelievable and extremely disturbing.

In early June 2011, Dr. Fowler and Dr. Ali e-mailed me a copy of the letter they had sent to Baltimore County State's Attorney Todd Slicenberger along with the amended detailed report signed by both doctors. This letter confirmed that Joseph was killed at the hands of another, Pete Coldwin and Joseph Miranda's death was officially a homicide.

Weeks went by and the doctors had not heard anything back from Todd Slicenberger. Dr. Ali informed me that he did get a call from the assistant state's attorney, Ms. Coffey, and she asked him several questions and also requested a copy of the deposition of Pete Coldwin. Dr. Ali told me on the phone that he had spoken with Ms. Coffey for about forty-five minutes and that he had worked with her before on other cases, even complicated ones.

In mid-July 2011 Dr. Ali replied to an e-mail I had sent him asking for an update on any response from the state's attorney's office. His reply said that there were issues and I should call him. When I spoke to him and

Dr. Fowler, they said they had received a letter from State's Attorney Todd Slicenberger saying he did not agree with their conclusion of homicide. Dr. Fowler told me that this was unprecedented and never had a state's attorney gone against and disagreed with the conclusion of manner of death confirmed by scientific doctors—medical examiners.

Dr. Fowler assured me that this was more than unusual and he and many, many others supported me. He said, "We stand strong on our conclusion of homicide and we will get this done." Dr. Fowler told me not to contact anyone at the state's attorney office and that he, Dr. Ali and a very helpful assistant attorney from the AG office had scheduled a meeting. He further explained that the assistant attorney with the Attorney General's office in Maryland would be submitting all of the documents to a court judge and would obtain the court order to have Joseph's death certificate changed to homicide. Dr. Fowler then said, "Adrienne, you will have two separate state divisions—the Office of the Chief Medical Examiner and the Department of Health and Mental Hygiene—along with the judiciary confirming homicide. Todd Slicenberger has no legal authority or medical or scientific credentials to disagree with the findings of the chief medical examiner for the state of Maryland and the medical examiner, Dr. Zabiullah Ali, who performed Joseph's autopsy. Joseph was murdered. If need be, we will have a meeting and present to Todd Slicenberger all of the facts and evidence, but it has already been forensically, scientifically and thoroughly documented for him and sent to him and he has no choice but to accept Joseph's death as homicide by assault and that the murder of Joseph is criminal." It remains completely unfounded and disturbing that Todd Slicenberger would not and will not make an arrest and charge Pete Coldwin with the murder of Joseph. It is quite evident that he did not want to go against the Maryland State Police, but it was not their case to initially even investigate. Joseph was killed in Baltimore County and it was the responsibility of the Baltimore County homicide detectives and Todd Slicenberger to do their jobs thoroughly and with integrity, but they did not. They devalued the precious life of my son and were more concerned with trial costs and cover-ups than performing their duty. How dare they put a price tag on the precious life of my Joseph or any other victim of violence? My family and I will not stand for it and pray that someone will get to the bottom of all of this corruption. We knew that God would reveal it in His way and in His time.

I had recalled at the May 24 meeting that I had with both doctors that they said Joseph's death was either first-degree or second-degree murder but not manslaughter. According to all of the facts, science, physics evidence and forensics, we knew that this was true. I felt sure that these good men would get the job done and I knew the confidence, respect and trust that Dr. Fowler had in an assistant attorney with the Attorney General's office in Maryland as well as his superior qualifications. I knew I had to be patient and let them do their necessary work. My heart told me that God was bringing all the answers and these malicious wrongdoers would be defeated and brought down. We would know victory and justice through God's great love, mercy and grace.

On July 20, 2011, five years after the day my Joseph went home to be with our Lord, all of us went to visit his gravesite. I took roses, sunflowers, hibiscus, "I love you" balloons and my message card to him. Others brought beautiful, vibrant bouquets and joined in sending love and remembrance to Joseph. I also brought with me two "Justice for Joseph" signs that I had made for the justice march we held around the Baltimore County courthouse in 2008. My mom, Bob, Rob, Scott, Matt and others were all present in honor of Joseph and we placed firmly in the ground just behind Joseph's headstone the two signs. One read in large red letters *Justice for Joseph* and the other read in large red letters *We will never stop* and had taped to it a very handsome picture of Joseph taken a few months before he was killed. The justice signs were taped very securely on the wooden stakes from top to bottom with duct tape and strong packaging tape. We opened the car door and played some of Joseph's favorite songs and music that he loved from the CD and Scott and Rob took pictures of us standing beside the justice signs, showing that we are still fighting for justice for Joseph and would never give up—never! We were still here five years later and would continue our crusade for as long as it took.

We all hugged and said our good-byes for now and I thanked everyone for coming. I then laid out a blanket and placed a chair under the cherry blossom tree for my mom to sit down on. I sat down beside my mother and read scripture from the Bible. It was a beautiful sunny day and we stayed for hours, feeling and absorbing all of God's peace, love, earthly beauty and promises in the word. We knew Daddy, Michael and Joseph felt our presence as we felt theirs. Father God opened up the heavens for us on that very day and wiped away our tears of joy through the pain inside of us. We went and said our prayers after a long while and gave kisses to our loved ones. I helped my mom back into the car and we headed home for the rest of the day.

I continued my communications with Delegate Pena-Melnyk, the FBI agent and others who had given me their absolute support. I could not wait to attend Sunday services at my church and worship with my brothers and sisters in Christ.

On the morning of Monday, August 1, 2011, I received a call from Teresa with Dulaney Valley Memorial Gardens. She gently said that they had received a few phone calls asking that the two signs for "Justice for Joseph" be removed from our family plot. I asked, "Teresa, why are they asking this? What is wrong with standing up for justice for your child?" Teresa said the three calls were from other families who said the signs made them "uncomfortable"; one said they found the signs "offensive." This was very hurtful to me and I didn't really understand why these people were bothered. Teresa was very kind and compassionate and said, "Adrienne, some people are just hateful, mean and cruel." I asked Teresa, "Do I have to pick them up today—right now?" She said, "No, of course not, just as long as you get them by Friday." I thanked her for the call and told her I would certainly be there by Friday to take the "Justice for Joseph" signs down.

On Wednesday, August 3, around five in the afternoon, I drove to the cemetery to pick up the signs. When I pulled up in front of our family plot, I could not believe my eyes! I saw that both signs were gone and as I walked up closer to Joseph's grave, I saw that the two wooden stakes were still in the ground. Someone had ripped both the signs off of the stakes, tape and all. I knew that the wooden stakes had been deeply and firmly secured in the ground and the signs were securely fastened to the wooden rods up and down the entire poster board. I started to cry, got in my car and left. I saw that no one was in the offices of Dulaney Valley Memorial Gardens because they closed the office at five.

When I got home, I phoned my brothers and told my mom what had happened. They were in disbelief. As soon as I got up the next morning, I called Teresa and asked her if she had removed the signs. She said, "No, why? Are they not there?" I told her what had happened the day before and she too could not believe it. She said that she would go and look for herself and I also asked her to please look in the trash cans because I was too upset to look to see if someone had thrown them away.

Teresa phoned me later in the day and said, "Adrienne, I agree with you. You can see the signs were ripped right off of the wooden taped rods." She said she even had Pat, their ground-maintenance superintendent, walk the entire property to see if they had been tossed aside somewhere and that Pat also looked in every trash can and all of the dumpsters. She said the signs were nowhere to be found. Teresa said, "This is despicable! This is personal, Adrienne, and I can't even imagine how you must feel." Teresa took notes and said she was going to talk with the owner of the cemetery about what had happened and that they, too, were concerned.

I still, even today, wonder who would be so mean as to take down justice signs for my beloved son. I wondered also what they did with his picture. I was still tending to my angel gardens around my home and always the white butterfly would appear. I could sense Joseph's presence and the love of my Savior. Over the years, there were many times when my flower beds and angel gardens would be desecrated. My beautiful flowers would be cut off right in the middle of the stems, my roses would be cut off, my angel statues would be broken and moved and the rocks that formed a cross for Joseph would be displaced. Whoever is responsible for these mean and cruel actions will have to look in the mirror and we all know what goes around comes around.

CHAPTER 22

MY COVENANT WITH GOD, MY ALMIGHTY FATHER

I do not let it bother me for I am with my Lord and He gives me great strength and comfort. I continue to plant and nurture my lovely angel gardens and sing praise to my Savior as I pray and find solace in His great love and mercy. *John 15:1–2 "I am the true vine and my Father is the gardener. He cuts off every branch in me that bears no fruit, while every branch that does bear fruit he prunes so that it will be even more fruitful."*

Every Monday evening I continue to study and grow deeper in relationship with my Lord as my life group meets at my home. I love my brothers and sisters in Christ and we are truly one in spirit and know that God has provided a safe and trusting dwelling for us. The ministry of life groups at Grace Fellowship Church is such a vital and significant reality of sharing our hope and faith with one another and finding the peace and wholeness of living out our lives together in God's love and presence. We are so blessed to be given this gift and the opportunity of allowing God to nourish our soul through His word. The purpose statement of my church is "God's grace growing in us, among us and through us—bringing the fullness of Jesus to all of life." I pray to be an ambassador for Christ and spread the good news of Jesus and the truth of the Bible to all I encounter.

On July 30, 2011, we had a beautiful celebration for our mom's eighty-fourth birthday. So many family and friends came to honor her and extend their love. Rob came and gave her a love gift and a beautiful card signed by both him and Joseph. My brother, Damian, came up from Florida and spent several days with us. He slept in your room, Joseph and said that he loved sleeping in your bed and was so very comfortable. I loved him being here too and he has never left my side through our entire journey. Damian is a wonderful, loving, caring and loyal brother and uncle. He has got our backs and has not missed a beat over the past five years. He, too, loves Jesus so much and he knows that all is in God's hands and He will deliver.

I am always in prayer and tell Joseph how I yearn to hold him in my arms again. He is with me every second of every day and our love never stops. We are never separated and I continue to carry him inside me from conception until the day I come home and hold him in my arms.

I tell Joseph, "Thank you for holding Mommy up and keeping me strong. We must thank Father God for all that he is revealing and bringing to me so I may be the instrument He has chosen to carry out his specific plan and purpose that is His alone." I will follow only Him and walk every step that he lays down before me. His Holy Spirit continues to guide me and is filling me up from head to toe. I am overflowing with His love, wisdom and guidance. On Sunday, after service, I was walking to my car. A kind gentleman was walking beside me and we started to talk. He had been a member of Grace Fellowship Church for many years. As we spoke, he looked into my eyes and said, "I see Jesus in your eyes." I smiled gently and said, "I cannot think of a more beautiful thing to be told from a fellow brother in Christ." We both bid each other a blessed day and went on our way.

On August 16, 2011, my son, Rob, turned twenty-seven. Wow, twenty-seven years old! We shared a wonderful dinner and I made Mom's homemade tuna casserole supreme. This dish was one of my sons' favorites. They both loved it and requested it often. Rob filled up his plate twice and actually so did Mom-Mom. I loved seeing my boys eat heartily and savor my cooking. We all sang "Happy Birthday" as Rob blew out his candles and made a special wish. We took pictures, opened gifts, smiled, laughed and really had a great time. My Rob has grown into such a fine, handsome, kind and caring gentleman and an incredibly intelligent young man. I love him so very much and am quite proud of all that he has accomplished.

On August 25, 2011, I was quite surprised to see a story in the *Baltimore Sun* paper about Joseph's death. I had no knowledge of it whatsoever and was shocked to see the headline that read *Police say 2006 case is closed and no charges will be filed against the Bobcat driver*. I thought how manipulative, twisted and totally misleading this story was to the citizens of Maryland and of course to my precious Joseph and our family.

I immediately called the *Sun* paper and left a message with the reporter asking that he please return my call as soon as possible. I said that it was extremely important that I speak with him. The crime reporter, Peter Hermann, called me back that afternoon. I introduced myself to him and asked," why he did not contact me to discuss and make me aware that a story about Joseph's death was going to be in the newspaper." He said that he was very sorry and tried to call but I was not there. I responded that he left no voice mail message for me and that the news story was missing truthful information and crucial facts. I said that anyone reading this would be very confused and that SA Todd Slicenberger was going against the medical examiners. I went on to tell him that Joseph's death had been confirmed a homicide by assault by the chief medical examiner in Maryland and his assistant.

When speaking with Mr. Hermann, I referred to the cover-up by the company and the magnitude of proven lies by Pete Coldwin, the killer. I said, "I have been working to obtain justice for Joseph for over five years now and you need to write a follow-up story that portrays the true facts, science, physics and evidence." He needed to give clarification so that those interested would realize all that had taken place and understand that while they have tried to keep beating me down, they would be exposed.

Although Mr. Hermann's story included holes and twisted, misleading comments from Todd Slicenberger, the MDSP and the Baltimore County detectives, he did get one piece of information accurate. In his story he said that Dr. David Fowler and Dr. Zabiullah Ali, the medical examiners, had confirmed Joseph's death correctly as a homicide. He wrote Joseph's death was now on the record as the eighteenth homicide in Baltimore County in the year 2011. Peter Hermann was an excellent reporter and I knew he wanted to get the story right. He asked if I would give him a few weeks before he would come to my home to interview me and then write a follow-up story. He agreed with how very important this was. I said OK and that I would be looking forward to meeting with him.

The hot summer days were getting a little cooler as September was approaching. My angel gardens were in full bloom and I loved sitting on my glider looking at their rainbow of colors. My precious roses, hibiscus, daylilies, hostas, vincas and impatiens were beautiful and I was surrounded by their splendid scent.

Today when I awoke, I prayed and wept for all of those who were taken from us on September 11, 2001. This entire week had been so very sad and heartbreaking. I remembered the morning well and exactly where I was when our nation was attacked by the evil acts of Osama bin Laden and his demons. My heart goes out to all of these families and their loved ones. Over three thousand innocent human lives were so maliciously and horrifically ended as the New York World Trade Center, the Pentagon and a fourth aircraft were turned into fireballs, leaving the ashes of these precious loved ones. True heroes were carrying through that day as they left behind this earthly world and entered into new life and the reality of everlasting life in God's kingdom. "Oh, how they do live on and we remember and honor them so dearly."

CHAPTER 23

My Penny from Heaven;
The Change Needed
from Humankind

On Tuesday, September 13, 2011, Peter Hermann, the *Sun* paper reporter, came to my home to do his follow-up interview with me. Bob, Joseph's dad, joined us. Mr. Hermann was also accompanied by a photographer who wanted to get some pictures. We introduced ourselves and then sat down at the kitchen table. I asked Peter to please excuse the documents and papers that were covering my kitchen table, but I said that he needed to see these reports, letters and documents for himself.

He thanked me for allowing him the time and giving him the factual details of what needed to be printed. He offered his condolences again and we thanked him. I started from the beginning, July 20, 2006 and explained all of what had occurred and what we had been exposed to by the lying, corrupt, manipulative and malicious state's attorneys, detectives, state agency employees and the owner and some employees of Outside Unliving.

Peter Hermann listened intently and took notes. He would often ask me questions and was very satisfied with my answers and what documents

I was able to show him for proof. He at times seemed to be in disbelief himself but could see everything I told him was true. In addition to the police reports, my research, photographs, measurements and medical examiner letters, I showed him my brief and record extract as well as the two house bills the delegate, I and my friend Ann got passed.

I also talked with him about Joseph and the kind of loving, caring and wonderful young man he was; so did his dad. We filled up with tears and Peter could see how sick and grief stricken we were. Peter understood the injustice and deceit we were forced to deal with. He knew we had the conviction to get the truth and justice for our son and that we would never stop. He asked about the penny that I wore around my neck and I shared with him that this was the one cent that was in Joseph's pocket at the time he went to the Lord. I told him Joseph never carried change—never—and this was my penny from heaven.

Peter thanked us for our time and for giving him the whole story that needed to be reported. We must have talked for almost five hours. We thanked him for listening and for his integrity in reporting the truth and clarification so that readers would better realize and be made aware of what actually occurred. He told us that he would need a few weeks to confirm some facts, write the story in completion, have it edited and then secure the date when it would go to print in the *Baltimore Sun*. We thanked him again and said we understood.

In the interim, I spoke with Peter several times on the phone just to see how he was progressing and if he had any other questions for me. He was solid in his facts and reporting and was working on when the *Sun* would be able to go to print and if it would be a front-page story.

On October 13, 2011, Peter Herman informed me that Joseph's story would be in Sunday's paper, on October 16, 2011 and that it would be on the front page and extend to almost an entire second page. The cover story on the front page would read in bold letters *A Call for Justice Ignored: Police and investigators refuse a mother's pleas to investigate her son's death, now ruled a homicide.*

I was so glad to learn that the truth would now be told and I knew that God was showing me His sign to never give up and keep on in faith and trust. I went and bought three copies of the paper—the only three left in the store. The story was, indeed, on the front page and under the bold heading was a picture of Bob and I sitting at our kitchen table in tears. There was also a picture of my son's beautiful face and smile. I read the story from beginning to end; the reporter had done a fine job. All of page 15 continued with the words that detailed the truth of how Joseph's life was brutally taken at the hands of Pete Coldwin. It explained how he lied and tried to blame the victim and how all the police involved, elected officials and Outside Unliving covered up the horrific crime committed against Joseph.

There were so many good people who wrote and sent comments to the *Sun* paper and showed us their support. Many phoned me and offered love and compassion and the support poured in. On the Internet you can search for "Adrienne Miranda, mother ignored" by Peter Hermann and see the entire three page story www.baltimoresun mother Adrienne Miranda ignored. My family and I knew we were well on our way to the revelation of the whole truth being unfolded and revealed through the light of God, our Almighty Father. I know, Joseph, that you look down from heaven and are living in peace and in paradise. You know that the Holy Spirit continues to guide me and how very much I pray to start your foundation. My Lord has shown me that our God is always good, always and that He will guide me as I pray to write my book, your book, giving all glory and honor to God.

On November 1, 2011, my mother and I started to prepare for our baptism at Grace Fellowship Church. Pastor Erich Becker met with us and explained the procedure and that there was a step-down ladder into the water. Everything was perfect and we had no worries. We had been a bit concerned because our mom has trouble walking and bending her knee. She had a knee replacement many years ago and we wanted to make sure she would be able to physically join in. We were able to watch a previous baptism into the water font and could see that she would be just fine. Pastor Erich also assured us that he and the other pastors would be right there to assist her. We were overjoyed and knew we were so blessed to be able to publically declare our love and faith in Jesus Christ, our one and only Savior, before our congregation. We also knew that our dad, our mem, Michael, Joseph and all of our loved ones would be right there with us.

On November 20, 2011, the glorious day of our baptism occurred. We had requested that Pastor Rusty Russey baptize us. He was so loving, compassionate and gentle and had been there in so many ways for my mom and me. He had prayed with me many times as I asked God to bring truth and justice for my son. Pastor Russey was also our life-group leader at that time and encouraged all of us to live together in relationship with Jesus and grow deeper in the Gospel truth. He is a holy and godly man and he will stay in our hearts always.

Prior to our baptism, we were to write our testimonials so they could be read aloud as each of us was submerged into the holy, sacred water to be cleansed and renewed in the Holy Spirit. My mom was the first to be called. She was eighty-four years of age at that time and was gleaming as she was led to the holy water by our loving and godly pastors. The church auditorium was filled to capacity as everyone listened to her loving and humble words giving praise to our Jesus and the many blessings that God had bestowed upon her. I was next and the tears poured from my eyes. I was so proud of my mother and knew how richly blessed I was to have been born to such loving, caring and special parents. There were about twelve of us being baptized that day and our joy was completely spread throughout while the Holy Spirit's presence was powerful. Each time a sister or brother in Christ was baptized, the congregation applauded and gave praise to our Father. Pastor Rusty took my hand as my testimony was being read aloud and facing me he said, "Adrienne, I baptize you in the name of the Father, Son and Holy Spirit." He then held my neck and I went back completely into the holy water and arose feeling completely cleansed and filled with the love of my Jesus. The joy and splendor of this holy, sacred and renewed life was amazing. You knew and felt you were absolutely in the light—His light—as you gave your life and all of yourself to Jesus. My heart said, "Joseph, I know you were right there with me shining down from heaven. I could feel you from heaven above and see your beautiful shining smile."

When all of us had been baptized, our head pastor, Danny O'Brien, made an altar call. He invited anyone and everyone who had been moved by the Holy Spirit to come to the holy font of baptism and repent, rejoice and give oneself to Jesus. His words were so beautiful, meaningful and truly genuine. His heart, soul and spirit for our Lord always came through so clearly. I was overjoyed to see my family, close friends and others truly captivated. Denise, my Lisa's mom, was so inspired and moved that she came up to the front wearing a dress, heels and stockings, ready to be baptized. It did not matter what you were wearing; our church provided and was waiting there for you with a fresh, clean towel to dry off after. They even gave everyone a baptism T-shirt in red for the blood of Jesus with scripture verse written on it. I was so happy for Denise and I loved her so much. I will always cherish this day and thank God for his unfailing love. It was an awesome day and God poured out His love and grace to all.

We all gathered together before we left church and embraced one another. My Rob was there and he hugged me and Mom-Mom tightly. He said how proud he was of us and it meant so much to me deep in my heart and soul. Grace Fellowship Church had made a CD for each of us to have as a keepsake of our baptism and my mom and I play it often. It is a blessed gift that I will forever treasure. Our friend, Shannon, happened to get an unbelievable picture of my mom just as she was being baptized and she sent it to us. God bless her for her loving kindness.

We had the photograph enlarged, framed and our Mom's date of Baptism and her testimonial words written on it. We presented our gift to her at Christmas and she was completely overjoyed. She hung it in her bedroom so she could see it always and especially at night while she said her prayers. Thank you, sweet Jesus, for your ultimate sacrifice and the love you so freely give to all. I adore you.

Thanksgiving Day, November 24, was wonderful. Our family gave many thanks and counted our blessings. Lisa and Dino, my brother, prepared a beautiful meal as we all prayed together before being seated at the table. There had been so much to be thankful for and we all knew our faith was continually deepening. November 25, 2011, was my nephew Joseph Vincent's twenty-first birthday. How we loved and honored him on this day, during his "rite of passage." Joe was so happy and smiling from ear to ear! We celebrated a joyful, special and treasured day with our Joe. I wrote to him a special letter that read "I love you, Joe". You are my wonderful, dear and caring nephew. You have such a big heart and are such an incredibly kind, thoughtful, bright and handsome young man; may God bless you always." Joe had been there for me completely and he was full of compassion. I knew he missed and loved Michael and Joseph, his cousins. He stays positive and believes justice will prevail.

On December 9, my birthday, my son Rob took me out for sushi. We sat at the large rotating sushi bar and everything looked so delicious. Rob helped me order and encouraged me to try some new dishes. I attempted to use the chopsticks and did OK, but I was no comparison to my Rob.

He and Joe were like experts when using chopsticks and they both loved sushi. Rob assisted with technique and demonstration; he was quite a good teacher. I tried to be a good student and I paid close attention. I even ate the "volcano"—wow, it was delicious. We had a great time and I loved being out with my Rob. I thank God for him every day.

On December 24, Christmas Eve, all of us attended church together. The service was beautiful, as always and we rejoiced at the birth of our Lord and Savior. My beautiful niece, Grace, sang the worship songs along with us and raised her precious arms up to the Lord. She was so happy and she knew how much Jesus loved her.

I visited the resting-place of my son Joseph on Christmas morning. I prayed, sang and wept beside your Christmas wreath, tree and flowers as I left my message card for you at your headstone. I prayed and sang to Michael and Pop-Pop too. I know all of you live in God's kingdom of heaven in eternal love, peace, beauty and joy. I also know that I will see you soon.

I said, "Joseph, you are with me each and every minute and justice, my love, is coming. God, our one and only Almighty Father, is bringing it. He will make it happen in His way and His time and for His purpose." I am God-centered and I put all of my faith, trust, hope, dependence and life in His hands.

CHAPTER 24

I MEET MY FBI FRIEND AND PROMISES ARE KEPT

On December 30, 2011, a promise from my very special friend and brother in Christ was answered. Today I met my earth angel who worked for the FBI and had been with me for many years. I knew this was a miracle that God made happen through His divine intervention. God is so great! We met just a few blocks away from my home at Dunkin' Donuts. I knew him as soon as I saw him even though I had not met him before. He stood up and allowed me to give him that special hug that he had promised me. I tried to hold back my tears as I held on to him and thanked him for all of the compassion, affirmation, kindness and concern he had given me.

We talked for a few hours and I understood even more about him. God had definitely put this good man in my path purposefully; there was no doubt. We shared a lot about many things and also about Joseph's case and his death. I still remained in contact with him and he was up to date with everything surrounding my journey. I knew it was time for him to get back to Bethesda, Maryland and I asked to give him one more hug before he left. He graciously complied and smiled.

As we said our good-byes for now, I asked him, "Will I see you again?" He turned and said, "You will see me at the trial for your son, Joseph."

This FBI agent and good and honest man stayed with me always. I knew that I would see him again, just as he said, at the trial for my son, Joseph.

It was now January 1, 2012. A new year—what would He bring? I continued to pray for resolution and revelation based upon the will of my Father, God. He had already shown me many miracles and I felt empowered to begin writing my book, *The Scent of My Son, In God We Trust* and to start Joseph's foundation. I realized that there were still several steps that needed to come to fruition and the assistant states attorney assigned to this task was hard at work trying to make them happen.

In early January I experienced a great deal of anxiety and difficulty with my computer. I had everything stored and backed up on my computer that related to Joseph's death and his case.

Then, for some strange reason, my computer started to operate very abnormally. It would suddenly turn off as I was searching and e-mailing. It would also not allow me to get on the Internet and then at times it would not come on at all. I had to contact customer service and explain the issues. It was a draining experience. I was told that the computer manufacturer had to remove everything off of my computer so they could perform a technical diagnosis.

I explained to them in detail the nature of my documents. I told them that my son had been killed, his death was a homicide and I could not lose any of the files and documents related to his death. I had to talk with so many technicians and was handed over to so many people; I started to feel as if something were getting lost in translation.

I finally spoke with two high-level technicians who understood and they told me they could remove my files and assured me they would be stored on my backup storage unit. They then said that once the virus was removed and the technical repairs completed, they would definitely reload my stored files back onto my computer. They said, "We promise you. You are at no risk of losing your files." That week my son came over and watched as they removed my files and loaded everything onto my backup storage unit. We could see that everything was, indeed, loaded and saved to my backup storage unit.

I continued to communicate with the lead technician for about three weeks. He then called me and said, "Ms. Miranda, everything has been done and the virus has been removed. We have also increased your megabytes and I am now ready to reload all of your files back onto your computer." I was so grateful and thanked him immensely. He instructed me to leave my computer on for the night and said that when I woke up tomorrow morning and went to my computer, I would see all of my files reloaded back onto my computer. I was finally at ease and knew that I could now continue with all of my work that still needed to be done.

The next morning I awoke and went downstairs to my office. I sat at my computer and went to my files. I looked at the screen and saw there was *nothing* there! I was in shock and could not believe it. I immediately called the technician and he was not in. I asked to speak with the other technician who had been aware of the problem and he was not in either. I left a message on the voice mail of the lead technician who had been helping me and explained that nothing was reloaded and that I had to talk with him immediately. I then called back and asked to speak to a supervisor. This person told me there was no one there by the name I mentioned and he would have to have someone else get back to me. I said, "What you are saying is untrue. I am giving you the proper name of the lead technician who has been helping me for over three weeks now and you are telling me there is no one by that name that works for your company?" He replied, "yes".

I could go on and on, but I will spare you the disturbing details. My son, Rob, who was a computer systems engineer, gave me the name of a company whom he said were experts at recovering and retrieving lost files. I phoned the Disk Doctors and spoke with a very intelligent and kind gentleman who listened to my entire ordeal. He said that he definitely thought he could help and we set up a time to meet. I took him my backup storage unit in order for him to test it and examine the device.

He later phoned me and said that the backup storage unit had been corrupted and the computer technicians had lost my files. He was certain. However, he did convey that he could recover the files but it would take

301

some time. He gave me a quote and I told him to please do the necessary work and how grateful I was to him. My computer was still not properly working after the technicians said everything was complete, so for a while I went to the Baltimore County Public Library to continue my work and my communications regarding Joseph's case.

I ended up having to purchase a new computer and I drove down to the Disk Doctors and took it with me. Finally, I met again with the Disk Doctors expert, Shahid, and he loaded everything onto my computer and set everything up for me. I will never forget this kind and wonderful man for giving me his expertise, undivided attention and heartfelt compassion. He is my friend for life and may God bless him always.

Throughout January, February and March, the AG assistant attorney was still working on getting all of the necessary paperwork in front of the Baltimore County Circuit Court judge. He had to actually create a "model" for people who had been confronted with the unprecedented circumstances that my family and I had endured for almost six years now. This attorney explained to me that the delay in preparing the "notice to respond" was because our case was in "unchartered territory."

He had now obtained additional papers from the circuit court that also needed to be filed and submitted prior to mailing out the "notice to respond." During this time, I was still working with Delegate Joseline Pena-Melnyk. I knew that she was in session and in committee to change specific laws. She, Spencer and Tim have been so diligent, hardworking and supportive and remained right by my side. I have the utmost respect and trust in them; they are truly phenomenal and their public service efforts and achievements are extraordinary. The delegate is a uniquely special lady and wrote to me to keep the faith and keep trusting in the Lord. She told me to be blessed and that I was a "good soul." She reaffirmed to me that once we have the changed death certificate that shows homicide by assault in hand, she will do whatever it takes to obtain justice for Joseph.

God has given me the strength, perseverance and guidance to stand firm in my faith and to listen and respond in the way he is telling me. I am following all of his instruction. I tell Him, "Here I am, Lord. My heart is completely open and ready to receive your call and meet you where you are so that your will and purpose are fulfilled. I love you with all of my heart, soul and mind; this is the first and greatest commandment." I am in my Father's will and glory and honor are His, His alone.

On March 9 I learned that the AG assistant attorney was still trying to complete his paperwork and court filings to the judge. He was finalizing the order for the judge in Baltimore County to sign and authorize the document. This week, however, the attorney general's office had problems with its Microsoft Word program and the AG attorney also had to be in court on some other court proceedings. He wrote to me that he would contact me early next week. I wrote back to him and said I understood and that I looked forward to hearing from him soon.

Today I also talked with mom, Catherine Miranda. We shared in beautiful conversation and I knew how very strong her faith and belief in our Lord was. She trusted in God our Father and tried to encourage me. She told me how much she loved Joseph and all of her grandchildren. She, too, was and is a wonderful grandma and often watched the children for us when they were young. I prayed Father God would bless her and always watch over her.

April 22, 2012, was Joseph's twenty-fifth birthday. I so often thought of him as that precious little boy and then that wonderful young man who had such love and gusto for life. His heart was full of love, tenderness and kindness. I visited his gravesite and brought my roses, prayers, balloons and message card to him. I sang "Happy Birthday" to my beloved son and knew he heard and could feel the deep and eternal love in my heart. He and Michael, who would have turned thirty-two on April 15, are at peace and know joy, happiness, heavenly love and bliss. They are at home together with their Lord and their loved ones. "I love you, my sweetheart angel boys," I said and I knew I would see them soon.

In May of 2012, I met with one of our senators. This man was a US congressman who was very well respected—rightfully so. He gave me time to talk with him and explain the circumstances that I was dealing with regarding the homicide of Joseph. This man was a good man and he truly and genuinely cared. He wanted me to call the office next week to talk further. I said that I certainly would, thanked him and gave him a hug. I knew God was present; He was right there and so was Joseph.

I called the office the following week and the congressman spoke with me briefly and then turned me over to his chief attorney. This gentleman was very kind and attentive. He listened carefully and then requested that I fax him all of the information that I had, including the facts of the case, letters and all pertinent information. I thanked him and said that I would be faxing him the next day. He said, "All right," and that he would be looking for the documents.

I compiled a total of over eighty pages containing crucial information and also wrote a cover letter to the congressman saying that further investigation into the actions and conduct of the police and law-enforcement agencies that investigated my son's death needed to be done. I also included a time line that contained all relevant and factual occurrences that had taken place since July 20, 2006.

I explained that Joseph's death was now confirmed to be a homicide by assault by the chief medical examiner in the state of Maryland and his assistant who performed the autopsy. The chief attorney received all of the information and wrote a letter requesting the same to the US attorney general and the special agent in charge with the Baltimore County FBI, the FBI headquarters for the Mid-Atlantic region. The FBI agent, Mr. Halk, called me about ten days later after receiving the package. When I spoke with him, he did seem aware of the many crucial facts that had been sent to him by the congressman's chief attorney. He asked me several questions and I answered him. I then asked him if he had reviewed the over eighty pages and he said, "Not really. I skimmed it." I said, "You really need to look at all of the documents so that you will understand the circumstances better." He then said, "OK, I will get back to you in two weeks." I waited over six weeks and never heard back from him.

Later, I phoned the congressman's chief attorney and asked if he could give me an update. At the conclusion of the senator's request, the AG at the federal level for Baltimore and the FBI said that they really did not know how to handle my son's case so they referred it to the US Department of Justice. They ended up saying there was nothing they could do at the federal level. The Congressman's chief attorney even took it to the ethics committee, the civil rights committee and the "hate crimes" committee. But they said, "No, nothing needs to be done at the federal level."

The chief attorney told me to keep it at the state level in Maryland and he wished me the best. I remain grateful for all of his efforts and his communications on behalf of Joseph, me and our family. I told Joseph, "Your voice will he heard, my darling son and it is only a matter of time."

During this time, the delegate Joseline Pena-Melnyk had informed me that House Bill 100 would go into effect in October 2012. She said that was the time we would move forward with the changed death certificate in hand stating manner of death (homicide) and how (by assault).

All of the evidence proved, without a doubt, that a horrific and hateful crime had been committed against my beloved Joseph.

It was now May and on Mother's Day, both Scott and John phoned me and told me how much they loved Joseph and would never forget him. I can feel Joseph's love through them. These two were Joseph's best friends since they were toddlers and throughout his years growing up. They are such wonderful, loving and compassionate young men and I pray God will always keep them safe and fulfill all of their hopes and dreams. They are true believers and they know Joseph lives on in heaven.

In June 2012, I finally gathered up enough hope and realized that I knew Joseph wanted me to go on with my life and find happiness. I knew how much he loved me and my Father in heaven was telling me the same. My dear friend and sister in Christ, Maria, encouraged me to go to a dance for fellow believers and that I really needed to start socializing more. I was hesitant, but I knew she was really trying to help me move forward.

On June 10, 2012, Maria and I did go to the event. We ended up having a wonderful time, talked, danced and met some really great people our age. I actually met the man, who would become my wonderful sweetheart, Bud Burrier. He was a real gentleman and came over to our table to introduce himself. We talked for a while, danced, talked some more and really felt a connection. At the end of the evening, he asked for my phone number and I gave it to him. I was very happy that I had gone to the dance.

Bud and I have grown to know each other so well over these past two years. I felt he had been sent from heaven for me and he has been right there for me, showing me love, compassion, support and kindness. He is a man of faith and a strong believer. Throughout these past two summer's he has been so helpful and he recreated the heart and cross garden that Luke had built for Joseph after his death. If you recall, some of my flower gardens and angel gardens had been desecrated over the past several years. In December, I had been weakened from an automobile accident and my neck and back were injured, so I was only able to work on my gardens for short periods of time.

Bud went and bought beautiful, large, white stones, dug out a heart in the dirt and then placed the large, white, shining stones in the ground. He also was able to restore the cross of stones that Luke had originally placed in the center. When it was complete, I was overjoyed. I watched as the sweat from Bud's face dripped down and knew that he put his whole heart into creating this for me and Joseph. The heart garden for Joseph was absolutely beautiful! In the spring and summer, Bud planted beautiful red impatiens for me throughout the heart bed and I still go to it to say my prayers daily. The guardian angel plaque hangs above it and was given to me by my sister-in-law, Lisa. Her gifts to me have been countless and so special and sentimental. I love everyone in my family so deeply and I pray that each of them grows deeper in his or her love relationship with Jesus; He wants our hearts and they are committed to their faith. I love all of my angel gardens and the beauty of their blossoms, colors, butterflies and fragrances. The perennials that you, Joseph, planted for me thrive and grow with each passing year and are a part of your and God's natural and divine love for His earth. How we are so richly blessed. The rainbows still appear and they are ribbons in the sky of God's glorious miracles. I have received many and I know they are sent from heaven above!

July 20, 2012, the anniversary of the day my baby went home to be with the Lord, was here once again. It had now been six years and Joseph lived on with me as we moved forward together. I visited his resting-place with prayer in my heart, song, "thinking of you" balloons, flowers, roses and my message card to him. I told my son how very much I loved him and that Jesus was telling me all that I had to do through his Holy Spirit. So many loved Joseph and he was sorely missed. "We are all praying for justice for you," I said, "and I know that God will bring it; it will come to pass."

It had now been almost a year that I had been back and forth with the assistant attorney with the Attorney General's office in Maryland. He had been working so very hard to get the death certificate legally changed and into the vital records division of Maryland. This very special gentleman was such an efficient and helpful attorney that I thank God for him every day.

Sadly, I learned that the assistant attorney had been taken sick and was hospitalized for a few weeks. He did return to work the first week in October. I had known that October 1, 2012, was the day that House Bill 100 would be enacted into law.

The second week in October, the assistant attorney phoned me. He was a very honest, diligent, hardworking and competent gentleman. He told me that he had been sick but was back at work and would have everything completed from vital records by October 12. I thanked him and was so grateful to him. I told him that I was so sorry he had been ill. He said that he was quite sick for a while but was feeling better. He also told me that he wanted me to know that he had put in his resignation at the attorney general's office after thirty years of service and said he was done and wanted no part of them. He said that October 31 would be his last day. I told him I understood and I prayed that he would find something and someone who were worthy of his work ethics, integrity and expertise. He thanked me and said that he wished me the best.

Dr. Fowler and Dr. Ali with the Office of the Chief Medical Examiner also e-mailed me telling me that my son's death certificate was corrected and ready to be put in my hands. I thanked them and then went to my knees in prayer. "Praise be to God," I cried. "All glory and honor are His!"

In mid-October I drove over to the vital records division for the state of Maryland to pick up my son's amended death certificate. I was feeling relieved as I was driving over to Reisterstown Road in Baltimore to finally have my son's corrected death certificate, which indicated homicide by assault, in hand. It was now official, confirmed, signed and legally filed in vital records for the state of Maryland.

So many wonderful, good, honest people of integrity stood by me and helped to make this happen. When I returned home, I phoned Delegate Pena-Melnyk as she requested and we discussed what the next steps would be. I knew in my heart and soul that we were well on our way to obtaining justice for Joseph. When the delegate and I spoke, she asked me to compile a very detailed time line of all of the most important events that occurred over the past seven years since Joseph's death and to provide names of the parties involved. I said, "All right, I will certainly do that," and she set up a time for us to meet at Starbucks near Annapolis.

I also asked her if she would like to have the over ninety pages that I had sent to the senator. She said for me to hold on to them for now but that she wanted a complete sequential summary of all that had taken place since July 20, 2006. I understood and said, "OK, I will prepare it."

When we met at Starbucks, we had a very productive meeting. She had already contacted the attorney general in Maryland and was requesting a time for us to meet with him. She actually spoke with his liaison of internal transactions between the AG, Mr. Duke Gunsler and the House of Delegates in Annapolis, Maryland, while I was sitting with her.

The delegate also reviewed the summary timeline that I had prepared and she was very satisfied with it. Her hope was to have the case taken away from the Baltimore County state's attorney, Todd Slicenberger and have our case escalated up to the state level. She did not think it would take too long, but she said she would contact me as soon as she had a date from the attorney general's office.

It was so good to see her and I thanked her again for all that she and her staff had done for me. I knew they truly cared and all along were doing the "right thing." That is the mantra of Attorney General Duke Gunsler:

to serve the people and "always do the right thing." Little did that happen for Joseph and our family. The AG prosecutors, you will see, did the exact opposite.

The holidays came and we all did our best to get through. We were overflowing with thankfulness and love for our Lord. However, at this time, we were very concerned for our mom because she had taken quite ill and was rushed to the hospital. She had to have emergency life-or-death surgery after her stay at a well-known elderly care facility. Throughout her stay there, she became extremely sick and the unspeakable negligence and lack of appropriate care led her to this consequence. We were all in deep and constant prayer for her. The surgery lasted about five to six hours and she was eighty-five years of age at the time. All of us gathered in love, deep heartache and earnest prayer for our dear and wonderful mom. The surgeon was excellent and very skilled at his profession. We knew that she was in good hands, but the situation was quite worrisome and upsetting.

.

CHAPTER 25

FATHER GOD'S
UNCONDITIONAL LOVE

Through the grace of God, our mother survived the surgery and the anesthesia. All of us gathered in prayer and thankfulness to our Lord. She was in the ICU for six days and the head nurse and her staff was so wonderful and skilled. They took excellent care of her and showed us such compassion and kindness. We will never forget them; they do God's work and it shows from their hearts.

My mom was released from the hospital after another two weeks and she needed long-term care. We looked at and visited several elderly health care facilities but were very disappointed. We had heard that Lorien Health Care at Mays Chapel was excellent and the staff really cared about their patients. When my sister-in-law Lisa and I took the guided tour at Lorien, we were so overjoyed. We loved everything about the facility and the staff was superb. We learned there was a waiting list and Mom's name was on it. We told Debra, our tour guide, that we would stay in prayer in hopes that a room would soon be available to her. We hugged Debra and thanked her for all of the time and kindness she extended to us. She was so very gracious answering all of our many questions and allowing us to see all the amenities that Lorien had to offer.

Lisa and I left feeling spiritually bound and telling each other, "Let's pray earnestly and ask our Lord to make a place for Mom at Lorien." The next day, sure enough, I received a call from Lorien telling me that a room did become available for our mother. We gave praise and thanks to our Almighty Father God and to this day our mom is making amazing progress. She was admitted to Lorien on December 31, 2013. I pray God allows her to see and hear justice for her beloved grandson, Joseph, while on this earth. If He chooses otherwise, she will know it from heaven above.

I told Joseph, "Mom is making headway for justice to be served and your voice to be heard." I know that my Lord is moving me forward every day in His will. This year will be seven years since Joseph was killed. In the Bible *seven* means complete and perfect. God's completion and perfect timing for his purpose and plan to be revealed will happen. He owns my heart and my trust and faith are in Him only.

On January 4, 2013, I met with Delegate Joseline Pena-Melnyk to take a file of essential documents to her office in Annapolis. I knew her plan was to turn them over to the attorney general's office for review. It was a rainy day and the delegate had been called into a very important conference. When I arrived I met with Spencer, her longtime aid. He knew exactly why I was there and what I was bringing to the delegate. I sat in the office while Spencer phoned the delegate and could hear her on speakerphone.

She again said that Kiercher Braun, the internal interim liaison between the AG office and the delegates in Annapolis, would pick up the documents and insure that they were given to the director of prosecuting attorneys, Mr. Don Barrett. I listened and said OK, but I was a bit concerned about the over 130 documents because I did not have time to make copies of all of them and they were crucial to Joseph's case. The delegate said it would be all right and that my documents would be in safe hands. I trusted her and her staff completely and Spencer confirmed as well that my documents would be fine and Ms. Braun would be sure to deliver them to Attorney Barrett. I watched Spencer put a thick rubber band around my file and lay it right on top of his desk. He said that Ms. Braun was scheduled to pick them up that same afternoon. I felt confident that these essential documents would be delivered as promised to the AG office. I thanked Spencer, gave him a hug and thanked him again for all that he had done. He said, "Adrienne, we will stay in touch for sure."

Meanwhile, Attorney Barrett from the AG office was e-mailing me through his assistant. He was well aware that the document package was on its way to him. He had told me by e-mail that he knew a lot had occurred and that he "wanted to know everything that I knew." The AG prosecution team had been in some discussion about my son's case and I knew that they had subpoenaed all of the police reports, photographs, witness statements and medical examiner letters.

I did write back to Attorney Barrett and said that I appreciated that he wanted to know everything that I knew and that the over 130 pages being delivered to him by Ms. Braun would help to achieve that. I continued, however, it was my understanding that he was allotting me two hours to present to him my son's case. I graciously said that while I appreciated the two hours and I knew he had told me how busy his office was, I could not possibly tell him all that I knew in two hours. I also said that I had sent the over 130 crucial documents to him "in good faith," knowing that they would be returned to me and that I felt sure these documents would help give him clarification and a substantial understanding of what had been going on and still continues to occur to this day.

It was now March 2013 and I had waited months to hear something regarding the review of my son's case and the death certificate that confirmed homicide by assault that was now recorded in vital records for the state of Maryland. We were so thankful that the case had been taken away from Baltimore County's state's attorney, Todd Slicenberger. We know that he was in violation of his oath of office and had committed other activities that he should be held accountable for.

On April 3, 2013, I finally heard back from Attorney General Duke Gunsler's office. At this time I was informed that the chief prosecutor, Mr. Don Barrett and five other excellent and experienced top prosecutors wanted to meet with me on April 10 at one in the afternoon. Also present would be a Maryland state trooper, Sha Bryan, who was very trusted and acted as the liaison between the Maryland State Police and the attorney general's prosecuting team.

I wrote back that I would be there and my sister-in-law, Lisa Gemma, would be accompanying me; God bless her loving heart. I said that I would be bringing some additional documents that I felt sure they had but that I would use as I presented our case and all of the factual circumstances and evidence.

CHAPTER 26

THE MEETING WITH THE AG OFFICE PROSECUTORS

On the morning of April 10, I awoke and reviewed once again the documents and my notes that I wanted to take with me. I prayed and I knew many prayers were being said for us. Lisa picked me up at quarter to noon. Once again, we placed my two boxes on the dolly and loaded them up in the trunk. I had my black satchel with me as well. I was eager to meet with these prosecutors and especially grateful that they were very experienced and had reviewed the factual science of Joseph's case and my essential 130 plus documents. Most importantly, I was extremely encouraged that they had in hand the confirmed death certificate showing and proving Joseph's death was "homicide by assault"; a definite and absolute crime was committed against Joseph and all of the proof was there.

We got on I-83 and headed to downtown Baltimore on Saint Paul Street. The traffic was not too congested and we made good time. Lisa and I were surprised to see that there was not one parking space in the Saint Paul Street parking lot as we drove around each level. We drove around one more time and through the grace of God, there was one parking space now open just in front of the entrance to the elevator door. We felt the Lord's and Joseph's presence and we looked at each other and smiled. We loaded up the two large boxes on the dolly and headed into the elevator entrance. We had to go down first to sign in and wait in the main lobby until they called us. We arrived at about half past noon and waited at least forty minutes, if not more.

We observed many people in business suits going in and out, we saw the mayor and some of her staff come in the main lobby doors and there were guards, of course. We stood anxiously waiting and then I went over to the receptionist and gently asked if Attorney Don Barrett knew we were here. She made a phone call and said, "Yes, but they will come down for you when they are ready." I said, "Thank you." Lisa and I stood for about another ten to fifteen minutes and then Attorney Barrett's assistant came down off the elevator and introduced herself. We followed her up to the nineteenth floor and she directed us into the conference room where all six prosecutors were seated along with the Maryland State Police liaison, Colonel Sha Bryan, who was seated toward the corner to the right of where I sat down. My sister-in-law, Lisa Gemma, sat down next to me, close to my right side.

The meeting opened and we went around the room and introduced ourselves. I was so grateful in my heart to finally be in front of men and women whom I believed would do the right thing and confirm that a horrifying crime had indeed been committed against my son and charges would be brought. Attorney Barrett led the meeting and started to ask me some questions. I answered everything that he asked with complete honesty. In addition to me asking if they had read Detective Rick Bishtall's entire police report and Antoine Ruberra's reenactment of the scene, I also showed them Pete Coldwin's deposition and pointed out where he admitted to physical contact with my son, calling it the "one-two" but saying that "it wasn't really violent or extreme—just a little bit." They all seemed a bit perplexed, so I stood up and handed the deposition to Attorney Barrett. He looked at it and just nodded.

I then asked Attorney Barrett if he had reviewed the over 130 pages that were given to him at his request. I was bewildered because he did not seem to really comprehend. He again just nodded. I said, "Everything was contained in that package regarding the killing of my son and the cover-up." He asked me why I believed there was a cover-up. Again, I was stunned by his question and said, "Are you sure that you read all of the crucial documents that you asked me to send to you prior to this meeting?" He said yes. I then said, "With all due respect, Mr. Barrett, you can believe whatever you choose to believe, but the evidence is all there. I would like to get to the facts, science, physics and evidence of what occurred on the day my son was brutally attacked and killed at the hands of Pete Coldwin, the so-called spotter."

At that time, one of the attorneys, a rather soft-spoken gentleman, said, "Ms. Miranda, can you show us what happened to your son because I do not really understand it?" I said, "Of course I will show you." I then took out the large map, the same that I used when I met with the medical examiners and placed it in the center of the table close to the attorney. I showed him and them in detail exactly where Joseph lay on the ground, how he was thrown into the reversing Bobcat to his death, the reverse movement, the measurement between the two left wheels of the earthmover and that what Pete Coldwin had claimed was a total lie. I told them that he pushed, shoved and propelled Joseph with force from behind right into the oncoming Bobcat to his death. I said, "It is all in Dr. Fowler's and Dr. Ali's conclusion of manner of death being homicide and how—by assault." The attorneys then asked a few questions and a few of them nodded in confirmation. I then added that Pete Coldwin had been observing the loading and unloading of the dirt from the Bobcat and saw the repeated motion at least nine times before Joseph ever arrived at the scene. I also pointed out and showed them how the dump truck had been driven forward after Joseph was killed to create an illusion that the Bobcat was moving forward but that that had been proven untrue. We knew the Bobcat backed up over Joseph and that he was already prone (lying flat on the ground and on his stomach) when the rear left wheel crushed his head, face and neck.

I showed them and read again Pete Coldwin's deposition where he admitted to physical contact with Joseph and that it was just a little bit violent, a little bit extreme. I asked Attorney Barrett if he had read the medical examiners' letters to State's Attorney Todd Slicenberger that confirmed Joseph's death was a homicide by assault. He just said, "yes".

I also showed MDSP detective Sha Bryan the police report by Senior Detective Bishtall and Trooper Ramarez who was the Spanish interpreter. He looked at it and could see clearly that Antoine Ruberra was telling the truth and that Pete Coldwin's statements were in total contradiction with Mr. Ruberra's. I told him that the Maryland State Police hid this report from our family and lied to us, telling us it did not exist. I asked him, "Why does he think they would do that?" He just shook his head back and forth and said, "Hmm, hmm, hmm, I don't know, Ms. Miranda. I don't know why they would do that."

I looked around the room at each attorney's face and did not know what to think. I had spoken with them and presented for four hours and I know that I was just as clear and concise as I was with the medical examiners. Attorney Barrett assured me that they would rereview everything that they had since January and that they understood all that was new and all that I had explained. I thanked them again and appreciated them for their expertise, time, concern and attention. I asked, "How will I learn of your decision?" He said, "We will communicate to you when we are finished with our investigation and review and see what directions we need to take." I asked about how long he thought it would take. He replied that he really could not say and that they were working on several cases at that time. He continued that he was not saying Joseph's case was any less important than the others but that they were all equally important. I said, "Of course, I understand," and to please contact me if they had any questions or needed any additional clarification as they reviewed my son's case—our case. "I am here to provide whatever you may need," I said. "All of the evidence speaks for itself and I am hopeful you will concur."

They all got up from their seats and quickly left the conference room. Attorney Barrett allowed me to shake his hand again and we said thank you and good-bye to the MDSP detective Bryan.

I gathered up my documents that I had shown them and placed them in my satchel. Lisa helped me put away the map and other files in my boxes. We then exited the conference room with the dolly and our feeling of relief, praying that these people had heard and seen what they needed to make the arrest and bring justice. We both felt that there could be no way that they would not return with confirmation of a crime committed against Joseph and prepared to make an arrest. The truth and facts had been clearly, completely and comprehensively shown and proven to them.

We got onto the elevator and Mr. Barrett's assistant escorted us down to the main lobby. She was kind and wished us luck. We then went down on the elevator to the parking garage and loaded up and got into the car. Both Lisa and I talked on the way home and agreed that they would surely return with a confirmation of first- or second-degree murder and take the next steps for accountability to be recognized. Lisa and I felt that our day in court was about to occur and were sure it was only a matter of time; Lisa told me that I had done a great job and explained articulately and clearly all of the facts, science, physics and forensics that proved our Joseph was viciously and brutally killed. I said,, "My goodness, they even have Joseph's death certificate that confirms homicide by assault, so how could they possibly say no crime was committed?"

We got home and pulled up into my driveway. Lisa helped me in with the boxes and we sat down for a bit. We hugged and prayed and knew that we were doing everything possible to bring justice for Joseph. After a while Lisa drove back home and told my brother Dino everything that took place. He phoned me and said, "Adrienne, keep the faith and you are doing everything that can be done." I was tearful, but I knew in my heart and in my soul it was true. I also talked with my brother Damian and he said the same and that I should continue to stay in prayer and that they were all with me and loved me. My Lord was my strength and my rock and He would continue to prepare me and guide me; in this I was certain.

During the next few weeks, Attorney Barrett and I communicated by e-mail. I did send him two additional postmeeting e-mails to further his clarification of all events and he did confirm that they were received. I waited patiently to hear from them on their decision.

I spoke and listened to God and His Holy Spirit. I remained in constant prayer and many family and friends were giving me much love and support. My pastors were there for me in prayer and reminded me always to trust only in the Lord.

April 22, 2013—Joseph's twenty-sixth birthday—was here. I knelt at my precious angel's headstone and asked God to keep carrying me. I asked for truth and justice and to be freed from the brokenness and heartache that ravaged me. I knew that the longing for my son would never cease and the lost hopes and dreams he had would never be, but I found refuge and solace in being given the justice he so deserved. Again the tears poured, but they were wiped away. My Jesus took them and lifted me up to stand strong. A new day was coming and I would always remain with him. Again I said, *John 15:5 "I am the vine you are the branches. If a man remains in me and I in him, he will bear much fruit; apart from me you can do nothing."* Once again I took my message card, roses and his "happy birthday" balloon to him. I sent kisses and love to my special three and knew that the Father, Son and Holy Spirit were leading me.

During this time I continued to stay in contact with Delegate Joseline Pena-Melnyk and she had encouraged me to contact and meet with my other delegates. I phoned all four of them, explained my circumstances and asked for a meeting. Two of them actually met face-to-face with me at Starbucks and were shattered and extremely concerned about my situation. They appreciated that I had shared all that had been happening and hoped I would obtain justice for Joseph. My Baltimore County delegates were sincere and I especially was hopeful that Delegate Liffertae would act on my behalf. He had e-mailed me and told me he was looking further into the facts and current actions and was going to speak directly with Delegate Pena-Melnyk and the US attorney for Maryland at the federal level. I very much appreciated his service and support on behalf of me and my family. I have not heard from him since last year, but I pray he is doing well and making progress.

It was now May 24 and I had heard nothing from Attorney Barrett with the AG office. It had been over six weeks since we met, but I felt sure he was leaving no stone unturned. It would be his duty to examine all of the evidence and certainly to use the confirmed death certificate of my son that indicated homicide by assault and was based on the facts and science of the case from the medical examiners' findings. House Bill 100, which was enacted into law on October 1, 2012, authorized the Office of the Chief Medical Examiner (OCME) to amend the cause of death on a death certificate at any time after issuance and in accordance with its adopted procedures. A record should be maintained that identifies the evidence upon which the amendment was based, the date of the amendment and the identity of the person making the amendment. Any amendments to death certificates beyond three years or more after the death shall require a court order.

This house bill in Maryland did help us to better understand all that the Assistant States Attorney who oversaw the OCME was confronted with as he worked so diligently to have Joseph's confirmed death certificate of homicide by assault recorded in vital records, proving that there was evidence a crime was committed upon Joseph. This states attorney is a very special, decent and good man who did the right thing. We thank God for him every day.

CHAPTER 27

THE STATE PROSECUTORS REJECT AND IGNORE THE MEDICAL EXAMINERS

On May 12, 2013, I was shocked and devastated to receive Attorney Don Barrett's letter. His letter read that no crime was committed against my son Joseph. He explained that after his review and reading the conclusions of the state's attorneys in Carroll County, Frederick County, Baltimore County and the Maryland State police and Baltimore County homicide squad, they would not conclude that Joseph's death was a homicide by assault.

The reason for several County jurisdictions review was because the Carroll County S. A. wanted someone to back him up even though he knew their investigation was grossly incomplete and their conclusions were impossible. He even knew that it had been brought to his attention that Joseph was not even killed in his jurisdiction but he was killed in Baltimore County. The Frederick County States Attorney is just west of Carroll County and she had no clue to what she was even reading in the police reports and made a huge blunder when she wrote that after her review of the case requested by the Carroll County States Attorney that

"Mr. Miranda said he was irritated" and she concurred with the findings of Carroll County. Well, Ms. Hemm, you are completely wrong and do not even know what you read that was right in front of your face. The police reports did not say that Mr. Miranda was irritated; the police reports stated clearly that *"Mr. Coldwin was irritated"*. Ms. Hemm acted more than stupidly and incompetently and for her to maintain the position as lead States Attorney Prosecutor for Frederick County is very scary and beyond puzzling. Of course Baltimore County became involved because that is the jurisdiction where my son was actually killed. If you will recall on the day Joseph was killed the Maryland State Police did not even do a GPS and they had questions about which county Joseph was killed in because the dividing county line runs right through the land where Joseph lay deceased. This property was and is owned by Jay Metvet, the owner of the land and the police allowed him to make the determination as to which county my son was killed in. All of this is unlawful and outside of police policy and procedure. Again, I had to jump through numerous hoops to finally get Baltimore County to agree to do a survey of the property. They finally did after I had done all of the research myself and could prove my son was killed in Baltimore County and the Maryland State Police should have never investigated or been involved in any way in the criminal death investigation of my son. Metvet wanted it this way due to his political connections in Carroll County and beyond. The bottom line is that the Office of the Chief Medical Examiner and his experts got it right. Joseph's death is confirmed homicide by assault. A serious and heinous crime was committed against our son. However, all of the coroner's findings and Dr. David Fowler's and Dr. Ali's conclusions were ignored and strongly opposed by States Attorney Todd Slicenberger in Baltimore County.

In fact, Attorney Barrett never mentions once the conclusions and confirmation of the Medical Examiners that Joseph's death is a homicide by assault. He totally dismisses their expert findings and all of the concrete evidence of the case.

Therefore, their conclusion was in agreement with Todd Slicenberger's—that Joseph's death was an accident. My family and I were outraged and once again in disbelief. Attorney Barrett did say in his letter that, while it was out of the ordinary for him to convey any emotion or opine, what this mother has been through given all of the circumstances of the case was almost unconscionable. He continued that Joseph's death was horrific and completely unnecessary. We were taken aback by "almost unconscionable"; it was and remains beyond unconscionable.

We again empahsize throughout his two-page letter that while Attorney Barrett referred to the county prosecutors and the police, he never mentioned the medical examiners and their findings in any way. He completely ignored them and all of their facts, science, physics and evidence that proved the truth that Joseph's death was a homicide by assault, a vicious attack.

I tried many times to e-mail Attorney Barrett because he would not accept my phone calls. He did at least respond to one of my e-mail communications when I asked him directly why he was ignoring me. Typically his e-mail responses were sent from his assistant, Ms. Monokasik, but this time I knew it was his own words that were written.

He told me that he was not ignoring me and I might have all the theories I chose to have but that they had reviewed the police reports and the county state's attorneys' decisions. Given their positions, he concurred with them and that was all they would do. I had asked him to please explain to me how he thought my son got to the ground lying flat on his stomach just before the Bobcat moved backward, crushing him to death? I continued that we knew Joseph did not fall or trip over his shoelace or stumble in any way—we knew this for fact and through the forensics and depositions. I asked why he was discarding the fact that Pete Coldwin assaulted Joseph and gave him the "one-two" and "wasn't really violent or extreme but just a little bit." I said, "These are Pete Coldwin's own words in his deposition. Why do you give no validity to them and to the true facts of the case?" I realized it was no use. Attorney Barrett was not going to answer my justifiable questions and he was finished. He was finished, but we were far from finished.

For many months I went back and forth with the attorney general's office, requesting that my over 130 crucial documents be returned to me as promised. The liaison, Ms. Kiercher Braun, was apparently still away and out of the country. Meanwhile, I contacted Delegate Pena-Melnyk and asked her if she knew anything about the document package since Ms. Braun had originally picked it up from the delegate's office in Annapolis, Maryland. The delegate informed me that once Ms. Braun returned, she would probably be able to find them right away.

I later received an e-mail from MDSP corporal Sha Bryan telling me that he had possession of my documents and that Ms. Braun was the one who handed the box directly to him. At this I was relieved. I asked if I could come to the AG office to pick them up. At first he said yes. Then a few days later, I was told that since the documents were picked up from the delegate's office in Annapolis, this was where they had to be returned. I said, "All right. Please let me know as soon as I may pick them up." I then received a phone call and an e-mail from Corporal Sha Bryan telling me that he had to go to Annapolis on other business but he would be glad to take my documents and deliver them to the delegate's office to save me the trip to Annapolis. I thought that was so very kind of him and I thanked him and wrote that it would be fine.

Later in the week, I contacted the delegate's office and asked if they had received my box of documents. They told me they had them and that the corporal had delivered them. I asked when would be a good time for me to come and pick them up. With that, I received an e-mail from Tim, the delegate's aid whom I had been working with and he offered to bring the box of documents to me in Lutherville, Maryland and save me the trip. He said that his daughter lived in Lutherville and he was up this way regularly. I said, "Tim, that would be great. I really appreciate it." He said, "No problem, Adrienne. I am glad to do it." We set up a time to meet at Starbucks in Lutherville off of York Road. Tim and I met and shared a cup of coffee and good conversation. He was so very kind and compassionate and a man of strong faith. We spoke of the case and he affirmed to me that the corruption and injustice throughout Joseph's criminal investigation was detestable. I, again, thanked him for all that he, Spencer and Joseline had done and said I would never forget them. Tim knew that there was more still to come and hoped and believed that justice for Joseph would in time prevail; he said, "It has to, Adrienne." I nodded and said, "It will; God will bring it." He knew that I was going to write a book and he really encouraged me. We finished our coffee, hugged each other and headed for the door. He asked where I was parked and I showed him. He said, "Let me drive my car up behind you and I will put your box of documents in the car for you." I said, "OK, great." I went to my car and opened the passenger door. Tim pulled up, stopped and got out. He reached into his car, lifted a large cardboard box and placed it on my front passenger seat. Once again, we hugged, wished each other well and said we would stay in touch.

I pulled out of the parking lot and headed home. I felt so relieved that I now had my very important documents back in my possession. I had set up some time to go be with my mom at Lorien Mays Chapel and I knew she was expecting me. I pulled up in my driveway and placed the box in my dining room, knowing that I would look at them later. "Praise the Lord," I kept saying and I was filled with peace and gratitude.

I visited with my mom; we played bingo with all the folk, shared some coffee with vanilla creamer and then chatted for a while back in her room. My dear mother was really trying and doing her best to keep a smile in her heart and overcome the severe depression she had been suffering with for so long. She loved to be around people and we knew that in time we would try rehab once again to see if we could at least get her legs moving. I love her with all of my heart and would do anything for her. Her faith has never wavered and God has blessed us with many miraculous events and gifts.

CHAPTER 28

MY CRUCIAL DOCUMENTS LOST OR STOLEN

Early the next morning, I went downstairs and put on a pot of coffee. I then went and opened the box of my documents. When I looked and saw three-ring white binders and some loose papers, I was astounded. I said to myself, "These are not my documents! What in the world is going on?" I immediately looked again at the words written in black on the side of the box: *Agency: Attorney General, Division: Criminal* and *Record Title: Miranda Death Investigation Review.* I was flabbergasted and started to look at what was contained in the binders. I knew for a fact that these were not my documents. As I observed the binders, there was one that I happened to quickly page through and I realized that the edge of one of the documents was very dark purple in color. I started to cry and realized that there were tabs in this binder and this tab read *crime scene photos.* I knew I could not bear to look at the horrifying and crushed face of my baby lying in a pool of his own blood. I did not think of this horrendous nightmare when I thought of my Joseph. I remembered him with his smiling, handsome and beautiful face and his loving and giving heart and soul.

I called my brother, Damian and told him what was in the box. He, too, was shocked. We agreed that something really strange was going on and wondered who had my documents. I started to read through the other binder and could see internal e-mails sent within the Maryland State Police about my son's criminal investigation. Lieutenant Rickerts, the head of the Westminster Barrack at that time, referred to my son's case as a "hot potato" and said, "This mother is not going away." He spoke of no criminal report being documented by Corporal Kitseng on July 20, 2006 and others asked why. Where was his initial report? He was the corporal who was assigned the case. There were also references to how they had to step up to the plate and how they would bring in a new homicide detective named Munn. The lieutenant said this would be his first homicide case but they needed to get these tasks done at some level. My heart was pounding and it felt like I was not going to come up for air.

It was now extremely hot and the summer sun was strong. July 20, 2013, the anniversary of my son's tragic killing, was present. This was seven years to the day. I cut some roses from my angel gardens and took my hibiscus and forget-me-nots to my son's gravesite. My message card was tearstained and I laid it on his headstone. I knelt at his resting-place and prayed and cried out to Jesus. "Oh, dear Lord, keep giving me the strength and perseverance to stand strong and carry out your will. I know that all that is happening is your way and for your purpose as you tell me to come and follow you. I do, Father. I do."

The more I read in the two binders, the more sickening it became. I called the delegate and Corporal Sha Bryan. I explained to both of them that the box given to me did not contain my crucial documents that were relevant to what happened to my son and asked "why"? Corporal Bryan told me that he did not understand but that was the box given to him by Kiercher Braun with the AG office. He then asked me, "Ms. Miranda, was there anything in the box that enlightened you further?" I said, "Yes, absolutely!" I told him they called my son's death investigation a "hot potato" as if no one wanted to touch it and that they said that this mother was not going away. They even referred to how no criminal report was written up by the investigating homicide detective on July 20, 2006, the very day my son was brutally killed. He was the MDSP trooper,

Corporal Kitseng, who was assigned the case and who lied several times at meetings and right to our faces. He was the one whom they later transferred into Internal Affairs after he drove over Senior Homicide Detective Bishtall's report that they first told me did not exist. MDSP corporal Bryan remarked, "Good, good. At least you have been more enlightened." I then said, "Corporal, where are my documents? They are my property and the state of Maryland has no rights to them." He just said, "All I know is I took to the delegate what was given to me from the AG's office." I said, "Can you help me? Will you go back and look again in their files and ask Attorney Barrett to please search?" He said he would do what he could and he would stay in touch.

When I spoke to Delegate Pena-Melnyk, she was very surprised. She confirmed that the box had been given to Justin, her aide and then Tim offered to bring the box to me to save me the trip. They never opened it either and certainly presumed that my documents would be returned to me as promised. I called and then e-mailed Attorney Barrett. He replied that they had checked the entire eighteenth floor where files are kept and that they did not have my documents. The delegate suggested that I contact Attorney Barrett and ask him if I could please come to view their investigative file of my son's case. She said to tell them they could have their guard or their attorney present as I looked to see if perhaps my documents were mixed in their file by mistake. I decided to do just as she suggested and wrote an e-mail to Attorney Barrett, but he never responded to me.

More days and weeks of struggling with this weird situation went by. I contacted Keircher Braun. She was now back from being out of the country and I explained the entire situation to her. She e-mailed me back saying that she knew nothing about where my documents were and that she never handed the box of documents to MDSP corporal Sha Bryan. Of course, I was in disbelief; someone evidently was not telling the truth.

The next day I left a message for Corporal Bryan to please return my call and I said why I was calling. It took him a few days, but he did call me back. He still maintained that Kiercher Braun did hand the box of documents to him. Well, we now knew those documents were the internal e-mails and some reports that the MDSP and Todd Slicenberger sent to Attorney Don Barrett and his prosecutors.

I talked with my friend with the FBI and explained everything. He said, "Adrienne, it is as if it were done by design; it is like someone or certain people purposely arranged this. We know that your documents are somewhere." I said, "Yes, my documents did not sprout wings and fly away and I find it hard to believe that they were thrown in the trash."

In August I phoned Lieutenant Mark Brook, the current superintendent for the Maryland State Police. I asked to specifically speak to him. His secretary asked me my name and said that she would pass on my message of how very important it was that I talk directly with him. A few days went by and I received a call from Sergeant Klybay. He left a message and said he was following up with me regarding my call to the superintendent and my Brother Damian's e-mail to him. He left his number and told me to contact him. The next day I phoned him and he was very professional, concerned and caring and listened as I detailed what was going on and tried to consolidate the facts and occurrences about Joseph's death and the medical examiner's ruling of homicide by assault. He asked me some questions and then focused on the loss of my crucial documents that had been temporarily turned over to the criminal division of the AG's office per their request.

He assured me that he would meet with Keircher Braun, talk with Detective Bishtall to learn more about the case and do his best to find my documents. He was also going to talk with Corporal Bryan to find out what he had to say about the box given to him by Ms. Braun. He did let me know that he had spoken with my brother, Damian, and he understood our dismay and how we felt. Each twist and turn was presenting more alarming and outrageous results. My brother and I stayed in prayer and kept on course in our belief that God would expose all in His way and in His time.

I heartfully thanked Sergeant Klybay for his prudent and timely response and it seemed we would get some results from his efforts. I was filled up a bit as I began to hang up the phone and he offered, "Ms.

Miranda, I am a parent and I cannot even begin to imagine what you are going through. I am very sorry for your loss and I will do my best." Sergeant Klybay was certainly a good, decent and compassionate gentleman and I expect he is and will become an even more outstanding role model for the Maryland State Police; God knows it is needed.

A few weeks went by and I had not heard back from Sergeant Klybay. I was hoping to hear from him and from Corporal Bryan. I decided to call and leave a message for the Sergeant. The next day Sergeant Klybay returned my phone call and said that he was very sorry but there was nothing he could do. I said, "Sergeant, what do you mean?" He went on to tell me that his bureau chief ordered him to not get involved and said, "That case is over and we are no longer any part of it." I asked him, "Who is his bureau chief?" He answered, "Lieutenant Colonel Don Calisin." I could not believe what I was hearing. I said, "He is no good." He was involved when Joseph was killed and at that time he was a major. He was also supposed to be present at the July 11, 2007, MDSP meeting held in Carroll County where they closed my son's case on an impossible scenario, a bevy of lies and a cover-up. However, for some reason he never showed up and Lieutenant Colonel Copsinger led the pack of corruption. Sergeant Klybay just listened and said, "Ms. Miranda, he is the bureau chief and head over everything within the MDSP. I wish you the best and if anything changes, I will let you know."

To this day my crucial documents remain lost or stolen. I have been repeatedly ignored and these prosecutors will not even call for a grand jury. They refused to accept or believe that the science, physics, forensics, deposition admissions and medical examiners' conclusion of homicide by assault inflicted upon my son, Joseph, had been proven and were based on facts and evidence. How could they be so isolated, indifferent and removed from the medical examiners for the state of Maryland? In our opinion along with the facts, science and repeated lies all of this adds up to undeniable cover-up and corruption.

CONCLUSION

We do not appreciate being ignored and rejected. All of law enforcement has completely disregarded all of the very valid and justified questions my family and I have asked of them. If that is how they exercise due diligence, duty and performance in their jobs, then I suppose that is their choice. The injustice surrounding us remains unending and deplorable. There must be resolution and revelation. I will continue to serve as His vessel.

Revelation 1:8 "I am the Alpha and the Omega," "who is and who was and who is to come, the Almighty." Vs. 19 "Write therefore, what you have seen, what is now and what will take place later.

In our hearts and minds, as well as with regard to our rights to a fair and balanced investigation of Joseph's brutal and horrific killing, we must know how they believe my son got to the ground and flat on his stomach just before he was crushed to death by a reversing Bobcat. We must understand their analysis, but they give us nothing. We already know what Pete Coldwin says is impossible. That is already certain and has been proven by the facts and evidence.

Even though Joseph's death certificate has confirmed that his manner of death is homicide and his cause of death is assault—an attack by another—these prosecutors maintain that no crime was committed. His death certificate is recorded in the division of vital record in the state of Maryland and his death has also been recorded as the eighteenth homicide in Baltimore County for the year.

We know all of the facts, science, physics, forensics and proof are there. We can read and we completely understand what happened to our son when his life was violently taken from him.

We have also witnessed Mr. Coldwin's deposition when he had no remorse whatsoever and repeatedly lied about the Bobcat saying it was moving forward instead of backward over Joseph and that Joseph jumped up on the top of the left front tire and then fell off, between and underneath a sixteen-by-nine-inch space of the undercarriage from the ground. Once again, Joseph had no broken bones or injuries below his neck. You could in no way survive this without broken bones to your feet, ankles, legs, hips, back and more. Joseph had none. A contortionist midget could not even do this in any physical way; it is totally and completely impossible. Mr. Coldwin also said in his sworn deposition that his one-two shove on Joseph was not really "extreme fighting or violent—just a little bit."

Are you kidding me? They say that a crime—an assault—that took my son's life was not committed against him by Pete Coldwin. What kind of legal parameters and criminal law are they following? My son deserves his day in court and so does our family. We are taxpayers of this state and do not give a darn if you think you may not win. It isn't about winning. It is about presenting all of the facts, science, physics, forensics and evidence in a court of law to get to the truth and justice; let a jury decide. That is why we have a judicial system. We are so hurt, devastated and exhausted from being beaten down over and over again.

The justice system in the state of Maryland has failed us. Trials happen every day in this state and across this country and the prosecutors do not always win, but at least they try with all of their presentations of facts, evidence, decency and sincere hearts to put on all of the evidence for the victim and his or her family. They work to bring justice and truth for the innocent victims and hold people accountable. Why are we being denied this? It is outrageous and beyond a disgrace.

There will be a public outcry and I ask, "What if it was your or their child?" Would this be understood and accepted by you? Would you just quietly go away and not be the voice of your beloved, innocent child?" I hardly think so, but I dare not even ask the question to these deceitful, sinister, cruel and callous people.

The perpetrator is a deceitful liar in more ways than one. People lie when they are covering up. Dr. Fowler and Dr. Ali, who performed the autopsy of my son, report and confirm all of this. Why are they dismissing and going against their expert autopsy and proven facts and evidence of the case. Why? It makes no sense. Why are they protecting Mr. Coldwin and that company? Why are they protecting the downright lies, distortions and outrageous and criminal misconduct of the Maryland State Police, Baltimore County Police, the three State's Attorneys (who are idiotic and want to cover up the egg on their faces for their own personal political aspirations) and especially Todd Slicenberger, who has treated us with bias and prejudice and is in violation of his own oath of office. Our civil rights have been more than violated and continue to be. Where are my stolen documents? Someone has them and they are my property, not the state of Maryland's. We will not accept this and we will continue to move forward.

These people are despicable and twisted and there is a reason that they, too, were protecting Jay Metvet, the police and his company. They all needed to be interrogated. It was a disgrace that not one prosecutor in this state would stand up for what was right and take action. Politics can certainly be a more than ugly game, but Father God will bring victory. The corruption is ongoing, but we will continue to march forward for justice in His name.

We sing out loudly, "Glory, glory, hallelujah, glory, glory, hallelujah, glory, glory, hallelujah, His truth is marching on."

MY SON ROB AND I TOGETHER ON CHRISTMAS 2011. I WILL ALWAYS
AND FOREVER LOVE BOTH OF MY SONS WITH ALL OF MY HEART.